Why OOP Using C++? Why The Beginner's Guide?

Object-oriented programming is fast becoming the dominant concept in programming design. C++, derived as it is from the solid and efficient coding offered by C, is an ideal language for the professional programmer to learn when approaching the object-oriented world. The Beginner's Guide to OOP using C++ leads you from your knowledge of C, through the enhanced capabilities of C++, into efficient programming with objects. You will find the examples and clear definitions will ease your entry into objects, and each chapter deals with a major component of C++ and objects. The Wrox learning system will give you confidence and the beginnings of expertise.

What is Wrox Press?

Wrox Press is a computer book publisher which promotes a brand new concept - clear, jargon-free programming and database titles that fulfill your real demands. We publish for everyone, from the novice through to the experienced programmer. To ensure our books meet your needs, we carry out continuous research on all our titles. Through our dialog with you we can craft the book you really need.

We welcome suggestions and take all of them to heart - your input is paramount in creating the next great Wrox title. Use the reply card inside this book or mail us at:

feedback@wrox.demon.co.uk

or

Compuserve 100063, 2152

Wrox Press Ltd.	**Tel:** 0101 312 465 3559
2710 W. Touhy	**Fax:** 0101 312 465 4063
Chicago	
IL 60645	
USA	

The Beginner's Guide to OOP Using C++

Laureen Romanovskaya
Sergei Svitkovsky
Tatyana Shapetko

Wrox Press Ltd.®

The Beginner's Guide to OOP Using C++

Published by Wrox Press Ltd. 1334 Warwick Road, Birmingham, B27 6PR UK
Library of Congress Catalog Number: 94-78397
ISBN 1-874416-27-3

Trademark Acknowledgements

Wrox has endeavored to provide trademark information about all the companies and products mentioned in this book by the appropriate use of capitals. However, Wrox cannot guarantee the accuracy of this information.

Borland C++ version 4.0 is a registered trademark of Borland International.
Microsoft Windows is a registered trademark of The Microsoft Corporation.
Lego (in UK and USA) is a registered trademark of Interlegal AG - Switzerland.

Credits

Authors
Laureen Romanovskaya
Sergei Svitkovsky
Tatyana Shapetko

Technical Editors
Julian Dobson
Ed Kenworthy

Series Editor
Luke Dempsey

Technical Reviewers
Jim Ditter
Francis Glassborow
Ian Wilks

Production Manager
Gina Mance

Book Layout
Ewart Liburd
Eddie Fisher
Greg Powell

Proof Readers
James Hare
Pam Brand
Simon Thomas

Translator
Alla Berezhnaya

Cover Design
Third Wave

For more information on Third Wave, contact Ross Alderson on 44-21 456 1400

Cover photograph supplied by Pictor International

About the Author

Laureen Romanovskaya works in NICEVT, a research computing center in Minsk, where she has been involved in the design, development and implementation of software including compilers and user interfaces.

Sergei Svitkovsky works for a company which specialises in software design for businesses.

Tatyana Shapetko also works on software design and development in NICEVT.

Thank You

We would like to thank Valentin Kazan, a former department head at the Computer and Development Institute, for his support and for allowing us the use of the computer facillites to prepare the manuscript. Thanks also to our colleagues E. Kozell, T. Russ, V. Doroshek, and V. Rybov for their constructive discussion and help.

SUMMARY OF CONTENTS

CONTENTS

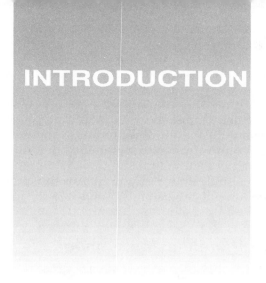

Introduction

What is an object? Well an object is a thing, it has features and it has properties. Let's have an example. A pool ball is an object. Its features are physical - it has dimensions, a color and mass, but it also has more abstract features - it represents points. A pool ball also has properties, although not many. For example, if pushed, then it moves in the direction you push it. If you hit it top left, you might get it to swerve left to right.

You can also think about the relationship *between* objects. A pool ball isn't much use without other balls (unless you live on the wrong side of the tracks!), a pool table, a couple of cues and of course a couple of people to play the game (and one or two beers).

But what has pool to do with programming? Well, quite a lot actually. Object-oriented programming is about taking real world objects and then describing them in a computer language. As with objects of the real world, the computer's objects may be purely abstract. That is, we could represent a thought in a computer (although neurologists may say that a thought is made up a physical objects called electrons). The idea is that we put into the computer a representation of the object we want the program to manipulate. We define the attributes of that object, and its reactions to different stimulii or properties. We also can define the relationship of one object to another.

Another feature of objects, just as Lego ™, is that you can create new objects by combining them with other objects. This is one of the most powerful features of object oriented programming.

But before we slam straight into any deep conceptualization about objects, let's have an overview of programming, and how it has led to objectification.

Evolution of Programming Languages

We will be dealing with both types and objects during the course of this book. There is a mismatch between the term 'typing' and the term 'object' which we need to be aware of. Historically, the term 'data type' appeared with the introduction of the first high-level programming languages (such as Fortran or Algol) and was associated with a computer representation of numbers (binary or decimal, fixed or floating-point) and the set of instructions used to perform arithmetic on these data types. The next generation of programming languages (such as PL/I, Algol-68 or Pascal) introduced the concept of manipulating 'abstract data types'. Object-oriented programming languages handle 'objects'.

We can consider that the concept of an 'object' is an extension and generalization of the concepts of 'data type' and 'abstract data type', and in consequence we won't adhere to the strict usage of these terms. Often the term 'data type' will be used for built-in types while the term 'object' will be used for user-defined object types.

Decomposing Programs

The change in the meaning of data type that came about due to evolution of programming languages is also evident in the development of the principles of splitting (decomposing) complex programs into simpler component parts.

For earlier generation programming languages (procedure-oriented), decomposition was based on identifying common algorithms and representing them as routine. For the next generation of languages (problem-oriented), the focus of decomposition moved to organization of data flows rather than algorithms, with a module used as a building block for a complex program. A module is a group of interrelated routines. Each module can be written independently of other modules, thereby allowing more than one programmer to be engaged in complex program design.

For an object-oriented programming language, objects with defined properties and interactions with other objects are used as a decomposition unit.

The above information about the evolution of programming languages is summarized in the following table:

Language Generation	Decomposition Unit	Approach to Abstraction	Design Method
Procedure oriented	Routine	Finding common algorithms	Top-down structured design
Problem oriented	Module	Defining abstract data types	Data flow organization
Object oriented	Class	Object classification	Object-oriented design

OOP and C++

The ways of expressing abstractions, access restriction and relations between classes are determined by the programming language used. We'll discuss these issues here, relative to C++. Let's move to an initial definition of what an object-oriented *programming* is.

Object-oriented programming is a programming technique which is based on representing a program as a collection of objects which form a hierarchical structure using inheritance. Accordingly, an object-oriented programming language must provide the facilities for expressing:

Object abstractions (abstract data types)

Access restriction to object

Inheritance-based hierarchy of objects

The C++ language, which we will be discussing in this book, is ideal as an object-oriented programming language because it meets all these requirements.

A Brief History of C++

C++ is an extension of C, and it allows you, the programmer, to write object-oriented programs. It was designed by Bjarne Stroustrup. The original C language was developed by Brian W. Kernighan and Denis M. Ritchie in AT&T Bell Laboratories in 1978 and gained popularity as a personal computer language. In 1989 the American National Standards Institute (ANSI) standardized the syntax of the language. The C language complied with the programming style of its time (structured programming statements, abstract data types) and allowed compact and efficient programs to be developed. However, as it turned out, it had the prerequisites needed for being transformed into an object-oriented language This was done by Bjarne Stroustrup in 1980/83.

First, classes were added to C and the language was called 'C with Classes'. The language was then refined, and virtual functions and operation overloading mechanisms added. This language version was referred to as 'C++'.

In 1990 a new version of C++ appeared which included multiply inheritance, abstract classes, refined function overload mechanisms, templates, and exception handling. This language version is taken by ANSI as a basis for standard C++ development. This is the language version we discuss in this book.

C++ is an evolving language (see Appendix A). Being an object-oriented language, C++ has been basically intended for the development of large program projects. A lot of care is taken to produce efficient implementations in order that time and space overheads don't exceed those of C.

A major advantage of C++ as an object-oriented language is the possibility of creating class object libraries to be used by programmers in other projects. Owing to the class hierarchy support and encapsulation feature, object-oriented programs can be more easily modified and expanded than programs written in other programming styles. Implementation of class methods can be modified without the users of the class libraries being aware of the change (except for the improvement in performance).

The language syntax is not significantly different from C which is a bonus for you as you don't have to learn C++ from scratch, but instead concentrate on the improvements to the language, and of course, object-oriented programming.

Brain, Taste, and Patience

As Bjarne Stroustrup said, you should have brain, taste and patience to write a good program. In practice, class design is an iterative process which will produce the desired result only after several passes.

Further, is it possible to solve a complex problem using only object-oriented methods, without using other (algorithmic, structured, data flow) design methods? Generally, the answer is no. However, it's best to embark on the design process using an object-oriented approach. You can then use the algorithmic decomposition and data flow methods (or other methods) to identify the behavior of objects. While in object-oriented programming you are dealing primarily with objects, the methods of those objects are still written as 'normal' sequential instructions.

What You Need

A knowledge of C will help you enormously when coming to objects in C++. And enthusiasm, a bit of perseverance, and the willingness to look afresh at programming design.

Conventions Used in this Book

Here are the styles we have used to help you find your way through the book:

▶ This is code which is important so we have shaded it:

```
Word w1 ("Week");
Word w2 ("end");
Word w3 ("ended");
```

▶ This is code which is either output or repeated or not essential to the example in hand:

```
Word();
Word(char*);
Word(Word &);
```

▶ This is how we have designed the introduction of new syntax which you will need to become familiar with:

```
class class_name
{
    class_member_declaration_list
};
```

▶ The words in italics in the above box are changeable, definition terms.

▶ *Try It Outs* take you through new ideas, and these ideas are then explained in *How It Works* sections.

Things you shouldn't ignore appear in these boxes.

Things which are background are in these boxes.

▶ Code which appears inside a sentence is picked out with `this_style`.

▶ And these are **important** words!

All these are designed to make your journey through this book as efficient and enjoyable as possible. We hope they help.

Tell Us What You Think

We have tried to make this book accurate, enjoyable and suited to the needs of the beginner to object-oriented programming. But what matters is what it does for you. We might never know unless you tell us. We at Wrox want to make books which meet real programming needs. Get in touch with us - call us, send back the reply card from the back of the book, or e-mail us at:

feedback@wrox.demon.co.uk
compuserve100062,2152

Code in the Book

All the source code in the book has been tested with Borland C++ 4.02, and where possible with Microsoft's Visual C++ 1.5. However, we do know that some of the programs don't compile properly with earlier versions of compilers (mainly Turbo C++ 3.0 or Borland C++ 3.1). This isn't owing to the code, but the compiler. These programs will work, but will need to be slightly modified. Just think how much fun you can have finding solutions to make the programs compile. Or, time to update your compiler?

One Last Thing - the Disk!

You'll find a disk inside the back cover which has on it all the source code from the book. To install the contents of the disk, change to the drive that the disk is in, for instance:

```
a:
```

then, simply type:

```
install  c:\disk
```

you can change `c:\disk` to any directory you want the code to be installed in.

CHAPTER 1

Objects and Classes - Your First Object-Oriented Program

This chapter aims to give you an overview of the key features of object-oriented programming. In the course of the chapter we'll introduce the key elements during the building of an initial program. Don't worry if we seem to be speeding ahead without taking time to explain in great detail - let's just get programming.

The problem we'll set ourselves is to count the number of occurrences of words in a random piece of text. We'll use a binary tree to order the words and then move on to define three objects, **WordTree**, **Word**, and **String**, which will help to define the scope of the problem and the operations we need to perform to go about solving it. We'll then use the objects to write a program.

Within this chapter we will be covering:

- Problem solving
- Abstraction
- Object behavior and the generic properties of objects
- Class definition
- A first object-oriented program

Problem Solving

Let's assume that you want to count the number of times certain words appear in a piece of text, using the power and efficiency of a computer. Such a program could be used to find out who authored a manuscript, if there is no conclusive evidence as to its author (this has been done with some of Shakespeare's plays).

As you'll see, when the objects used by a program are expanded, the scope of its application expands too. For example, if the object used is a character rather than a word, counting the number of character occurrences in a file can be used as a basis for selecting an optimum compression scheme.

Getting back to the problem, let's use the following text:

'Taking a new step, uttering a new word, is what most people fear most'.
Fyodor Dostoyevski, *The Diary of a Writer*

How would you count the occurrences of words in the text without a computer?

You'd probably take a blank sheet of paper and write down the first word 'taking' on the left, and put a 1 to its right to indicate that the word occurred only once in the text:

Taking 1

You'd then pick the next word and compare it with the words written on the sheet of paper. If there was no match, you'd add the word to the end of the list with the number 1. If there is a match, you'd increment the number of words by 1. You'd then repeat this until the end of text was reached.

The procedure results in a list of words and numbers:

taking	1
a	2
new	2
step	1
uttering	1
word	1
is	1
what	1
most	2
people	1
fear	1

The Simplest Approach to Problem Solving

Although we've taken only a short fragment of text, you might have noticed that as the list increases in size, looking for a particular word becomes a bit tiresome. Imagine strafing through Hamlet to find out how many times the word *alas* appears! Further, the list we created is in no particular order, and this makes the search slower.

The most natural and usual way of ordering words is in alphabetical order. However, if you try to arrange the words alphabetically when you write them on the paper, you could soon face the problem of insufficient space, as you could never know in advance how many lines to leave between words.

Binary Trees

Fortunately, computer science possesses well-defined techniques for ordering objects, for example, using a hashing algorithm or constructing a graph. For ordering words, we'll use the binary tree technique.

Generally, a tree consists of a root node, attached to other nodes each of which usually has two descendent branches, pointing left and right. In a binary tree, the number of branches any node possesses can't exceed two, hence the name. A node without any incoming branch is called a root node, or a tree root, and a node lacking any descendants is a terminal node.

Building a Binary Tree

Let's build a binary tree.

▷ Select the first word 'taking' and write it down on a sheet of paper in the middle of a line. This is the root node of the tree (see figure below). It has two descendent nodes:

Tree Root Node

▷ Then, pick another word in the text, and compare it with the word of the root node. If the word alphabetically precedes the node word, move along the left-hand branch of the node and add a new node using the word.

▷ If the word alphabetically follows the one in the node, move along the right-hand branch and add a new node with the word to this branch.

▷ If the word matches the one in a tree node, increment the word count for the node by 1, otherwise, add a new node and place the word there.

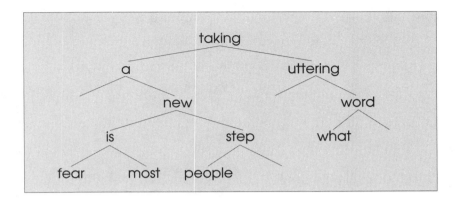

Complete Binary Tree

For each successive word, start searching with the root node in the tree and move along the left or right-hand branch, depending on whether the word alphabetically precedes or follows the one in the node - and if it matches, increment the node count by one.

Note that if you traverse the tree vertices going first left and then right, when you arrive at a particular node for a second time, and write the word down, you will obtain the alphabetically sorted list of words in the text with the count of occurrences for each word. Here is a sample of this process based on the words 'is fear most':

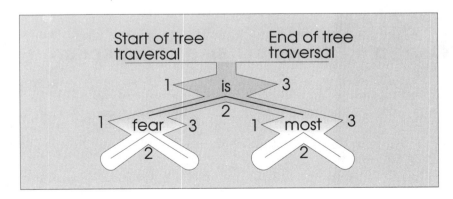

Traversing the Tree Left to Right

The completed list of words, in alphabetical order and with their occurrence count, is shown below:

a	2
fear	1
is	1
most	2
new	2
people	1
step	1
taking	1
uttering	1
what	1
word	1

Alphabetically Sorted List of Words

Thus we've determined the problem to be solved. Having discounted the simplest solution (that of a simple list with no sorting) as far from being the best one, we can move to using a binary tree to alphabetically order the words, and this is a widely used technique in programming. From this point we can move onto a further level of planning, using the object-oriented approach to problem solving. We'll discuss this approach in the next section.

Determining Objects Using Abstraction

Everything in the world is an object. The Beginner's Guide you are reading now is an object. The computer you use to run a program is also an object. Although the book and computer are both objects, we can distinguish between them without any difficulty. An object can be defined as a real or abstract entity, which has behavior and functionality in the correct context.

When we talk about a book, we don't imply that the book is thick or thin, fiction or scientific, paperback or hardback. Without wishing to be too Platonic about this, the word 'book' is an abstract notion implying that any object referred to as a book has some common properties inherent to only this object type. For example, it is possible to get books on tapes, or on CD-ROM, neither of which are books in the sense that they have pages made of paper. Yet they do share the idea of what a book is, that is, a place where ideas are written for other people to read.

> Plato argues that the 'ideal' is the thing as an abstract ('heavenly') concept, and that the embodiment of this 'ideal' is the 'things' themselves, real earthly books, real earthly CD-ROMs and so on (though claims that Plato knew anything about CD-ROMs are an exaggeration). And to think we computer scientists thought we'd got there first!

Common Properties

Looking for common properties between objects is not (generally) an easy task. For real world objects, the way of ordering these objects is known as scientific classification. The whole history of science can be considered as looking for either the properties of the objects, or an adequate classification for the objects being studied. You may well recollect the attempts of classifying species of animals by Darwin after his trips on The Beagle, or the ordering of the chemical elements by Mendeleyev.

One approach to classifying objects is grouping by categories. This process implies that all objects with a specific property, or set of properties, form a category or a class of objects. For example, this can be a class of mammals in the animal kingdom, or a class of geometric figures in geometry.

However, there are times when the objects have no pronounced properties and require more sophisticated methods for their classification.

Abstraction

You may well be wondering what classification methods in science have to do with object-oriented programming (let alone what Plato's got to do with anything!). But just as with Plato's musings in Greece, or Darwin's plowing the high seas to the Galapagos, any programming requires a thorough investigation of the problem. In object programming, using a process called abstraction you can find objects and the behavior of these objects.

Abstraction is the process of determining what the objects are and what their properties are. For physical objects this is usually quite an easy task, but for the less physical, like an idea, the process is more difficult.

Levels of Abstraction

The level of abstraction used will vary, depending on what you are trying to achieve. For example, we might imagine a beginner to programming would know that a personal computer consists of the following basic units: a central processor, a monitor, a keyboard, and a floppy or hard disk drive.

Personal Computer Structure at the Top Level of Abstraction

An electronic engineer who is designing a processor must know that the processor consists of main memory, an ALU, and a bus acting as common connection between peripheral devices. The ALU, in turn, consists of registers, control circuitry, and other elements (see opposite) which interact to provide the operations of the ALU. The same is true of other computer components.

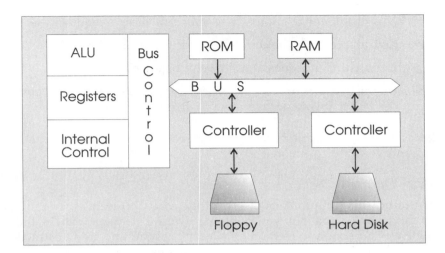

Personal Computer Structure at a Lower Level of Abstraction

As you can see, virtually any object is made from a complex hierarchical system of smaller objects. Each level represents a certain level of abstraction, allowing the internal details of the object to be hidden. This diminishes the system's complexity and facilitates its comprehension at every level of abstraction.

Actions performed on objects belonging to different hierarchical levels are clearly of different levels of refinement. For example, a driver of a car knows that turning the ignition key will start the car. However, for the mechanic, this simple action encapsulates a lot more detailed operations within the engine.

Objects for Programs

This same process also applies to programming with objects. You, the programmer, have to decide on the level of abstraction, as well as which objects are required within your program. You also need to decide on the relationship between the objects and what the objects do. The difficulty of this task is dependent on the nature of the problem you are trying to solve. Sometimes the objects required are obvious, and don't require much in the way of thought (such as designing an address book program). However, most of the time you'll find that you don't have such luxury, and you won't be surprised to learn that there are whole books dedicated to designing objects.

Thus, an object-oriented approach to program design requires the following:

> Key abstractions (object classes) for an application

> Hierarchical relationships between object classes

> Object behavior which manifests itself in the operations performed on the object involving a change in the state of the object.

This is a rather difficult concept to understand, but is fundamental to programming, object-oriented style.

Application Domain Dictionary

Let's return to our problem of counting word occurrences in a fragment of text, and try to find out which objects we are dealing with in the problem. The simplest method of object analysis and key abstraction identification is the use of an application domain dictionary. An application domain dictionary is a list of the verbs and nouns that relate to the problem in hand. The nouns are the objects, and we're able to determine the relationship between the objects (nouns) from sentences. The verbs tend to act upon nouns and this gives us the behavior of the objects. With this in mind, let's review the problem description, paying attention to the nouns and verbs used therein. Nouns can be the candidates for object classes, and verbs can be the candidates for operations performed on those objects.

> You should take into account, however, that a natural language isn't adequate for precisely representing a problem, therefore the list of object classes and operations will be strongly dependent on problem definition. The method is only applicable as an initial approximation, and may need to be followed by another process which qualifies the object classes and operations to be performed on them.

Restating the Problem

Here is the problem one more time.

We want to count the number of occurrences of words in a fragment of text, using a binary tree. Each word is a node of the binary tree, with the left-hand branch containing those words which are alphabetically before the node word. The right-hand branch contains words which are alphabetically after the node word. The first word is the root or first node.

When reviewing the description of word occurrence counting problem, you might well notice that there are three key nouns:

- Word
- Node
- Tree

These will be the candidates for object classes in our problem.

Look at the following combinations of these nouns:

- Word in a tree node
- Left-hand branch of a node
- Right-hand branch of a node
- Word occurrence counter
- Root word node

These combinations will help us to identify the dependencies between the objects and their properties. You will see that the object 'word' is both the object selected from the text and the one placed in the tree node. Hence the class object 'node' uses the class object 'word'. In addition, the tree node has two branches (left and right) as well as the occurrence counter for the word in the node. And, finally, the object 'tree' consists of 'nodes' and has a node called the root.

Thus we are dealing here with the three interrelated classes of objects.

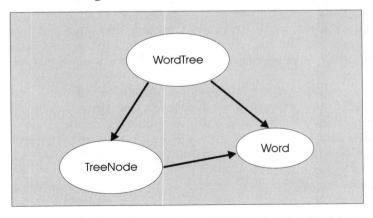

Dependencies Between Class Objects in the Problem

Class Names

When selecting a class name, you should take care that it represents the object's identity as closely as possible. The convention we'll use for the class name is to begin with an upper-case letter. You should also keep in mind that C++, like C, distinguishes between upper and lower-case letters, so that **Word** and **word** are not identical.

Creating a Model of Object Behavior

We've said before that an object must have a set of properties. The properties of an object determine its state - this, along with the object's behavior, is the key characteristic of the object. The properties of an object are usually static - that is, all occurrences of that object contain the same properties. The actual value of each property changes dynamically for each occurrence of the object, independently of all other occurrences. So if we have two occurrences of a **Word**, then both have the same properties (the actual string that is the word), but each occurrence is a different string. Thus, though the **type** of data is the same for all occurrences of the same object, the actual **data** changes.

Let's look at the properties inherent to the objects of classes **Word**, **TreeNode**, and **WordTree**.

Word Object Properties

The **Word** class object is a character string, and it represents the word we'll be counting the occurrences of. As with an object in the *real* world, any object in a program comes to existence at its creation, that is, when it's allocated some space (large enough computer memory area to accommodate it). The life of an object within a program comes to an end when its space is deallocated.

When a **Word** class object is created, it should be allocated the amount of space needed to represent the whole character string up to a blank (we won't take punctuation marks into account for a while). Therefore, the object characteristic, word length, will be very useful. The word length can be used when a program requests storage for a **Word** object.

Let's denote the above characteristics of the **Word** class object as **theWord** and **wordLen**, respectively. These are the static properties of the **Word** class object. **wordLen** is an integer, and indicates the number of characters in the current string.

Owing to the fact that words differ in length, we can separate the sequence of characters which form the word from the **Word** class object. You can do this by associating a pointer to the sequence of characters with **theWord** property, rather than to the sequence of words itself. The figure below shows the relationship of a 2 byte pointer **theWord** to the character string. The next two bytes (or 4 bytes) is the string length **wordLen**. The whole figure is a representation of classes of our class **Word**.

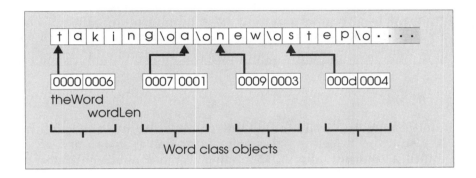

Memory Representation of a Word Class Object

The TreeNode Object Properties

Let's have a look at the properties of a **TreeNode** class object.

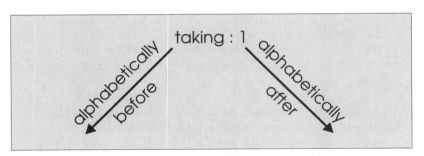

A Word Tree Node Structure

As you can see, the **TreeNode** class object contains a word from the input text, a word occurrence counter for the text (represented by an integer, separated from the word by a colon), and two arrows pointing to the left-hand and right-hand branches going out from the node. Each branch points to a node of similar structure.

Don't worry if this form of data organization looks unusual and complicated to begin with - we can easily find similar structures in the real world. For example, a tree has a root, branches and leaves. In the real world, trees are growing: buds appear in place of leaves, and these give rise to new branches. The root is the part of the tree *from which* branches grow, but *to which* no branch grows.

> The leaves of the tree have been referred to as nodes in our discussions so far, but sometimes they are referred to as vertices. You may also have noticed that programming trees have their roots in the air. Modeling computer science on the real world has its limitations, as well as its inversions.

Recursion

Notice how each node in our tree points in turn to two other nodes in the structure, which are also pointing to similar nodes, and so on. This is called a recursion, that is, the defining of one notion in terms of itself.

Recursion depends upon a certain condition defining the termination point, or else the process would continue indefinitely.

Recursion: An Example

Let's take an example. When you encounter an unknown word while reading a text in a foreign language, you might consult a dictionary to find the meaning of the word. However, when reading the explanation in the dictionary, you may well encounter another unknown word. In order to define this new unknown word, you then look up another entry in the dictionary, having marked the place you had reached in the first definition.

The process could continue *ad infinitum*, or until you had found the definition of the original word which was clear to you. In the latter case, you would then be able to return through the incomplete explanations (incomplete in terms of your understanding) until the initial word in question was reached. This, too, is a recursive operation.

Let's return to the properties of our class **TreeNode**. Firstly, each tree node is associated with a **Word** class object. Secondly, each node has a word occurrence counter for the text. We'll refer to it as **count**. Finally, there are two pointers: one pointing to the left-hand branch (referred to as **left**) and another pointing to the right-hand branch (referred to as **right**).

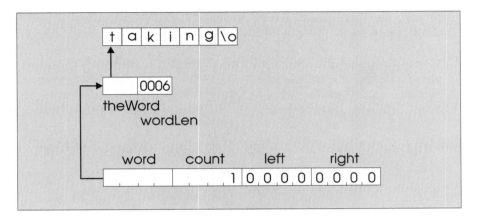

A Tree Node Representation

The tree node definition as noted previously is recursive, that is, the class object **TreeNode** contains a pointer to an object of the same class:

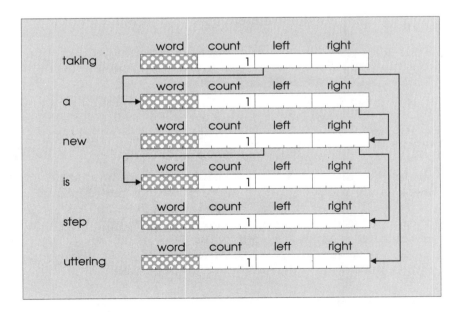

Representation of a TreeNode Class Object

Note that the design of the **Word** class object used by the object **WordTree** is now no longer relevant.

Finally, the class object **WordTree** has only one characteristic of its own - the pointer to the root note of the tree.

We've discussed the characteristics of objects for our classes **Word**, **TreeNode** and **WordTree**. We must now have a look at the behavior of the objects and determine what operations are to be performed on them and how they will affect object states (dynamic values of object properties).

Defining Operations to be Performed on Objects

Let's go back to an informal description of the problem to be solved: counting the number of occurrences for words in a text using a binary tree. As you saw, the minimum you have to do is the following operations:

▶ Get the next word from the input text

▶ Compare two words

▶ Add the word to the tree

▶ Display the word count.

Also, you should be able to create an object (that is, allocate a memory space for the object and assign a value to it) and destroy an object (that is, release the space occupied by the object when it's no longer needed).

We'll enter the text which is to be analyzed from the keyboard, and display the resulting count on the screen. The key combination *Ctrl+Z* will denote the end of text entry.

Getting the words from the keyboard consists of receiving the input text character by character until a blank is encountered (for simplicity, we won't use other punctuation marks in the program). The entered characters form the value of the property **theWord**, and their count becomes the value of the property **wordLen** of the **Word** class object. Thus we've defined how the **Word** class object will change its state as a result of the 'get a word' operation.

The next step is to define the meaning of the 'compare the two words' operation. In fact, we need at least two operations to define the dependencies existing between the two words: they are either equal, or the first word is less than the second one. If the first word is equal to or less than the second, that is, if the == and < comparisons fail, then obviously the first is greater than the second. The comparisons clearly must result in either true or false.

> **In C++, as in C, the true value is represented by a non-zero integer, and the false value by a zero.**

For the operation 'add the word to the tree', we must define how the state of the **TreeNode** object will change. We've already described the algorithm for this operation:

> Once the next word is retrieved, beginning from the tree root, search the word tree for the word.

> If the next word retrieved matches the node word, increment the word count by 1.

> If the next word retrieved is less than the node word, check whether the node has the left sub-tree (pointer **left** is non-zero).

> If the left subtree exists, proceed with the recursive operation until a node with the non-zero pointer **left** is encountered.

> We must then create a new class object **TreeNode** for this word, and set the **left** pointer of the preceding node to the new object.

> If the word retrieved for a certain level node is greater than the one in the node, move along the right-hand branch and down on the right branches recursively as described above.

Thus the change in the **TreeNode** object state resulting from the 'add the word to the tree' operation consists of the following:

> If there is no matching word in the tree, a new **TreeNode** class object is created.

> If there *is* a match, the word count is incremented by 1.

To conclude this section, to display the results we traverse the tree left to right, starting from the tree root. We then step down along the left branch to reach the next node, and so on, until the empty **left** pointer is encountered. At this point we actually go back to the same node for the second time, display the word and the word count from the node, and move along the right-hand branch.

Therefore, we move from one tree node to another, successively getting into each of them three times but retrieving the word only on the **second** arrival to the node. The following figure shows the traversal of a tree fragment ('is fear most') starting from the word *is*.

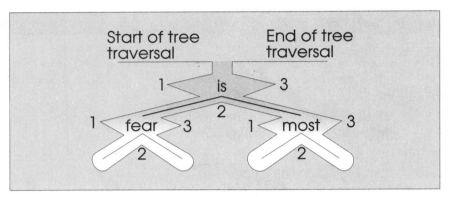

Traversing the Tree Left to Right

Generic Properties of Objects

It's clear that, for a problem to be analyzed in an object-oriented fashion, a solution must be designed before getting near the computer. This process is dependent on the programming language used for the actual implementation. For example, in our case, we have to some extent discussed using pointers within the nodes, but pointers are not available in all languages. Your analysis is always going to depend ultimately on the language you are going to use. However, you are a C programmer, learning to program C++.

At this point we'll introduce some key concepts of object-oriented programming, all of which we'll return to more fully later in the book.

Abstraction

As we've already said, the key aspect of object-oriented analysis and design is the abstraction of the class objects and construction of their behavior model as close to the real world problem as possible. Abstraction is based on identifying the properties inherent in the objects to the required level of detail, and ignoring the irrelevant properties.

Object Behavior Model

The process of creating an object behavior model consists of describing operations to be performed on the object and operations which one class object can perform on another class object.

Encapsulation

With the object-oriented approach, you focus your attention on external features of an object. The internals of the object are normally hidden and protected against any influence from other objects. This object-oriented design concept is referred to as encapsulation (or access restriction) which complements the abstraction concept. Generally, access restriction ensures that only specific operations are allowed to dynamically vary the values of class object properties.

However, without interaction between different class objects, we could never model the behavior of real world objects. Think of the classes **Word**, **TreeNode**, and **WordTree** - we demonstrated one type of relation between classes: the relation of use. The **TreeNode** class *uses* the **Word** class. The **WordTree** class *uses* the classes **TreeNode** and **Word**.

Inheritance

There are relationships between classes. A common relationship is the one where one object completely incorporates another object and gains access to the properties of this object. This kind of relation between objects is referred to as inheritance. Inheritance can also occur when a new object incorporates two or more objects. This kind of inheritance is referred to as multiple inheritance.

The principles of access restriction and hierarchical inheritance are competing with each other as the protection mechanism sets up the stringent access limits, while the inheritance feature requires free access to the state and operations of the incorporated object.

The inheritance mechanism is one of the key characteristics of object-oriented programming, and will be discussed in more detail in Chapter 8.

Polymorphism

Another important feature of an object-oriented programming language is polymorphism which can be described as 'many forms' for a single operation. Polymorphism allows you to assign the same name to operations on different objects. The desired operation implementation is selected dynamically, depending on the object being used.

Typing

As you'll see later, a good object-oriented programming language must also be strongly typed, that is, all expressions are verified for types. This implies that an object must be explicitly declared and that conversion rules are defined for the objects involved.

Class Definition With C++

When discussing object-oriented design we used the term *class* to mean a set of objects with common properties. While being related, the class and the object are different terms that should be clearly distinguished from each other. A *class* is an abstract description of the properties of objects belonging to the class. An *object* is an instance of the class that is allocated some space in computer memory.

Let's now declare the first of the three classes of our C++ program for counting word occurrences, **Word**:

```
// Word class definition

class Word {
    private:
        char * theWord;
        int wordLen;
    public:
// Constructors
        Word();
        Word(char *);
        Word(Word &);
// Destructor
        ~Word();
// Selectors
        char * IsWord();
        int IsWordLen();
        int IsEmpty();
// Assignment one word to another
        Word & operator = (Word &);
// Compare two words
        int operator == (Word &);
        int operator < (Word &);
};
```

As you can see, the class definition begins with the word **class** followed by the class name (**Word** in our program) and then by the class member declaration list enclosed in braces **{** and **}**. The class definition ends in a semicolon (**;**) placed next to the closing brace.

Keywords

In the class definition, you can see individual members with the labels such as:

private:
and
public:

These words are the reserved words or keywords in C++ which have a fixed meaning and can't be used as programmer-defined names for program properties and objects (we'll give you a full list later in the book).

The words **private** and **public** (as well as **protected** which isn't used in the example but exists in C++) specify the accessibility (access restriction) of properties listed in the appropriate section.

Thus, the keyword **private** specifies that the properties are only inherent to these class objects and inaccessible to other class objects, that is, they are hidden to an outside viewer.

Alternatively, the keyword **public** specifies that access to this class properties is unrestricted. Generally, declarations of operations, which a programmer uses to manage objects of this class, are placed in the public section.

The keyword **protected** is used in relation to the inheritance mechanism in the hierarchy of classes, and implies that the base class properties declared **protected** can only be used in the base class, or its direct derivative, but they are inaccessible to other classes.

Class Member Declaration List

A class member declaration list can contain declarations of class data members and class member functions. A class data member is associated with the properties of class objects and member functions implement operations performed on the class objects.

Thus in the class **Word** we have declared the data members **theWord** and **wordLen** in the **private** section:

```
private:
    char * theWord;
    int wordLen;
```

The declaration is very similar to that which you have probably already used in C with **struct**s. The difference between the **struct** and **class** is in the inclusion of methods in **class**es which does not occur in **struct**s.

> We must say at this point that we are talking of C **struct**s, not C++, as C++ allows **struct**s to have methods and access modifiers.

The fact that the data members **theWord** and **wordLen** are declared in the **private** section means that access to data is restricted solely to operations of this class. The declaration of these operations follows the data member declarations next to the label **public**.

TreeNode and WordTree Data Members

Before proceeding to the use of class member function (operation) declarations, let's consider how the properties of other classes of interest are declared.

In the **TreeNode** class member list, the following data members are declared:

```
class Word {
...

// TreeNode class definition
class TreeNode {
   private:
      Word * word;          // Pointer to word
      int count;            // Word count
   public:
      TreeNode * left;      // Pointer to left subtree
      TreeNode * right;     // Pointer to right subtree
...
};
```

As you can see, a class data member can be an object of another class but the class must be already defined by the time it's used. As with **struct**s, an object of the class being defined can't be a member the same class, but you can have a pointer to this class object:

```
public:
    TreeNode * left;        // Pointer to left subtree
    TreeNode * right;       // Pointer to right subtree
```

Unlike declarations of the **Word** class data members, data members **left** and **right** are in the **public** section as they must be accessible to add a word to the tree.

Finally, the only data member in the **WordTree** class is a pointer to the tree root:

```
class Word {
...
class TreeNode {
...
// WordTree class definition
class WordTree {
    public:
        TreeNode * root;
...
};
```

Class Member Function Declaration List

Let's go back to the definition of our **Word** class. In this class, the data member declarations are followed by those of class member functions that can be used to perform operations on objects.

```
// Word class definition

class Word {
    private:
        char * theWord;
        int wordLen;
    public:
// Constructors
        Word();
        Word(char *);
        Word(Word &);
// Destructor
        ~Word();
// Selectors
        char * IsWord();
        int IsWordLen();
        int IsEmpty();
// Assignment one word to another
        Word & operator = (Word &);
// Compare two words
        int operator == (Word &);
        int operator < (Word &);
};
```

In its simplest case, the function declaration has the following syntax:

```
return_value_type  function_name  (argument_type_list);
```

This is obviously the same as how functions are used in C.

Constructors and Destructors

Each of our classes comprises the declaration of the function whose name coincides with the class name. This is a special kind of class member function called a constructor. A similar declaration with a tilde (~) before the function name is a function called a destructor.

These member functions are used to create (as with constructor) or destroy (as with destructor) the specific object of the class.

Generally, the constructor is called automatically whenever a class object declaration is encountered in the code, while the destructor is called when the object's life span comes to end. Constructors make it possible to assign an initial value to the object of the class.

The three member functions of the **Word** class are constructors (whose names coincide with the class name) and they only differ in the argument type. They allow you to create and initialize a **Word** class object when there is no information available, when a pointer to a character string is passed, or when a reference to another **Word** class object is passed.

```
// Constructors
    Word();
    Word(char *);
    Word(Word &);
```

Function Overloading

This ability of C++ to use the same name for functions that differ in their parameter list is called function overloading. C++ decides which function to call depending on the parameters passed.

The following declaration of a member function relates to a destructor:

```
// Destructor
    ~Word();
```

The following group of declarations for member functions have names which begin with the word **Is** (**IsWord**, **IsWordLen**, and **IsEmpty**). We'll refer to these functions as selectors - they are used to query the state of an object without changing it.

```
// Selectors
    char * IsWord();
    int IsWordLen();
    int IsEmpty();
```

Finally, there are the three member functions that define the operations affecting the object state:

```
// Assignment one word to another
    Word & operator = (Word &);
// Compare two words
    int operator == (Word &);
    int operator < (Word &);
```

This is another feature of C++: the ability to design your own operators. We'll be discussing all of these new features in a lot more detail throughout the book. We have mentioned them here so that you get an idea of how powerful C++ is.

TreeNode and WordTree Member Functions

In the **TreeNode** class, there is an **Increase** function which increments the word occurrence count for the node. In addition, there are constructors, a destructor, and the selectors **IsWord** and **IsCount**.

```
class TreeNode {
   private:
      Word * word;            // Pointer to word
      int count;              // Word count
   public:
      TreeNode * left;        // Pointer to left subtree
      TreeNode * right;       // Pointer to right subtree
   public:
      TreeNode();                // Constructors
      TreeNode(Word &);
      ~TreeNode();            // Destructor
      void Increase();        // Increase count of word
      Word * IsWord();        // Get a pointer to word
      int IsCount();          // Get a word count
};
```

In the **WordTree** class, there are three functions declared:

- **Add**   For adding a word to the tree

- **Print**   For displaying the result of counting the word occurrence in the text

- **Destroy**   For releasing the memory occupied by the word tree upon completion of the program being run

```
class WordTree {
   public:
      TreeNode * root;
   public:
      WordTree();
      ~WordTree();
      TreeNode * IsRoot();
      TreeNode * Add(Word &, TreeNode *);
      void Print(TreeNode *);
   private:
      void Destroy(TreeNode *);
};
```

In addition, there is a constructor, a destructor, and the **IsRoot** selector.

Comments

As you may have guessed, in our C++ code, a line that begins with two slashes (//) represents a comment. The comment is contained between the // and the end of a line. If a comment can't be accommodated on one line, you can continue it on the following line, having marked the beginning of the line with two slashes. This is different to the standard C comments, which are still available for you to use.

Class Member Function Definition

As we mentioned earlier, we need to define the operations which are to be performed on the objects of our classes.

All we've done so far is to declare the member functions of our classes. The next task is to implement these member functions so that they will perform the tasks that we have designed them to complete.

Normally, a class member function definition is placed outside the class body enclosed in braces, hence the member function definition must include the reference to the class name where the function belongs.

The class name is placed before the member function name and is separated by a pair of colons (::) as, for example:

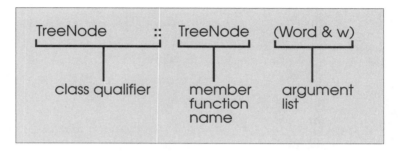

Syntax of a Member Function Definition

Here is a definition of the member function that is a constructor for the **TreeNode** class object:

```
// Constructor to create a node with word
TreeNode :: TreeNode (Word & w)
{
    word  = new Word(w);
    count = 1;
    left  = right = NULL;
}
```

We won't go into detail here about the statements used in the definition of member functions for our classes - the majority of them should be easily recognizable to you as C programmers. This particular constructor assigns a pointer to a **Word** object to **word**, using **new** which is the C++ equivalent of **malloc**, sets **count** to 1 and the **left** and **right** pointers to **NULL**.

The definitions of **Word** class member functions are as follows:

```
// Definition of Word class member functions
// Constructors
Word :: Word()
{
    theWord = NULL;                 // Create dummy word
    wordLen = 0;
}
```

35

```
Word :: Word(char * s)     // Create word from character string
{
   int Len;
   Len = strlen(s);
   theWord = (char *) new char [Len + 1];
   strcpy(theWord, s);
   wordLen = Len;
}

Word :: Word(Word & w)     // Create word from word (duplicate word)
{
   wordLen = w.IsWordLen();
   theWord = (char *) new char [wordLen + 1];
   strcpy(theWord, w.IsWord());
}

// Destructor
Word :: ~Word()
{
   if (theWord != NULL)             // Prove if word exists
      delete theWord;        // before deleting
}

// Get pointer to word
char * Word :: IsWord()
{
   return theWord;
}

// Get the length of the word
int Word :: IsWordLen()
{
   return wordLen;
}

// Does word is empty
int Word :: IsEmpty()
{
  return (theWord[0] == '\0') ? 1 : 0;
}

// Assignment operator
Word & Word :: operator = (Word & w)
{
   if (this != &w) {
      int Len = w.IsWordLen();
      if (theWord != NULL)
        delete theWord;
      theWord = (char *) new char [Len + 1];
      strcpy(theWord, w.IsWord());
```

```
        wordLen = Len;
    }
    return * this;
}

// Relation operators
int Word :: operator == (Word & w)
{
    if ((strcmp(theWord, w.IsWord()) == 0) &&
        (wordLen == w.IsWordLen()))
        return 1;
    return 0;
}

int Word :: operator < (Word & w)
{
    if (strcmp(theWord, w.IsWord()) < 0)
        return 1;
    return 0;
}
```

There is quite a bit of code here, and all of this is just for one class. Fortunately, there's very little here which won't be recognizable to C programmers.

Overloading

Notice that there are definitions of functions:

operator==
operator<
operator=

in the **Word** class.

The first two operators check the operands for the 'equal' and 'less than' conditions, while **operator=** denotes an assignment. In C++, however, these operators are defined for built-in data types; for example integers, as in the case of **count = 1**. We're using the same representations for operations performed on the objects of our class. This is referred to as redefining the semantics (meaning) of operators, or operator overloading.

You can overload both operators and function names. Overloading is one of the ways of implementing polymorphism in C++, but many C++ programmers would argue that this is not true. Overloading is about selecting from a number of functions within the same scope.

Polymorphism is selecting the scope depending on the type of the object. Polymorphism is related to the hierarchy of classes and the dynamic selection of a function during program execution. This mechanism will be detailed in Chapter 9.

Let's define member functions of the **TreeNode** class:

```
// Definition of TreeNode class member functions
// Constructor to create dummy node
TreeNode :: TreeNode()
{
   word = NULL;
   count = 0;
   left = right = NULL;
}
// Constructor to create a node with word
TreeNode :: TreeNode(Word & w)
{
   word = new Word(w);
   count = 1;
   left = right = NULL;
}

// Destructor
TreeNode :: ~TreeNode()
{
   if (word != NULL)
      delete word;
}

// Increase word count
void TreeNode :: Increase()
{
   count++;
}

// Get a pointer to word
Word * TreeNode :: IsWord()
{
   return word;
}

// Get a counter
int TreeNode :: IsCount()
{
   return count;
}
```

These are the member functions of the **WordTree** class:

```
// Definition of WordTree class member functions
// Constructor
WordTree :: WordTree()
{
   root = NULL;
}

// Destructor
WordTree :: ~WordTree()
{
   if (root != NULL)
      Destroy(root);
}

// Add a word to the tree
TreeNode * WordTree :: Add(Word & w, TreeNode * p)
{
   if (p == NULL)
      p = (TreeNode *) new TreeNode(w);
   else if (*(p->IsWord()) == w)
      p->Increase();
   else if (*(p->IsWord()) < w)
      p->right = Add(w, p->right);
   else
      p->left = Add(w, p->left);
   return p;
}

// Print a wordtree
void WordTree :: Print(TreeNode * p)
{
   if (p != NULL) {
      Print(p->left);
      cout << p->IsWord()->IsWord() << " : " << p->IsCount() << '\n';
      Print(p->right);
   }
}
// Private member function to destroy
void WordTree :: Destroy(TreeNode * p)
{
   if (p != NULL) {
      Destroy (p->left);
      Destroy (p->right);
      delete p;
      }
}
```

This concludes all the function definitions for our program. We can now use all of this to write our program - that is our next project.

Counting Word Occurrences - the Program

Let's look at our program:

```
#include <iostream.h>
#include <string.h>
#include <ctype.h>
```

```
// Word class definition
...
// TreeNode class definition
...
// WordTree class definition
...
```

```
// Our program for counting word occurrence

Word GetWord()
{
  char buf[40];

  cin >> buf;
  Word w = buf;

  return w;
}

void main()
{
  Word w;
  WordTree * tree = (WordTree *) new WordTree;

  for ( ; ; )
  {
    w = GetWord();
    if (!w.IsEmpty())
      tree->root = tree->Add(w, tree->root);
     else
       break;
  }
  tree->Print(tree->root);
  delete tree;
}
```

As you can see, the program is very much like any other C program, with only a few minor differences.

The **main()** function definition is preceded with the **GetWord()** function definition, which isn't a member of any class. It gets the next word (that is, the keyed-in text to be analyzed for word occurrences) from the input stream **cin** and places it in a temporary buffer (40 characters in size).

This is expressed by the statement:

```
cin >> buf;
```

This statement uses the **>>** operator which is a predefined overloaded operator to get a word from the keyboard, as defined in **IOSTREAM.H**. This functionality of the operator is only apparent when you use it with **cin** (or related input streams from **IOSTREAM.H**); at all other times it's still the bit-shift operator. After a single execution the **GetWord** function returns the value of the **Word** class object.

Notice how member functions of the classes are called in the same fashion as accessing data in a struct. This is not by accident - you have to keep in mind that C++ is an extension of C, and not a completely new language.

For example, the **Add** function call appears as follows:

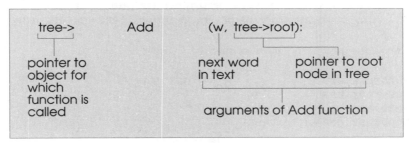

The Add Function Call

The result of the program is shown below:

```
taking a new step uttering a new word is what most people fear most^Z
a : 2
fear : 1
is : 1
most : 2
new : 2
people : 1
step : 1
taking : 1
uttering : 1
what : 1
word : 1
```

The code above does contain things that may not be obvious or familiar to you as a C programmer. Don't worry - as you work through the book, the new features of C++ will be explained in a lot more detail and you will soon learn how to write good object-oriented programs in C++.

Dividing a Program Into Separate Files

The complete program text including the class definitions, the class member function definitions and the proper program, is provided on a companion disk in two versions: as a single physical file **????.CPP** (which we have used in text above), and as several files, to demonstrate an approach to decomposing the program into separate physical files.

The program parts are divided into files as follows:

▶ The class definition is placed into the file with the class name and the extension **.HPP** (where **H** in the file extension stands for header, and **PP** stands for Plus Plus in the C++ name)

▶ The class member function definition is placed into a file with the class name and the extension **.CPP** (which, wait for it, stands for C++)

▶ The text of the word occurrence counting program is placed in a file with an arbitrary name, for example, **????** and the extension **.CPP**.

Thus, our program could consist of 7 files:

```
WORDTREE.HPP
TREENODE.HPP
WORD.HPP
WORDTREE.CPP
TREENODE.CPP
WORD.CPP
????.CPP
```

In order that the contents of these files become visible (and hence to provide the interface), the files must be added with special format directives which ensure that the right file is included in the right place within the code. These are include directives whose syntax is either

```
#include   "file-name"
```

or

```
#include   <file-name>
```

The difference between the two formats is irrelevant for the time being. We need to place the **#include** directive at the top of our program (before the **GetWord** function definition) so that we can use the classes **WordTree**, **TreeNode**, and **Word**. Besides, we must also include the **iostream.h** predefined in the C++ implementation, to input data from the input stream **cin**.

```
#include <iostream.h>
#include "word.hpp"
#include "treenode.hpp"
#include "word.hpp"
Word GetWord {
...             function body
}
int main ()
{
...             function body
}
```

Similar **#include** directives must be placed at the beginning of each file with the extension **.CPP**, which contains the member function definitions for our classes.

Because of the **#include** directive, the program will have added the appropriate header file as if it has been installed here. The action is performed by a preprocessor that makes up part of the compiler.

Summary

The first thing you should do when faced with the task of writing a program is to find an appropriate way of solving the problem away from the machine. This can then lead object analysis and object-oriented design upon the problem in hand.

Object-oriented design should take into account abstraction, access restriction, and hierarchical features of C++.

▶ Abstraction provides the mechanism for defining class objects that will be manipulated by the program. This is done by identifying the key properties of the objects and modeling their behavior with operations.

▶ Access restriction allows you to hide the irrelevant details of the internal structure of an object, and thereby reduce the complexity of the problem.

▶ A hierarchy of abstraction levels can be developed and mapped to the required object classes.

C++ is a language well-suited to object-oriented programming, and this makes it easier to implement object classes and the operations to be performed on the objects. All the mechanisms of object-oriented languages are implemented in C++, including providing protection and access to any class members, the ability to derive one class from another and let it inherit the parent class properties, and redefine operator semantics via overloading.

In the next chapter we will discuss the differences between C and C++ in more detail, and show how C++ makes programming in C++ a lot easier than it is in C!

CHAPTER
2

The Differences Between
C and C++

As we mentioned in the introduction, C++ was developed as an enhancement of C, and as such, inherited C's system of built-in types and operators. Some of C's constructs were enhanced to make C++ more reliable and convenient when used as a procedural language. There are, however, more significant changes that make C++ a new language, and one well suited to object-oriented programming, rather than simply an improved C.

This chapter will concern those C++ features that belong to the category of C improvements and you will cover:

▶ C++ as an enhancement of C

▶ C++ as an object-oriented language

C++ as an Enhancement of C

Tokens

A C++ program consists of one or more files. A token is the smallest unit of text which is meaningful to the compiler. Both C and C++ recognize five kinds of tokens:

> Identifier
>
> Keyword
>
> Literal
>
> Operator
>
> Other separators

Identifiers

An identifier is a sequence of letters and digits of any length (but see foreground box below!). The first character must be a letter. An identifier can also contain an underscore (_). Identifiers can be used for naming objects, classes, class properties and actions to be performed on class objects. It's worth remembering that if you want to have a well-designed program, you should use meaningful identifiers rather than mere sequences of characters. This stops you straining your memory over what is stored in object **tttt** in a weeks time, for example. Besides, using meaningful identifiers saves you from unnecessary commenting and documentation. Clearly, an object identified as **SUM** will probably contain a sum!

> There is actually a length limit to identifiers - all compilers have such limits, but as the limit is normally beyond that which most programmers will ever need, it's not usually something you'll need to worry about unduly!

Keywords

The following table lists all reserved keywords which mustn't be used as normal object names.

C++ Keywords	
asm	new
auto	operator
break	private
case	protected
catch	public
char	register
class	return
const	short
continue	signed
default	sizeof
delete	static
do	struct
double	switch
else	template
enum	this
extern	throw
float	try
for	typedef
friend	union
goto	unsigned
if	virtual
inline	void
int	volatile
long	while

As you might well have noticed, the list of C++ keywords is much longer than that of C. Let's briefly review the purpose of the new keywords:

'New' Keyword	Purpose
class	Lets you create a new abstract data type. The **class** word is used in a similar way to the **struct** keyword.
new and **delete**	These offer dynamic storage allocation and deallocation.
friend	This is used to denote both functions and classes that have access to **private** members of the class.
inline	This is a function specifier, used to define a function which is substituted for the call.
operator	Lets you redefine any built-in operator for the user data type.
private, **protected** and **public**	These specify the level of access to class members.
template	This is used to define a family of classes or functions.
this	This is a pointer to a class object.
try, **throw** and **catch**	These are used to define exception handling.
virtual	This is a function or class specifier in a hierarchy of classes to be redefined.

Comments

Good commenting harms no one, in fact, comments are essential to maintaining code. Future changes are made much easier if good and relevant commenting is present. Both C and C++ allow comments to be placed anywhere in a program with just one restriction: they can never break an expression or a token. There are two kinds of comments in C++.

1 The first one you no doubt know from C. The pair of characters /* starts the comment, and the pair of characters */ terminates it. To

put it another way, any text between the pairs of characters **/*** and ***/** is treated as a comment. These comments can't be nested.

2   The second kind of comments is C++ specific. A comment starts with two slashes (**//**) and extends up to the end of line. In other words, what comes after **//** is treated as a comment.

```
int b; /* Old comment representation,
    extends to more than one line */

int b; // New comment representation,
   // extends to the end of one line
```

In rare cases, character sequences in a C++ program can be interpreted in a different way by C and C++.

For example:

```
b = a //* division by 10*/10;
++a;
```

With the comments stripped away, you can see the statement to be interpreted by C++ as

```
b = a++a;
```

From the point of view of C, the resulting operator will be

```
b = a/10; ++a;
```

From the point of view of C++, the division sign and the first occurrence of the comment-opening pair of characters **/*** are integrated as **//**, while the remainder of the line is recognized as a comment.

Constants

The representation and type of numeric constants in C++ is the same as in the C language:

- **3**   - decimal integer constant
- **03**   - octal integer constant
- **0x3** - hexadecimal integer constant
- **3.0** - floating point constant

Floating point constants in C are always of type **double**. The type used for numeric integer constants depends on constant size. In the above example, all integer constants are of the type **signed int**. In the C language, a type modifier **l** or **L** can be used to change the type of integer constant by default. For example, **3L** represents the constant with the type **signed long**. Two new modifiers have been added to the C++ language: **u** and **U** for integer constants, and **f** and **F** for floating point constants. **U** and **u** modifiers convert the type of integer constant to **unsigned**. **F**, and **f** modifiers convert the type of floating point constant to type **float**. For example:

```
0xFF00ul - is unsigned   long
5.2f - is float
5.2 - is double
```

Declaring Variables

Any object of a C++ program must be explicitly declared before being used. This is the same as with C, where before you can reference an object, you must give it a name, a type (or class), and allocate memory to it. The difference in C++ is that you can declare an object anywhere in the program. With C, declarations must be placed at the beginning of the block. However, it's more natural to declare an object when it's needed, rather than trying to foresee every required object at the beginning of the block. Here is the normal syntax for C++:

```
for (int i = 0; i < MAX; i++)
     string1[i] = string2[i];
```

Basic Types and Modifiers

Both C and C++ share the same basic types: **int**, **float**, **double** and **char**. The same modifiers act on these basic types: **signed**, **unsigned**, **long**, **short**, **const**, **volatile**, **static**, **register** and **extern**.

C++ adds some new modifiers to the following list:

New Modifier	What It Does
public, **public,** and **protected**	These three work in conjunction with classes, and are used to change access rights to class members, to both their data and methods.
friend	Other functions or classes can gain access to the private members of a certain class with this modifier.
inline	This modifier causes the compiled function code to be inserted at the point of call, rather than inserting a call to the function. This is a bit like macro substitution for functions.
virtual	This is a modifier for class methods and is part of the class polymorphic mechanism.

Derived Data Types

Like the C language, C++ lets you derive an infinite number of types. However, these derived types are combined out of basic types and modifiers, and follow the following rules:

Derived Type	Rules for Use
array	An array of objects of a specified type is defined by brackets (**[ ]**).
pointer	A pointer to an object or function of a specified type is denoted by an asterisk (*****).
reference	A reference to an object of a specified type is denoted by the ampersand symbol (**&**).
constant	This is a fixed value of a specified type. It's denoted by the reserved word **const**.
class	A class contains a sequence of various type objects, a set of functions to operate on objects of the class, and specifiers of access restrictions to class members. It's defined by the **class** keyword.

(Continued Over)

Derived Type	Rules for Use
structure	This is a kind of class which, by default, has public access restriction, and has public inheritance. It's defined by the keyword **struct**.
union	This structure allows only one object type to be stored at any one time. It's defined by the **union** keyword.
pointer to class member	This identifies class members. It's defined by the symbols (::)*.

As you can see from the above list, C++ has some new derived types that are not available in C. Let's take a closer look at these new types.

References

A new data type, reference, has been introduced into C++. A reference allows you to define an alternative name for a variable.

The syntax of a reference declaration is as follows:

```
type & identifier1 = identifier2;
```

Actually, this declaration assigns another name *identifier1* to a variable with the name *identifier2*. The reference must always be initialized in the declaration, and its value can't be changed later. For example:

```
int a, b;
int & alt = a;    // alt is a reference to a
alt = b;          // a = b;
alt++;            // a++;
```

Reference declaration resembles a pointer declaration except that the **&** operator is used instead of *****. Using the fragment of code above, if we were to declare a pointer:

```
int * point = &a;
```

then the following conditional expressions will always be true:

```
*point == alt
```

and

```
point == &alt
```

A reference can be treated as a constant pointer that is always dereferenced, and therefore it needs no dereference operation (*) to be performed upon it.

If two or more references are declared in the same declaration, the **&** operator must precede each identifier, as shown in the following code:

```
float & fl1 = f1, & fl2 = f1;
```

The reference declaration doesn't create a copy of the object but only introduces an alternative name for it. Thus, ordinarily the following conditional expression:

```
&alt == &a
```

will always be true.

There are two exceptions to this rule, and they cause a copy of the object to be created in temporary storage by reference declaration:

1   When a reference to a constant is declared. In this case an internal working variable is generated with the value of the given constant and then the reference is initialized with this variable. That is, given this declaration:

```
char & refchar = '\0';
```

the compiler will build the following:

```
char temp = '\0';
char & refchar = temp;
```

This use of a temporary variable increases the safety of your code. This can be shown by considering the following code fragment:

```
char & refchar = '\0';
refchar = '\n';
char ch = '\0';
```

Many compilers optimize the constants and allocate matching constants to a single storage area. If the reference to constant **refchar** didn't use a temporary variable we would change constant **'\0'** by the statement **refchar='\n';** and it wouldn't be possible to use the former constant anywhere else in the program, and the declaration **char ch = '\0';** would result in **ch** being equal to **'\n'**!

2 When a reference is initialized to a variable of different type:

```
unsigned int ui = 20;
int & refi = ui;
```

is interpreted in the following way:

```
unsigned int ui = 20;
int temp = (int) ui;
int & refi = temp;
```

When a copy of the object is created in temporary storage, the compiler usually issues an appropriate warning message.

Declaring Functions

C++ requires that you explicitly declare every function you are going to use. Every declaration of a function must be complete, and must include the types of all parameters and the return value. Unlike C++, C is less severe. Thus, if the C compiler comes across an undeclared function call, it generates its prototype assuming that the function returns an **int**. Also, the C language lets you use the syntax:

```
char  func();
```

without recognizing this as an error when encountering the **func()** call with the arguments. This is due to type checking being performed at call-time.

C++ also tolerates this kind of declaration but treats it as a declaration of function that takes no arguments. Therefore, an error message is issued in response to the call:

```
func (10); // Error
```

Function Scope

In C++, function declarations have the same scope as variables. Thus, if a function has been declared in a block, the declaration will be local to the block. Trying to call the function from outside the block causes the compiler to issue a function prototype omitted message, as you can see from the following coding:

```
#include <stdio.h>
int i = 0x38;
main()
{
  printf("i = %d\n", i);
  {
    char fun(int);
    char c;
    c = fun(i);
    i = i + c;
  }
  (void) fun(i);  // Error: Function fun()
      // must have a prototype
}
char fun (int a)
{
    char rez = (char) a;
    printf("fun( %d) = %c\n", a, rez);
    return rez;
}
```

Passing Arguments to Functions by Reference

In C++ the opportunity to pass arguments to functions by reference has been introduced. It can be used in two situations:

- Passing large structures to the function to avoid copying the argument into the stack.

- Passing the argument to be modified by the function to the function.

In both cases you could use a pointer and pass either a pointer to the structure (in the first case) or a pointer to the argument to be modified (in the second case) to the function. But the use of the pointer involves these additional overheads:

- The given parameter must be dereferenced in the function body.

- In the function call, an argument address rather than the argument itself must be passed.

These inconveniences are removed with the use of reference as a parameter.

Chapter 7 discusses the use of references for passing arguments to a function, and also discusses its usage during operator overloading.

Passing Arguments by Default

Another addition in C++ is the ability to supply default values for one or more parameters in the function declaration. When such a function is called, parameters may be omitted and the default argument is used instead.

The default values are specified in the parameter list of function declaration in the following way:

```
void funct(double m, char ch = '*', int i = 2);
```

It's important to remember that the default arguments must be placed after all the other arguments in the argument list. This is because the arguments of the function call are resolved positionally. The following kinds of calls are acceptable for the **funct** function declared above:

```
funct(2.5, '\', 10);
funct(2.5, '\');
funct(2.5);
```

These calls

```
funct(2.5, 20);
funct(2.5,,20);
```

are illegal. The legal call is:

```
funct(2.5, '*', 20);
```

The default value can be submitted for an argument either in the function declaration or function definition, but must comply with the following rules:

▶ The default value can be defined in only one place: either in the function declaration or function definition.

▶ The default values for a function must be defined and visible (in scope) before a call to the function with an incomplete argument list is made.

The following fragments of program will run in both cases. The first case is where the default argument value is specified in the function declaration.

```
int f(char, double = 3.14);
void f1();

main()
{
    f('*');
    f1();
}

void f1()
{
...
    f('\\');
}

int f(char c, double pi)
{
...
}
```

The second case is where the default argument value is specified in the function definition.

```
int f(char c, double pi = 3.14)
{
...
}

void f1();

main()
{
    f('*');
    f1();
}

void f1()
{
...
    f('\\');
}
```

Note that there is no need to use a parameter name when defining the default values of arguments (see the first of the above cases). But you should be careful when initializing pointer or reference type arguments. For example, in the declaration:

```
void save(char *, char * = "Welcome");
```

a space must be inserted between `*` and `=` characters, otherwise the pair of characters `*=` will be interpreted as a compound operation sign and an error message will be output. The same is true when declaring a reference as a default argument.

Inline Functions

A C++ function can be **inline**. This means that the function call is substituted with the function body. To define such a function, use the **inline** specifier:

```
inline double Sum(double d, double w)
  { return ( d + w); }
```

The syntax of an **inline** function is a normal function definition with all restrictions as to scope and type checking applied. An **inline** function is merely another implementation of the function call. Imagine a chapter of a book which refers the reader to Table 2b, earlier (or later) in the chapter - and then imagine the reference being replaced by the table itself. This is essentially how an inline function works. The function call is replaced by a single instance of the function code. A copy of the function code substitutes the function call. This reduces the control transfer (to/from) overhead, including the costs of register saving/restoration, parameter copy, and so on, making the resulting program faster, but larger.

Rules for Using Inline Functions

When you define and apply **inline** functions, you need to adhere to the following rules:

- You must define and declare an **inline** function concurrently before the first function call.

- It's more reasonable to define only small functions as **inline**, since large functions expand the compiled code and increase compilation times.

> You should bear in mind that the **inline** keyword is only a hint to the compiler that you would prefer the function be inline. It is up to the compiler to make a final decision. The compiler takes into account whether the function is large or small, and what statements form the function body. A function with a loop statement can't be made inline. Moreover, if a function that has been declared **inline** contains recursive calls, only the first call can be expanded inline.

Normally, the compiler issues a warning message for a function declared **inline** whenever it can't be expanded inline.

Overloading Functions

C++ allows the same name to be used for different functions within the same scope.

This feature is very useful when the same actions must be performed on different data types. In a C program, the programmer is forced to invent a unique name for every function and ensure that the appropriate function is called for particular data. Function overloading allows the process to be simplified.

In C++, several functions can be given the same name provided that their signatures differ. A function signature is determined by the number and types of its arguments. Consequently, overloaded functions must differ in the number of arguments or argument types:

```
void swap(int &, int &);
void swap(double &, double &);
void swap(char &, char &);
```

Here are three instances of an overloaded function declared with the same name. Each is to perform the same action, namely, swapping the values of two variables, but manipulating different data type. All three functions could then be implemented as follows:

```
void swap(int & a, int & b)
{
   int temp = a;
   a = b;
   b = temp;
}
```

```
void swap(double & a, double & b)
{
   double temp = a;
   a = b;
   b = temp;
}

void swap(char & a, char & b)
{
   char temp = a;
   a = b;
   b = temp;
}
```

You can now use the **swap()** function without having to worry about the data types involved, or having to remember what they called the different functions. This is particularly useful if this is part of a larger project where several programmers are working on different sections.

Using C Functions in C++ Programs

C++ allows function overloading using a feature called function name encoding (or name mangling). Name mangling ensures complete type checking on all functions, whether or not they are overloaded.

Name mangling is a process of generating a unique name from the given function name and the passed parameters. This is done so that the object file contains unique function names, otherwise the linker will fail. For example, the function **swap(int &, int &)** would be mangled into **swapii(int &, int &)**, and **swap(char &, char &)** into **swapcc(char &, char &)** (these mangled names are not *true* names, as different compilers have different methods of name mangling). The C language compiler doesn't support name mangling. Thus, to link object code with C function calls (that is, functions compiled with a C compiler) you need to tell the compiler that the external function is an unencoded C function.

The Extern Specifier

Therefore, to prevent the compiler from mangling the name of a C function, you must apply the **extern "C"** specifier when declaring a function written in C or in other programming languages. For example:

```
extern "C" void strcpy (char *, const char *);
```

If there are several functions you don't want to be mangled, then you can use braces:

```
extern "C"
{
    void strcpy(char *, const char*);
    int strcmp (const char*, const char*);
}
```

These declarations can be only global.

Declaring Structures, Unions and Enumerations

Unlike C, C++ allows you to use the name of user-defined types without explicit use of the **typedef**. Technically, this is placing the type names together with other names in the same name space. C uses different name spaces for types (as it does for other names). This means that without an explicit **typedef**, C doesn't understand the name as a particular type.

For example, the following C code

```
struct comp
{
...
};
struct comp obj;
```

declares an object named **obj** of the **struct comp** type. Since the names of types and variables are allocated different spaces, you must specify the **struct** keyword for the type name so that the compiler knows where to look for the name.

The common name space gives you, as a C++ programmer, more flexibility when using identifiers.

Thus, for the same type of structure named **comp**, you can declare an object as

```
comp obj;
```

without using the **struct** keyword. An exception is in the case where the type name coincides with the variable name. The **struct** keyword can't be omitted for such objects. Consider the following fragment of a program:

```
struct str
{
   char s[5];
   int n;
};
...
void f()
{
   char *str;      // Local variable str
   struct str String;
...
}
```

In the second block, the local variable **str** overloads the type name **str** (from the structure declared at global level). In this case, the keyword **struct** makes the compiler treat **str** as a type name.

Unnamed Enumerations and Unions

In C++ you can use unnamed enumerations and unions. An unnamed enumeration is an alternative way of defining symbolic constants. For example:

```
enum { FALSE, TRUE };
```

That code defines two symbolic constants **FALSE = 0** and **TRUE = 1**. Both constants have type **int** and can appear wherever constants are required. But symbolic constants defined through enumeration differ from similar constants defined by the keyword **const**, in that the former constants have no storage allocated to them, and therefore, we can't apply the 'address of' operator (**&**) to them.

Unnamed **union**s (also known as anonymous **union**s) are convenient to use when defining variable parts of a structure. There was no such feature in C. For example, the definition of structure **Person** in C may look like this:

```
struct Person
{
   char *name; // Name
   char *address; // Address
   int swh;    // Family status
   union
   {
      char *wife; // Name of wife
      int age; // Age
   } fam;          // Variable name of union type
} men1;
```

and the field **wife** can be accessed in the following way:

```
men1.fam.wife
```

In C++ this structure, and the access to the fields, is made much simpler through the use of unnamed **union**s:

```
struct Person
{
   char *name; // Name
   char *address;   // Address
   int swh;      // Family status
   union
   {
      char *wife; // Name of wife
      int age; // Age
   };          // Variable name of union type
} men1;
```

Now, access to the name of **wife** will be:

```
men1.wife
```

That is, using unnamed **union**s allows one additional level of qualification to be avoided.

Bit Fields in Unions

Another C++ extension enables you to use bit fields as **union** members. In C, bit fields were only allowed in structures. The same restrictions apply to bit fields in **union**s as they do in structures. Namely, it's impossible to get an address of a bit field, declare an array of bit fields, or declare a function that returns a bit field. When using bit fields in **union**s, remember that every such field starts from the beginning of the **union**, and a single field is only available at any one time. For example:

```
union mt
{
   char ox;
   unsigned a : 2;
   int b;
} x1 = {0x3533};
```

As a result, the variable **x1** is allocated 2 bytes of storage and the low order byte is initialized to 33. The expression **x1.a** takes the value of 3.

63

The following figure shows the storage representation of the **union**.

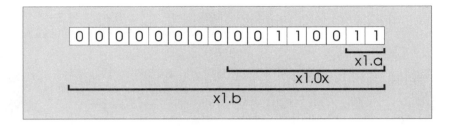

Storage Representation of Union With Bit Fields

> You should take care when using bit fields because they are machine dependent and therefore produce code that isn't portable.

Static Variables in Structures

In C++, unlike C, a structure member can be a **static** variable. In such a case, only one copy of the structure member will be stored for all objects of this type. For example, look at the following code:

```
struct Stock
{
   char type;
   double netto;
   static int count;
};

Stock sk1;
Stock sk2;
```

The memory allocated for every object of **Stock** (**sk1** and **sk2**) will be enough to contain values of **char** and **double** types. A single member **count** of type **int** will be created for all objects of **Stock**. In other words, **count** will contain data which is accessible to all **Stock** objects, and **&sk1.count == &sk2.count** will be true.

A **static** structure member may be accessed in two different ways:

1   Qualifying the structure member by the object name through member selection operator, for example, **sk1.count**.

2   Qualifying the structure member by the structure type name through scope resolution operator, for example, `Stock::count`.

This second route is possible because the `count` member is unique for all objects of `Stock` type.

There is one problem with the fragment of code above, and that is the declaration of `static` for the `count` variable effectively tells the compiler that the variable is external. This then requires you to make a second declaration of the variable, otherwise the linker while give you an error. The declaration is in the same form as any other declaration, except that you must specify that the variable is part of the structure. You can also initialize the variable at the same time. The only limitation is that the declaration must appear in the same scope as the structure declaration. The general form of the declaration is as follows:

```
member_type structure_type_name :: static_member_name [= initiator]
```

Therefore, the correct declaration of a structure containing a `static` member is as follows:

```
struct Stock
{
   char type;
   double netto;
   static int count;
};
int  Stock :: count;
```

If the program using structure type objects with `static` members has been broken into separately compiled files, the declaration of `static` members must be performed only in one of these files.

Dynamic Memory Management

If you have any experience in C programming, you'll be well aware of how often objects have to be created dynamically. Using dynamic memory allocation you can make code more concise and flexible - objects are created whenever you need them, and then deleted when they are no longer needed.

In C, you used the functions `malloc()`, `calloc()`, `realloc()` and `free()` to perform these tasks. However, they are very cumbersome and when used, could easily lead to mistakes. To manipulate dynamic memory in C++, two new operators were introduced:

> **new** operator for memory allocation.

> **delete** operator for memory deallocation.

By using the **new** operator, memory can be allocated for a single object of any type including user-defined types. The result of the operator is the same as for `malloc()`, and will be a pointer to allocated storage, or a null pointer if an error occurs:

```
// Space allocation for a single element of type int
int *ip = new int;

// Space allocation for an array of 20 type str elements
struct str
{
    char name[40];
    int m;
};
str *pstr = new str[20];
```

The difference between `malloc()` and **new** is that **new** returns a types pointer, freeing you from the necessity of casting the pointer returned by `malloc()`.

The storage obtained by the **new** operator will remain allocated until it's explicitly freed by the **delete** operator. As with C, you must free up allocated memory before exiting the program, otherwise the memory will remain allocated, and therefore unusable for any other program. The **delete** operator has the following format:

```
delete pointer;
```

The **delete** operator can free only that storage which has been allocated earlier by the **new** operator. *pointer* is a pointer to the storage being freed.

```
f()
{
    int *first = new int[5];
    int mas[5];
```

```
    delete first;  // Deallocation of storage for 5 elements of type int

    delete mas; // Error: mas had not been allocated by new operator
}
```

A reference to dynamic memory can be defined using the **new** operator. This is its syntax:

```
type & identifier =  *  new type;
```

The dereference operator * must precede the **new** operator, because the result of **new** operator is a pointer, while a reference can be initialized only with a variable; for example:

```
double & number = * new double;
```

To deallocate dynamic storage referred to by the variable **number**, use the **delete** operator in the following way:

```
delete & number;
```

Operator **&** is needed because the operand of the **delete** operator must be a pointer.

Type Conversion

As you know, certain operators convert the value of an operand from one type to another depending on the operand type. To do this the compiler, whether C or C++, uses the same set of type conversion rules. The idea underlying these conversions is that of promoting operands from lower types to higher types before the expression is evaluated. For complex expressions the result is influenced by the order of the evaluation, which in turn depends on the precedence of operators.

In C, a great deal of freedom is allowed in pointer handling. In particular, it is permitted for a pointer to an **int** to be assigned to a pointer to a double, for example:

```
int a = 5, * pa;
double * pd;
pa = & a;
pd = pa;
```

While such program fragments are allowable in C, C++ is more strict in this respect and doesn't permit the mixing of pointers of different type, unless the correct type conversion is used. In addition to the standard C conversions, C++ defines further rules for pointer conversions:

▶ Any constant expression giving zero as a result can be converted to a pointer. Such a pointer is referred to as a null pointer.

▶ Any non-constant pointer can be converted to a pointer to void (**void** *).

▶ A pointer to a function may be converted to a pointer to void (**void** *). Such conversions are only possible when the sizes of the pointers are equal.

In addition to implicit conversions that are automatically performed by the compiler, both C and C++ let you use an explicit type casting operator. Unlike C, the C++ language defines two forms for this operator.

The first form is a standard one that you know from the C language:

```
(type)  expression
```

The second form is a functional one that is defined solely in the C++ language.

```
type  (expression)
```

For example:

```
(double) x;  // Standard form
double (x);  // Functional form
```

Apart from standard conversions, and the type casting operator used for built-in data types, C++ lets you define your own set of conversions for class objects. For example, you can specify conversions from a built-in to a user-defined type and vice versa. You can also define conversions from one user-defined type to another. For this you can use a special member function of the form **operator()** or a constructor function with a single argument. The object conversion from one class to another is discussed in more detail in Chapter 7.

Input / Output

The C++ language offers a new I/O library: **IOSTREAM**. We'll discuss here only its most basic capabilities: output to the screen and input from the keyboard.

To display information on the screen, we use the object named **cout** and the operator **<<**.

For example:

```
cout << "Value";
```

will display Value on the screen, while:

```
cout << x;
```

displays the value of **x**.

The output stream is designed so you can write the two operations as a single statement. In other words, you can concatenate the **<<** operators:

```
cout << "Value"<< x;
```

If you wish to start a new line, then with **cout** you have three options. You can use a string containing the carriage return code, the carriage return character, or the pre-defined variable **endl**. The following three lines are equivalent:

```
cout << "Value" << x << "\n";
cout << "Value" << x << '\n';
cout << "Value" << x << endl;
```

With **cout**, the order of the elements that form the output is more natural than with **printf()**.

Input is accessed with the **cin** object and the **>>** operator. It would be enough to write:

```
cin >> answer;
```

to input data from the keyboard into the variable **answer**. **cin** can handle any variable type which needs input specifiers (as with **scanf()**), making it a lot easier to use:

```
#include <iostream.h>

main()
{
   char text[20];
   int integ;

   cin >> text;
   cin >> integ;
}
```

As with output, you can concatenate several input operators to form a single one:

```
cin >> text >> integ;
```

To use the stream input/output operators, you need to specify the **#include <iostream.h>** in your program. This file declares the objects **cin** and **cout** and defines the overloaded operators **<<** and **>>**. Note that the new input/output library doesn't prevent you from using all the C input/output functions in C++.

C++ as an Object-Oriented Programming Language

All the above can be treated as enhancement of C. There are, however, some fundamentally new features. Let's briefly review them.

Classes

To implement a mechanism for abstract data types, C++ introduces the new concept of **class**. A C++ class resembles a C structure, with the exception that the class can contain not only data but functions to operate on data.

The declaration begins with the **class** keyword. Data and functions defined in a **class** are referred to as data members and function members respectively. All class members are accessed as **private** by default. That is, you can't access a class member outside the class scope. To make a class member accessible, you must define it as **public**. This section of the declaration normally includes function members which can access the members in the **private** section. The class members located in the **public** section can be accessed in a normal way (normal in terms of C): either by the name operator (**.**) or by the pointer operator (**->**).

The type name following the **class** keyword represents the new type introduced by the user. This name can then be used to declare variables (objects) of given type.

The **class** body is enclosed in braces and ends with a semicolon. It contains the declarations or definitions of class members:

```
class myclass
{
    int count;
    char * name = "My name";
public:
    void printname();
    void printcount();
};

mycount object1, object2;    // declares two objects of the class mycount
```

Constructors and Destructors

A further difference between C++ classes and C structures is the technique used for initializing the objects.

There is a special class member function, called a constructor, which initializes objects of a C++ class. Constructors have the same name as the class they belong to. This function can be called explicitly or implicitly to initialize data members during the declaration of an object.

As the member functions are still normal functions but with restricted scope (they may only use elements of their own class), they are subject to all the normal function rules. They may be overloaded - that is, you can declare multiple functions with the same name but different signatures within a class definition. This, too, applies to constructors.

In addition to constructors, there is a special function defined by a class called a destructor. This function name has the same name as the class, but is preceded by a tilde(~).

For example:

```
~myclass() {}
```

A destructor is called automatically whenever an object goes out of scope.

When declaring constructors and destructors, you must apply the following rules:

1 Constructors and destructors don't have return values.

2 Constructors can be overloaded.

3 Destructors have no arguments and hence can't be overloaded.

this Pointer for a Class Member Function

A class member function is a member function which obeys all the rules defined for the function. The only difference between a class member function and an ordinary function is that any class member function receives the implicit **this** pointer as one of its arguments. The **this** pointer is a pointer to the class object by which the function is called.

To show this, the **printname()** function of **myclass** could be implemented in either of two ways - the following is the first way:

```
class myclass
{
   int count;
   char * name = "My name";
public:
   void printname()
   {
      cout << name;
   }
   void printcount();
};
```

This is the other way:

```
class myclass
{
   int count;
   char * name = "My name";
public:
```

```
    void printname()
    {
        cout << this->name;
    }
    void printcount();
};
```

Operator Overloading

Any class can define special class member functions which allow class objects to perform arithmetic operations. These are called operator functions. An operator function has the name **operator op** where **op** is the symbol of the specific operator. In the example used in Chapter 1 we used this mechanism to overload the operators **=**, **<** and **==** of the **Word** class.

```
// Word class definition

class Word {
...
// Assignment one word to another
    Word & operator = (Word &);
// Compare two words
    int operator == (Word &);
    int operator < (Word &);
};
```

Operator overloading is detailed in Chapters 7.

Friend Functions

In a class, you can declare friend functions in addition to member functions by using the **friend** keyword. This allows the specified function access to the class members in the private section. You can declare as a **friend** any global function, any member function of another class, or another class as a whole. For example:

```
class B;    // Forward declarations
class C;

void function()

class A
{
    friend void function();    // Global function is friend of class A
    char function_A();
```

```
};

class B
{
// Member function function_A of class A is friend of class B
   friend char A::function_A();
};

class C
{
   friend class A;    // All member functions of class A are friends of
class C
};
```

You should note, however, that by introducing **friend** functions into a class, you violate a major principle of object-oriented programming, that is, hiding data and accessing data members only via member functions. Therefore, you should avoid using unnecessary **friend** functions in a class. They are very useful in certain cases, but we'll leave that until we discuss it in Chapter 5.

Pointers to Class Members

C++ provides one more data type that is not available in C: a pointer to a class member. This is fairly different to the 'ordinary' pointers you've gotten used to.

Try It Out

Let's look at the following example:

```
class myclass
{
public:
   int count;
   void printcount();
};
```

The class we're considering contains two members: one of type **int**, and the other a **void** function without arguments. With the conventional pointer declaration rule, you must specify the type of data which is to be pointed to. For the class under consideration, you can declare two types of pointers, a pointer to the **int** data item and a pointer to the function. Moreover, both the data item and the function are members of the **myclass** class, and you need to take this into account when declaring a pointer to the class member. To do this you need to use the scope resolution operator (::) to indicate the class:

```
int myclass::*pd;    // Pointer to type int data member of myclass class
```

Now you must initialize the pointer. As an example you can use the following:

```
pd = &myclass::count;    // Address of count data member
```

Also you can declare and set a pointer to the member function `printcount()`:

```
// Pointer to member function printname of myclass class
void (myclass::*fp)() = &myclass::printcount;
```

How It Works

The result of this is that a pointer contains an offset of a member relative to the class origin, rather than the address of the object member. To use this pointer you need to use two new dereference operators `.*` and `->*`.

Operators .* and ->*

Let's look at a short example which will demonstrate the rules for applying the new operators:

```
#include <iostream.h>

class myclass
{
public:
    int count;
    void printcount();
};

void myclass::printcount()
{
    cout << count;
}

void main()
{
    myclass example, *pointer;

    pointer = &example;
```

```
    int myclass::*pd;    // Pointer to type int data member of myclass class
    pd = &myclass::count;    // Address of count data member

// Pointer to member function printname of myclass class
    void (myclass::*fp)() = &myclass::printcount;

    example.*pd = 10;

    (pointer->*fp)();
}
```

As you can see, there must be an object name or a reference to an object on the left-hand side, and a pointer to the class member to be referred to on the right-hand side of the **.*** operator.

```
object_name.*pointer_to_member
```

The left-hand side of **->*** must be a pointer to an object, and the right-hand side must be a pointer to the class member to be dereferenced.

```
pointer_to_object->*pointer_to_member
```

To conclude the section, note that these operators obey all class member access rules.

Scope Resolution Operator ::

We've already used the following syntax:

```
class_name::member_name
```

This syntax uses the operator **::** , the scope resolution operator. For example, the definition of the **printcount()** function is:

```
void myclass::printcount()
{
    cout << count;
}
```

and uses the operator **::** to refer the **printcount()** function to members of the **myclass** class. However:

```
&myclass::count
```

defines that the address of the **myclass** member **count** will be taken.

In this syntax the operator `::` is binary. However, there is also a unary scope resolution operator in C++:

```
:: variable
```

This operator lets you access a global variable even if it's hidden by a local redefinition of the variable:

```
#include <iostream.h>

int count = 1;

void main()
{
    int count = 2;

    cout << count;      //prints the local variable
    cout << ::count;    //prints the global variable
}
```

Inheritance

A program can contain many object types which are able to share common properties. These common properties can be placed into a separate type to be included later in other types. However, this can lead to a duplication of information. Moreover, if one of the properties in the common set differs in any way from what your program requires, you would ordinarily have to either create a new common type, or else not use the common set at all.

C++ solves this problem by inheriting the features of another class, whereby you can add new properties to an inherited class or replace the old properties. A class used to derive a new class is referred to as a base (or parent) class. A new class can both inherit all the properties of the parent class and retain its own properties.

Inheritance is closely related to virtual functions. Virtual functions allow base and derived classes to have different functions with the same name. The choice of which function is actually used isn't made until the program is actually running.

Class derivation, virtual functions, and multiple inheritance will be fully discussed in Chapter 8.

Templates

In addition to inheritance, C++ allows you to define a generic class or function as a template. This lets you construct a family of related classes or functions for a desired data type. An individual class or function is constructed by template instantiation. To a great extent, instantiation resembles a function declaration or call. A function is declared, and its parameter types are substituted by actual arguments in the function call.

To define a generic class or function, the **template** keyword is used. For example, you can use the following syntax to define a class template:

```
template <class T> class Figure
{
...
};
```

The word **Figure** is the name of a class template. The **T** denotes the class template parameter to be substituted with a specific type name when constructing an instance of the class. For example:

```
Figure<Circle>
```

is the name of a specific template class where the **T** parameter is substituted with the name of the other user-defined class **Circle**. You can use this kind of class name anywhere that an ordinary class name can be used.

Similarly, you can define a function template instead of a set of essentially identical functions that differ only in argument type. The specific function is automatically generated by the compiler wherever it encounters a function call, with the required actual arguments using the type of those arguments.

Exception Handling

Exceptions are errors that are generated not by the program, but by the environment in which the program is running. One such example is if you tried to open a file on a floppy disk when there is no disk in the drive. This is an error which most C programs handle by some sort of exiting from the program.

Exception handling provides a cleaner way of handling these sort of errors, (and in the case of a floppy disk, allows recovery from such an error). C++ provides support for exception handling by introducing three new constructs denoted by the keywords **try**, **catch** and **throw**.

The **try** keyword is used to designate a compound statement or a program block where there is the possibility of an exception occuring. With the **try** block defined, the compiler ensures that any 'thrown' exception is caught.

To deal with an exception, we must specify our own exception handler and identify it by the **catch** keyword followed by a list of exceptions to be handled by the handler.

The **throw** construct is used to identify and raise an exception within a **try** block. In effect, throwing an exception means that an object of the exception-defining class is constructed. The exception handler uses a copy of this object to find out the cause of the problem.

The exception handling mechanism will be discussed in Chapter 11.

Summary

In this chapter we have covered most of the differences between the two versions of the language, if only briefly. The C++ language can be assessed from two standpoints: as an improved C and as a new object-oriented programming language.

C++ allows you to define operations to be performed on user-defined types, rather than just involving data as in C. This utilizes operator overloading to allow arithmetic expressions involving these user-defined types.

Function overloading and templates can be used in C++ to implement similar actions on different data types with functions of the same name.

New operators allocate or deallocate memory for class objects and built-in types.

To facilitate passing arguments, C++ offers a new data type: reference. A reference is normally a dereferenced pointer.

A function can be defined **inline**. This lets you reduce the overhead connected with calling functions.

The C++ language provides a class inheritance mechanism that lets you derive new classes without duplicating information. Inheritance is closely related to virtual functions and dynamic binding.

C++ supports exception handling.

In the next chapter we will be taking a closer look at user-defined types, and in particular, classes.

CHAPTER 3

Classes - User-Defined Types

In this chapter, we'll return to a topic previously mentioned, that of classes.

Unlike built-in types, with their predefined operators, classes don't have any operators. Instead, we have to define our own operators to act on these objects. Operators or operations can be expressed by member functions or with overloaded operators (this is similar to built-in types).

In this chapter we will explain in more detail how to build classes and add the required functionality to those classes.

The topics that will be covered are:

- Writing your own data types using classes
- Accessing members of the class instance
- Using arrays
- Writing operators for your classes

Built-in and User-defined Data Types

We can consider C++ to have been derived from the C language (with some minor reservations). As such, C++ inherits its properties from C in the same way as one class can be derived from another. This means that C++ inherits C's system of types, although it has some features of its own.

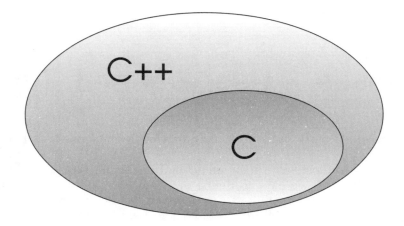

Hierarchical Relation Between C++ and C

A crucially new feature of C++ is its ability to define new data types via a **class** definition. These new types comprise of data and operations. The operations allow the classes to be manipulated as built-in data types. Therefore, there are two categories of data types in C++:

1 Built-in data types from C.

2 User-defined classes.

The built-in data types are divided into fundamental and derived types. The fundamental types have fixed names that are the C++ language keywords. The following figure is a simplified diagram of the different data types available in C++.

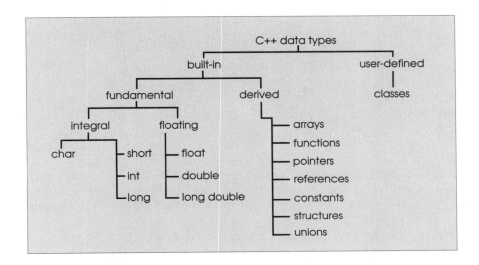

Simplified Diagram of Data Types

For the built-in types, the following predefined operators are provided:

Predefined Operators for Built-in Types

+	–	*	/	%	^	&	|	~
!	=	<	>	+=	–=	*=	/=	%=
^=	&=	|=	<<	>>	<<=	<<=	==
!=	<=	>=	&&	||	++	––	,	–>
()	[]	.	?:	new	delete sizeof

For user-defined class objects, there are also these predefined operators:

Predefined Operators for User-defined Objects

–>*	.*	::	new	delete	sizeof	=	()

As you might have guessed, the list of predefined operators for the user-defined class objects is much shorter than those for the built-in types! This can be easily explained. The compiler can't know every single user-defined type, and therefore it can't know how to add them together. So, if the + operator linking two integer variables denotes the addition of two numbers, the result produced will also be an integer representing the sum of operands.

The problem is that we would still need to know what could denote the addition of, say, two of the **Word** class objects that we defined in Chapter 1. With user-defined types the arithmetic operators are dependent on the implementation of the class, so the compiler can't define these operations for you. Unfortunately, you have to do the work, and define the operators.

Even the pre-defined operators for classes can have problems. Let's go back to adding two **Word**s together. We'll assume that the + operator has been defined to concatenate the second operand to the first, and increment the **wordLen** variable. If you define the following three **Word**s:

```
Word w1 ("Week");
Word w2 ("end");
Word w3 ("ended");
```

then by evaluating

```
w3 = w1 + w2;
```

you will find that for **w3, theWord** points to **Weekend** and **wordLen** equals 7.

Although the = operator, is predefined for class objects (as noted above), it performs only a memberwise copy. We can show this graphically in the figure opposite:

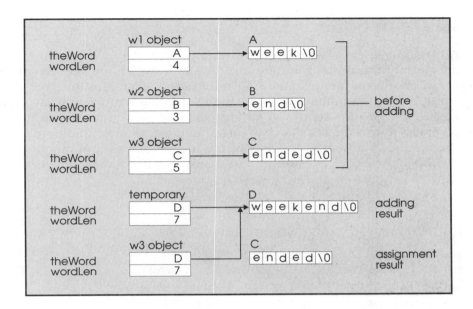

Memberwise Copying Word Objects

Garbage

At first glance, everything seems to be in order: the values of **w3** have changed to the desired values. You might well notice, however, that the initial value of **w3**'s **theWord** remained in memory (although its address is now lost). This causes part of the memory to be lost to the system, because it's assigned, but never removed (and is known as **garbage**).

To avoid this, you'd need to re-define the = operator to perform the equation properly and in a non-memberwise fashion. In other words, for the **Word** member, we would have to de-allocate the old value, then allocate enough space for the new word, then copy the temporary value to this space, rather than change the pointer.

This kind of restriction on the default = operator means you also have to be careful when using it with initialization. However, special functions called constructors can be used for initializing objects of user-defined classes. But, we're getting ahead of ourselves, so let's get back to our class definitions.

Class Definitions

A class is a user-defined type. The concept of a class allows you to implement both abstraction and encapsulation, which are the key concepts of object-oriented programming. These concepts allow you to have classes which match the problem you are trying to solve through it's data and methods. They also allow you to hide the internals from the rest of the program, restricting the external access to those members that are specifically indicated as being available to the programmer. Encapsulation is a bit like being a member of an exclusive country club, where you only know the names of a few of the other members.

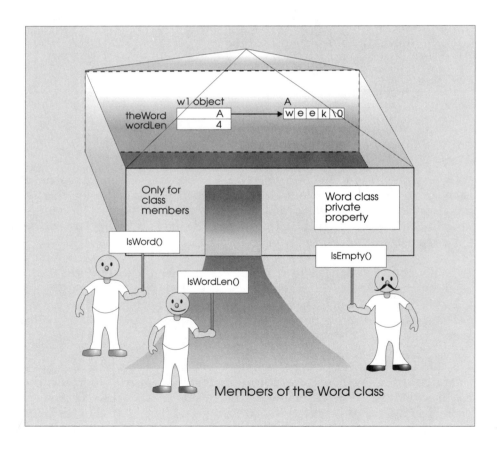

Concept of Access Restriction

A **class** is the building block of an object-oriented C++ program. To be more precise, classes are an extension of the user-defined types of **struct** and **union** that are available in C. In fact, in C++, **struct**s and **union**s are extended to allow functions to be declared as members (unlike in C).

Structures and Unions Vs Classes

The major difference between a structure or union and a class is that the members of a structure or union are public by default, whereas they are private for class. Generally, programmers don't rely on the default access rights of members, but specify the access for all members. This means that the **class** and **struct** keywords are interchangeable in the program (but you don't gain any advantages from doing this, and could lose readability). These extensions to structures and unions to maintain the theme between user-defined types, **struct**s and **union**s have most likely been kept in C++ for the sake of compatibility between C++ and C programs.

> The aim of this book is to take you as a C programmer, and change your procedure-oriented programming habits to object-oriented programming concepts. That's why at this point we won't discuss defining new data types through structures and unions, because you should be familiar with them already. We'll look at classes as a mechanism for defining new object types and we'll treat structures and unions as containers for data only, and even then not that often!

You can use class objects the same way as built-in types, that is, assign values, pass to a function as an argument, or return values. Other operations have to be defined before you can use them to act upon the class.

Let's recall the simplest syntax for class definition:

```
class class_name
{
    class_member_declaration_list
};
```

In Chapters 8 we'll cover more complicated declarations based on inheritance, but for now this will do us.

The *class_member_declaration_list* includes the declarations of data and functions that are members of the class. The members are private by default, which means that the only other members of the class can access the members. To change this we need to use the **public** keyword to define those members which are to be accessed from beyond the class. We can use **private** to emphasize those members which are strictly for internal use. Therefore we can modify our syntax to be as follows:

```
class class_name
{
private:
      private_class_member_declaration_list
public:
      public_class_member_declaration_list
};
```

Let's look again at the definition of the **Word** class from Chapter 1. Using this class as an example, we can demonstrate many properties of classes as data types.

```
// Word class definition

class Word {
   private:
      char * theWord;
      int wordLen;
   public:
// Constructors
      Word();
      Word(char *);
      Word(Word &);
// Destructor
      ~Word();
// Selectors
      char * IsWord();
      int IsWordLen();
      int IsEmpty();
// Assignment one word to another
      Word & operator = (Word &);
// Compare two words
      int operator == (Word &);
      int operator < (Word &);
};
```

In this example, only the data members are **private** while every member function is **public**. We could declare member functions as **private** and data member as **public**, but then although the data is open to us to use, we can't get at the functions at all. Normally, you use public functions to access other members which are private, whether they are data or other functions. In other words, private member functions can only be used by other members functions of the same class.

> Note that making your data members **public** isn't good practice. The idea behind hiding the data is to stop programmers accidentally changing it. Generally, if you need to access the data directly, then use a **struct** instead - remember, you can still have member functions.

Class Object Declaration

You should have realized that by merely defining a class you don't produce an object of that class. Just as the word **int** is used for integers, you have to declare a variable as an integer to get some space from the computer:

```
int a =1;
```

This means that the variable **a** has the properties of being an integer and all the operators that are defined for integers can now be used on it. In the same way, the class definition will allow you to associate the properties of this class object with the class name.

Try It Out

Now, we can declare a variable of this type:

```
#include <iostream.h>
#include <string.h>
#include <ctype.h>

#define MAXSIZE 20
// Word class definition
class Word {
...
};

// Definitions of the Word class member functions
...
```

```
void main()
{
   Word w1;
   cout << w1.IsWord() << '\n';

   Word w2("Week");
   cout << w2.IsWord() << '\n';

   Word w3(w2);
   cout << w3.IsWord() << '\n';

   Word w4 = "Week";
   cout << w4.IsWord() << '\n';

   Word w5 = w2;
   cout << w5.IsWord() << '\n';

   Word w6 = 1;    // Oops, this is an error!
}
```

The first five declarations of instances of **Word** are fine, and result in space being assigned to program for the variables. The final declaration is invalid because we're trying to assign an **int** to a **Word**, and this results in a type mismatch error from the compiler.

How It Works

The first three declarations are all valid because we declared three constructors for the **Word** class:

```
Word();
Word(char*);
Word(Word &);
```

which ensures new instances of **Word** are initialized As you can see, we have overloaded the constructor so that we can initialize an instance of **Word** with different types - in this case, without a parameter, but with a pointer to a null-terminated string or another **Word** instance.

The **Word()** constructor initializes the data members of the instance created to zero, that is, the **theWord** pointer is set to **NULL** and the **wordLen** to zero. This constructor acts when **w1** is declared and results in a blank line being output by the **cout** (**w1.IsWord** returns the pointer to the string, but in this case that pointer is **NULL** and results in nothing being displayed).

```
Word w1;
cout << w1.IsWord() << '\n';
```

The **Word(char*)** constructor comes into play when **w2** is declared. The constructor obtains the length of string **"Week"** and sets the **wordLen** data member to the same length. Then the constructor gets memory for the **"Week"** string using the obtained length plus 1 byte for the terminating null character and copies the **"Week"** string there. **cout** then displays the string on screen.

```
Word w2("Week");
cout << w2.IsWord() << '\n';
```

The **Word(Word &)** constructor acts when **w3** is declared. The constructor sets the values of an object being created to the appropriate values of the **w2** object. Again, **cout** displays Week on screen.

```
Word w3(w2);
cout << w3.IsWord() << '\n';
```

For **w4** and **w5** declared, the **Word(Word&)** and **Word(char*)** constructors are used respectively. And again, the output from the two **cout**s is **Week**.

```
Word w4 = "Week";
cout << w4.IsWord() << '\n';

Word w5 = w2;
cout << w5.IsWord() << '\n';
```

We've dealt here with the two forms of calling the initialization operator: functionally (for **w2** and **w3**) and by operator (with the **=** sign).

Typecasting

With the final declaration, as we have already said, the attempted declaration results in an error. However, it is worth spending a little more time on it. With the line:

```
Word w6 = 1;
```

there is an object of type **Word** on the left and an **int** type constant on the right of the assignment operator. The reason this doesn't work is that we have no constructor that takes an integer. This is basically a cast - the compiler has to be told how to cast from an **int** to a **Word**. To perform the operation, you should use the type casting class member functions. The **Word(char*)** constructor is, in effect, the member function that converts the **char*** type to the **Word** type.

As we have no constructor with an **int** as the parameter, this line results in an error.

Constructors and typecasting constructors in particular will be discussed in more detail in Chapter 6.

Classes and Derived Types

You can create derived types with a new class in the same way as with built-in types. For example, using the **Word** class as we previously defined it, we can create:

▶ An array of class objects:

```
Word words [20];
```

▶ A reference to a class object:

```
Word & wref = w2;
```

▶ A pointer to class object:

```
Word * poin = & w3;
```

▶ A function returning an object or a reference to a class object:

```
Word & f(Word &);
```

▶ Or a structure or union with a class object as its member:

```
struct wstruc
{
    Word w;
    int count;
} cnt;
```

As you can see, once we have declared a class, we can use it just like any of the built-in types.

We'll look at the use of an array of class objects under *Array of Class Objects* later in this chapter.

Public Constructors

By now you have learned that to initialize class objects you can use special member functions called constructors. You should keep in mind, however, that for you to be able to use them when declaring an instance of the class, the constructors should be **public**. If they're not public, your program won't have access to them and so won't be able to use them.

This doesn't mean, however, that you can't then use the class, as the compiler will generate a constructor for you. This happens for all classes that don't have constructors defined. This constructor is very limited, and really only reserves enough memory for the class, in much the same way as built-in data types. It's then up to the programmer to initialize the class instance. But, this is only half of the story. Now we have our class instance, we need to discuss what happens when we no-longer need that instance.

Deleting Class Objects: Destructors

When you declare an instance of a built-in variable, you needn't worry about destroying the instance. The rules applied are just the same that you are used to for C programs. The instance of the built-in type remains in memory until the variable goes out of scope. This obviously occurs when the block of code that the variable was declared in is exited.

The same rules are applied to class instance. However, just as with dynamically declaring built-in data types, if the **new** operator has been used to allocate memory for the object being created in the class constructor, the memory needs to be returned to the system when the instance goes out of scope.

With classes, this can be done by defining a special member function, a destructor, in the class. As we have used the **new** operator in the **Word** class to allocate memory for the string in **Word**'s constructors, we must give this memory back before any instances of the **Word** go out of scope. We do this with the destructor **~Word()**:

```
// Destructor
Word :: ~Word()
{
    if (theWord != NULL)        // Before deletion,
        delete theWord;     // test if the word exists
}
```

Unlike constructors (which can be overloaded), there can be only one destructor. It has neither arguments nor a return value. If a destructor has been defined for a class, the compiler will call it before the instance of the class goes out of scope. Like constructors, if there has not been one declared, then the compiler will automatically generate one for you - but again, don't expect it to do much.

Let's look to see what would happen if there were no destructor to deallocate the memory we have assigned for the instances of the **Word** class. Suppose you declared three objects of the **Word** class in a block:

```
{
    Word w1 ("Week");
    Word w2 ("end");
    Word w3 ("ended");
}
```

The code execution would result in the three objects created in the memory as shown in the figure below.

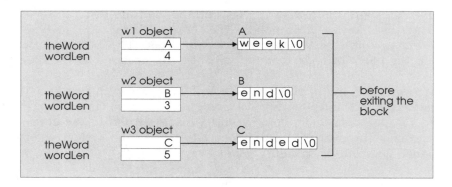

Three Word Objects in Memory

Data items **theWord** and **wordLen** forming the contents of the **Word** class object are the built-in types, **char** and **int**, and are allocated memory automatically by the compiler. However, for the string representing the word, we have to obtain memory by the **new** operator on our own.

On exiting the block, memory occupied by the pointers **theWord** and **wordLen** for all local objects will be automatically released. However, memory obtained by the **new** operator won't be released unless you do it yourself.

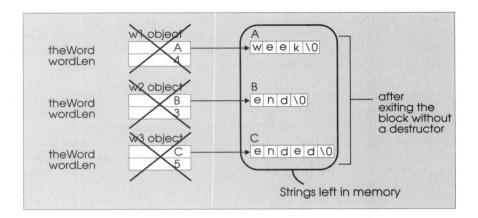

The Result of Not Using a Destructor

Again we are up against the 'garbage' problem, which we need to resolve by coding a destructor with the **delete** operator:

```
// Destructor
Word :: ~Word()
{
   if (theWord != NULL)       // Before deletion,
      delete theWord;   // test if the word exists
}
```

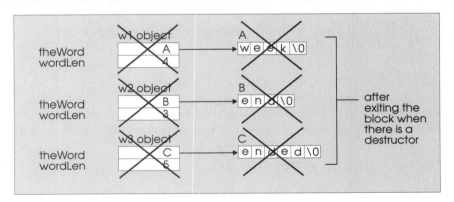

Result of Using a Properly Coded Destructor

Knowing that the destructor is automatically called for local objects on exiting the block, you can instruct it to perform other additional actions if necessary. For instance, a class which handles items stored in a file may write the instance to disk before going out of scope.

The impact of 'garbage' isn't drastic on most modern computer systems, as memory size is fairly large. All the memory used by a program should be released back to the computer when the application terminates - but not every time! You should never rely on the computer to do what you want it to *by itself* - if you dynamically allocate memory, then always release the memory before the program terminates.

Class Data Members and Member Functions

As we have already said, encapsulation is the amalgamation of data and the operations to be performed on that data in a class. The declaration of the class members, both data and functions, has to be done before an instance of the class can be used. There are a couple of points that need to be kept in mind:

1 Data members are declared as ordinary variables except that their explicit initialization is not allowed.

2 Member functions declared in a class specify a set of operations to be performed on the objects of the class. Member functions of a class have the privilege of accessing all members of the class without restriction.

Static Specifier

Every instance of a class has its own copy of data members unless the **static** specifier is used for a class member. In this case, there will be a unique instance of static data which is common to all instances of the class.

Member Selection Operators

Like ordinary structures, class members are accessed via the member selection operators (. or ->). This is also pertinent to a member function - it can only be called when you specify the instance of the class it is called for.

In our example of counting word occurrences in Chapter 1, you can see this in the call of the **IsEmpty** function for instance **w** of the **Word** class:

```
w.IsEmpty()
```

or in the call of the **Add** function and the reference to the data member **root** of object tree in the **WordTree** class.

```
tree->root                 // Reference to data member root by
                           // pointer tree to WordTree class object

tree->Add(w, tree->root)   // Call of member function
                           // Add by pointer tree to
                           // WordTree class object
```

Inside or Outside the Body?

It's possible to define member functions of a class either inside or outside the class body.

In our example, all the definitions of the member functions for the classes **Word**, **TreeNode** and **WordTree** are located outside the class body. When defining a member function outside the class body, you should specify the name of class that the member function belongs to before the name of member function to be defined. The class name is associated with that of the member function by the scope resolution operator **::** as in:

```
Tree Node * WordTree::Add(Word & w, TreeNode * p)
{
...
}
```

Inline Functions

You can also define a member function within the class body. For example, you could have the **Word()** constructor definition placed where it is declared:

```
class Word
{
...
    Word()
    {
        theWord = NULL;
        wordLen  = 0;
    }
};
```

97

These functions are called inline. Just as for ordinary functions that are defined with the keyword **inline**, the compiler includes the code to implement the function at the point of function call, thereby eliminating the function call overhead.

An **inline** function can also be defined outside the class body. To specify the function as inline, you should include the keyword **inline** before the implementation:

```
class Word
{
...
    Word();
};

inline Word :: Word()
{
    theWord = NULL;
    wordLen = 0;
}
```

The keyword **inline** is not specified in the function declaration.

> Use inline functions to define small simple functions, otherwise the gains in using the `inline` keyword tend to be outweighed by the losses.

Private and Public Class Members

To protect the internal data of a class from occasional outside tampering, you should declare it **private**. Taking the **Word** class definition:

```
class Word
{
    int wordLen;
    char * theWord;
...
};
```

the following code fragment would not compile.

```
Word w1;
w1.wordLen = 10;    //Error as this attempts to access a private member
```

Only member functions of a class can refer directly to private data members of the class. When writing the code for a member function, you don't have to qualify which class the member belongs to. Also, unlike when you are access the members externally from the class, you don't specify the instance of the class either (for obvious reasons). This can be seen in the **Word()** function of the class **Word**:

```
Word :: Word()
{
   theWord = NULL;
   wordLen = 0;
}
```

This restriction applies not only to methods that modify the class, but to the member functions that only read the values of private data members. If you need the value of internal data, it is safer to define an appropriate member function called a **selector**, rather than make these data members public. Names selected for these member function normally represent the kind of a request: **IsWord**, **IsEmpty**, and so on, but it is up to you.

Generally, we can divide the operations defined for objects of a class into the following groups:

- Constructors
- Destructor
- Modifiers
- Selectors

You already know what the constructors and destructors as used for.

- Selectors are used to provide access to private data members without modifying their states.

- Modifiers are used to perform operations that alter the values of data members in a class.

The member functions of a class that don't alter the state of an object could be considered safe. To guarantee their safety, we can use the keyword **const** when declaring a member function.

Const Class Members

In C++, the keyword **const** can be used both for declaring a built-in type object and for class objects you define yourself.

As you know already, when you use **const** with a built-in type, once the variable has been initialized, you are unable to change its value. For example, the following line:

```
const char* name = "John";
```

declares the pointer to the constant with the value **"John"**, while:

```
char * const cname = "Bill";
```

declares the constant pointer to a character string.

What is the difference between these two declarations? In the first case, the pointed-at value is constant but the value of the pointer itself can be changed. In the second case, the value of the pointer is constant, that is, it always points to the same byte address and you can never change that address. However, the value pointed to can be changed.

You can also declare a class instances as constant. For example:

```
const Word w1("Week");
```

Member functions of a class which don't modify the object class state can also be declared constant. For example, you can declare constant the member functions **IsWord**, **IsWordLen**, and **IsEmpty** of the **Word** class. To do this, the word **const** is written between the parameter list and the member function body in the function definition. If a member function is defined outside the class body then **const** must be specified in the function declaration as well:

```
class Word
{
...
   char * IsWord() const;
   int IsWordLen() const;
   int IsEmpty() const;
};
```

```
char * Word :: IsWord() const
{
...
}

int IsWordLen() const
{
...
}

int IsEmpty() const
{
...
}
```

This stops the functions from changing the contents of the class.

Handling Class Objects

In C++, a major attraction of using classes is the capability of the language to define classes in the same way as built-in types. This means that you can create the derived types with a class, such as pointers, references, arrays, structures, and unions, or other classes. You can also pass instances of a class as arguments to a function and receive them as a value returned by a function.

When building a class, you usually define a number of operations to manipulate the classes data. These operations are defined as public member functions of the class, and this ensures that the private data is hidden from the programmer.

However, for built-in data types, there are many pre-defined operators: additive, multiplicative, comparative, bitwise, logical, and so on. With C++, you have the option of re-using these operators for the class by overloading the operators. You should take care though - if you do overload an operator, make sure that you do it logically. For instance, don't use a * as a search operator for a string, as it will just make the program confusing.

Redefining Operators

To redefine an operator, you must declare the class member functions using the following syntax:

```
type operator op (argument_type_list);
```

The **op** denotes the operator which can be any legal C++ operator, excluding the following:

.   .*   ::   ?:

The rules governing operator overloading will be discussed in more detail in Chapter 7. For now, note that we have already used the overloading feature for the following operators

=   ==   >

to assign, test for equality to or greater than for the **Word** class of Chapter 1.

Operators **.** and **->** are used to select a class member the same as for a structure or union, and their meanings are the same. If we want to access a member from an instance of the class, we use the **.** operator, placing the instances name (variable) on the left-hand side, and the members name on the right.

For example, in the definition of the member function **operator == ** for the **Word** class we used the operator for selecting the member functions **IsWord()** and **IsWordLen()** of the instance of the **Word** class **w**:

```
// Relation operators
int Word :: operator == (Word & w)
{
    if ((strcmp(theWord, w.IsWord()) == 0) && (wordLen == w.IsWordLen()))
        return 1;
    return 0;
}
```

Pointing

We use the **->** operator when we have a pointer to an instance of a class, and like **.**, the left-hand side is the instance's name, and the right the member name. You can see this from the following code fragment:

```
Word * pointer, w("Weekend");
pointer = &w;

cout << pointer->IsWord();
```

Therefore, to access any public member of a class, whether it's data or a function, you use the same syntax as for structures and unions. In C++, we can declare not only the pointer to an instance of the class, but also a pointer to a class member, as well as a pointer to a pointer to a class member. Before using these pointers, you should initialize them in the same way as ordinary pointers. The syntax for declaring a pointer to a member comes in two forms: the first is for data members, while the second is for member functions:

```
type class_name::*pointer_name;
type (class_name::*pointer_name)();
```

The type should match either the data type or the return type of the function. You can then initialize the pointer in the usual way with the address of operator, but placing the **&** before the *class_name* rather than the member name:

```
pointer_name = &class_name::member_function;
```

Of course, you can combine the two lines into one:

```
type class_name::*pointer_name = &class_name::member_function;
```

To dereference the pointers, use these operators:

Operators to Dereference Pointers

.*   To dereference a pointer to a class member
->*   To dereference a pointer to a class member pointer

These operate in the same way as the **.** and **->** operators, except you are using a pointer to a member, rather than the member directly.

Let's look at how the operators can be used using our old favorite, the **Word** class:

```
#include <iostream.h>
#include <string.h>
#include <ctype.h>
```

```
#define MAXSIZE 20
// Word class definition
class Word
{
...
};

// Definition of Word class member functions
...

int main ()
{
   Word w1("First");          // Word class object

   Word * wpoi = &w1;         // Pointer to Word class

   int (Word:: * pf1) ();     // Pointer to member function of
                              // Word class without arguments
                              // which returns the int value

   pf1 = &Word::IsEmpty;      // Pointer pf1 is initialized to
                              // member function IsEmpty

   cout << (w1.*pf1) () << " is result of IsEmpty call";
   cout << " through .* operator\n";

   pf1 = &Word::IsWordLen;    // Pointer pf1 is set to another
                              // member function (IsWordLen)

   cout << (w1.*pf1) () << " is result of IsWordLen call";
   cout << " through .* operator \n";

// Another example of invoking the same function

   cout << (wpoi->* pf1) () << " is result of IsWordLen call";
   cout << " through ->* operator\n";
   return 0;
}
```

The result of executing the program will be:

```
0 is result of IsEmpty call through .* operator
5 is result of IsWordLen call through .* operator
5 is result of IsWordLen call through ->* operator
```

Implicit Pointer this

Let's look at the definition of **IsWord**, **IsEmpty** and **operator=** functions of the **Word** class:

```
// Get the length of the word
int Word :: IsWordLen()
{
    return wordLen;
}

// Does word is empty
int Word :: IsEmpty()
{
    return (theWord[0] == '\0') ? 1 : 0;
}
```

Although we haven't passed any arguments when we call the functions **IsWordLen** and **IsEmpty**, a result is still obtained. But which instance of the **Word** class is used to obtain the results? Obviously we use a **.** when we call the function to associate the instance to the function. However, how does the function (**IsWordLen** or **IsEmpty** in this case) know which object it is operating on?

Remember, unless we specifically make the function inline, there is only one copy of the function code in the compiled code. In C++, this is implemented through the **this** pointer which is implicitly passed to every member function of a class as one of the function arguments. The **this** pointer points to the class instance for which the member function has been called for. We can explicitly use **this** in the body of the member function, but only in the member function - **this** is an invalid pointer anywhere else in the program. We could therefore rewrite the **IsWordLen()** function to be as follows:

```
// Get the length of the word
int Word :: IsWordLen()
{
    return this->wordLen;
}
```

However, being implied, this would be unnecessary in this case. Let's now look at the body of the **operator=** function for **Word**:

```
// Assignment operator
Word & Word :: operator = (Word & w)
{
   if (this != &w)
   {
      int Len = w.IsWordLen();
      if (theWord != NULL)
         delete theWord;
      theWord = (char *) new char [Len + 1];
      strcpy(theWord, w.IsWord());
      wordLen = Len;
   }
   return * this;
}
```

This function operates on two instances of **Word**, the one pointed to by the implicit **this** pointer, (that is, the instance to which a value is assigned), and the one which is passed as an argument. The return value is the assigned **Word** instances pointed to by this, so we dereference this and pass it back. As you can see, we actually use this twice: the first time we use it to check to see if the programmer has done something such as the following:

```
Word w1("Weekend");
w1 = w1;
```

in which case we don't actually want to do any work, just pass the value back. As you can see, without this, it would be impossible to write a function in this way, as you would have no way of returning the result.

Array of Class Objects

Let's rewrite our word counting program to use an array of **Word**s instead of a **WordTree**. This will allow us to find out whether an object-oriented program is difficult to modify.

Try It Out

This time we'll apply a different approach to problem solving. Having obtained a word from the input text, we assign its value to the first (null) element in the **Word** array. Then we retrieve another word and compare it against the words that have been placed earlier in the array. If the words match, increment the word counter for this array element by 1, otherwise place it in the next element available. When the input text terminates, print out the obtained array. As you might guess, the words will be printed as they appear in the input text rather than in alphabetic order.

In Chapter 1, we used a binary tree which we implemented with the classes **TreeNode** and **WordTree**. These classes are no longer required. Instead, we'll define a new class, called **WordArray**, with two data members, an array of **Word**s and an **int**. The size of the **Word** array we will set using a macro **MAXSIZE** and the integer will contain the current number of words in the array.

We will also need some functions to act upon this data:

Functions Required to Act on an Array

IsFound   To test whether or not the word is in the array.
Add   To place the word in the next array position available.
Print   To print the counting result.
WordArray Use a constructor to set the initial value of the integer to zero.

The definition of **WordArray** class takes the following form:

```
// WordArray class definition
class WordArray
{
private:
   Word words[MAXSIZE];
   int top;
public:
   void Add(Word);
   int IsFound(Word);
   void Print();
   WordArray();
};
```

Since the array has to contain not only the word, but also the counter for the word, we need to alter the **Word** class to contain this counter and give it some methods to gain access to the count. The methods must firstly increment the count, and then return the value of the counter. The new **Word** class is shown on the following page (we've highlighted the changes from the previous version):

```cpp
// Word class definition
class Word
{
private:
   char * theWord;
   int wordLen;
   int count;
public:
   Word();
   Word(char *);
   Word(Word &);
   ~Word();
   char * IsWord();
   int IsWordLen();
   int IsEmpty();
   void Increase()
   {
      count++;
   };
   int IsCount()
   {
      return count;
   };
   ...
}

// Definition of Word class member functions
// Constructors
Word :: Word()
{
   theWord = 0;    // Create dummy word
   wordLen = 0;
   count = 0;
}

Word :: Word(char * s)   // Create word from character string
{
   int Len;
   Len = strlen(s);
   theWord = (char *) new char [Len + 1];
   strcpy(theWord, s);
   wordLen = Len;
   count = 1;
}

Word :: Word(Word & w)   // Create word from word (duplicate word)
{
   wordLen = w.IsWordLen();
   theWord = (char *) new char [wordLen + 1];
   strcpy(theWord, w.IsWord());
   count = 1;
```

```
}
...
// Assignment operator
Word & Word :: operator = (Word & w)
{
   if (this != &w)
   {
      int Len = w.IsWordLen();
      if (theWord != 0)
         delete theWord;
      theWord = (char *) new char [Len + 1];
      strcpy(theWord, w.IsWord());
      wordLen = Len;
      count = w.IsCount();
   }
   return * this;
}
```

The remaining member functions of the **Word** class are appropriate to the changes we are implementing in the program.

How It Works

The figure below shows how **WordArray** uses memory.

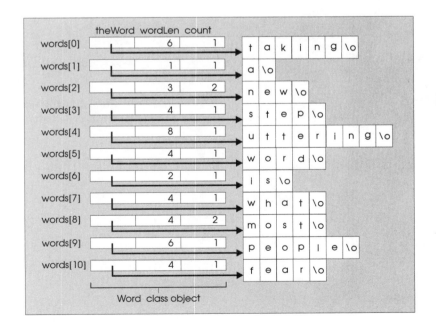

Representation of the WordArray in Memory

Let's define member functions of the **WordArray** class:

```cpp
// Class WordArray member function definition
void WordArray :: Add(Word w)
{
   if (!IsFound(w))
      words[top++] = w;
}

int WordArray :: IsFound(Word w)
{
   for (int i = 0; i < top; i++)
      if (words[i] == w)
      {
         words[i].Increase();
         return 1;
      }
      else
         continue;
   return 0;
}

void WordArray :: Print()
{
   for (int i = 0; i < top; i++)
      cout << words[i].IsWord() << " : " << words[i].IsCount() << '\n';
}

WordArray::WordArray()
{
   top = 0;
}
```

The **GetWord()** function is still applicable as well, and doesn't need any modifications. Also the **main()** function remains almost the same:

```cpp
...
// Our program for word occurrence counting
Word GetWord()
{
   char buf[40];

   cin >> buf;
   Word w = buf;

   return w;
}

int main()
```

```
{
    Word w;
    WordArray warr;
    for ( ; ; )
    {
        w = GetWord();
        if (!w.IsEmpty())
            warr.Add(w);
        else
            break;
    }

// Print word array
    warr.Print();

    return 0;
}
```

> The entire program appears as file **CHAP3_2.CPP** on the disk.

Using the same text as Chapter 1, we would get the following output:

```
taking a new step uttering a new word is what most people fear most^Z
taking : 1
a : 2
new : 2
step : 1
uttering : 1
word : 1
is : 1
what : 1
most : 2
people : 1
fear : 1
```

Let's take a closer look why it was so easy to implement the **Word** array. Notice that there was no need to define the operators **[]**, **=**, and **==** for the elements of the array. The reason is quite simple. Remember that for an array of say **int**s, **array[i]** is the same as ***(array + i)**. In other words, reference to an array element returns a instance of the type of the array. So for our class array, using **words[i]** returns the **Word** pointed to by **words+i**. With this in mind, it should become obvious that the assignment and comparison operators used are that which we have already defined for the class **Word**.

If we hadn't used one of the defined operators for **Word**, such as **>**, then the compiler would have generated an error, which we would have had to solve by either implementing the operator for **Word**, or changing the comparison so as not to use that particular operator.

Overloading Operator Functions

For the built-in basic data types of the language, arithmetic, relational, assignment, and other operators are predefined. However, as you could see from counting the occurrences of words, these operators are useful for the classes that we write ourselves. We don't have to use operators, we could just as easily define normal functions to do the task, but this leads to code which is difficult to read. Remember the functions from **STRING.H**? Instead of having to use **strcat()** with two character arrays, we could use our **Word** class with some modifications to do the same thing using the **+** operator. So if we define the **+=** operator for **Word** we would move from this:

```
strcat(string1,string2);
```

to the following:

```
string1 = string1 + string2;
```

or even this:

```
string1 += string2;
```

You should take some care with overloading the operators for our own classes. For instance, what does the following code fragment do?

```
Word word1("Weekend"), word2("end");
int found = word1 * word2;
```

It is only the fact that the variable is called **found** that would give you a clue to the fact the ***** operator is to search for an occurrence of **word2** in **word1**! The problem is that it's not obvious from the code. So make sure that you re-define the operators in a logical fashion for your classes.

Now, how do we overload the operators? Well, you have seen the syntax already, but to refresh your memory:

```
type operator op (argument_type_list);
```

The **op** denotes the operator which can be any legal C++ operator, excluding the following:

.   .*   ::   ?:

Restrictions When Overloading Operators

There are some restrictions when overloading operators:

- You can't define a new symbol, for example, @ for the operator. This is because the compiler knows neither the priority of the new operator in relation to existing operators, nor the order to evaluate the operands.

- You can't overload an operator for the built-in data types. That is you can't change the meaning of the + operator for integers, for example.

- You can't define an additional operator for the built-in data types, for example, the array adding operator. In this situation, you should define a new class to implement the notion of an array and then define the add operator for the class.

- Overloaded operators keep their original precedence.

- You can't change the operator syntax. Any operator must be overloaded as it has been defined in the language: unary as unary, binary as binary, prefix as prefix, and postfix as postfix.

Rules of Operator Overloading

Thus, you can overload an operator for which at least one argument is an instance, or a reference to an instance of a class. The operator function must be defined as a member function of the class it operates on, or as a friend of the class.

Let's now pay attention to the argument list for operator functions. If we consider the operators we defined for the **Word** class, there is only one argument in the list. However, these operators are binary (that is, they contain two operands) and will be overloaded as binary. What is used then as the second (or to be more precise, the first) operand? As we have already said, as the operator function is a member of the class, when we call the function, the pointer **this** is passed as well. So how does this work with operators? Well, let's consider the following line:

```
w1 == w2;
```

The compiler effectively translates this into:

```
w1.operator==(w2);
```

Now, it's more obvious how the pointer gets passed to the operator function.

It should be noted that if you have overloaded the assignment operator **=** and the addition operator **+** for a class, this doesn't mean that you can use the compound assignment operator **+=** for the objects of the class. You have to specifically overload the **+=** operator before you could use it.

Unary operators obviously don't take any arguments, as the **this** pointer is sufficient for the operator to act on the class, as we shall see later.

Summary

In this chapter we have covered all the basics of writing your own data types using classes. We have shown how to access the members of a class instance, using both the instance and pointers to members of the class instance.

We have shown how to use these new types, in particular how to use them in an array. To demonstrate this, we re-wrote the word counting program from Chapter 1.

We have also shown how to write operators for your classes to allow you to use them in a logical form.

In the next chapter we will have a look at functions which work upon classes.

Functions for Classes

In this chapter we'll continue discussing the topic we introduced in Chapter 1, and which we continued with in Chapter 3, namely class functions or methods. Functions are used to implement the operations you want to be performed on your classes. There are three concepts associated with the use of a function: declaration, definition and call. Functions can communicate by passing information as arguments and return value. In C++, unlike C, function arguments are type-checked, improving the reliability of your programs.

As examples of functions, we'll create classes, and also the code to implement a simple calculator that uses data arranged in a stack. We'll also revisit the functions from the word counting program of Chapter 1.

In this chapter you will cover:

▶ Function basics

▶ Writing a simple calculator program

▶ Using functions of the same name

▶ Passing function arguments by reference

▶ Using default parameter values

Function Basics

Although none of this is going to be new to you, we'll have a look at function definition and calling in C++. We'll use this to introduce the calculator program, simply because, as you will see, it uses both member functions for the classes we need, and also normal C functions.

Calculator Properties

For the simple calculator we'll write in this chapter, you'll need a function to return the priority for an operator. For example, if you want to calculate the value:

123 + 12 * 542

you can't perform addition before multiplication because the priority of operator * is higher than that of sign +.

Using the calculator, we'll perform addition (+), subtraction (-), multiplication (*) and division (/), and properly handle parentheses to change the normal order of precedence. We'll specify the precedence of the operators as follows:

Operator	Priority
(	0
)	1
+	2
-	2
*	3
/	3

What we need is to write a function which returns the priority of the operator. We'll call this function **isPriority** and define it as follows:

```
int isPriority (char c)
{
    int ret;
    if (isOperator(c))
      switch(c)
      {
          case '(': ret = 0; break;
```

```
        case ')': ret = 1; break;
        case '+':
        case '-': ret = 2; break;
        case '*':
        case '/': ret = 3; break;
    }
    else
        exit(ERROR);
    return ret;
}
```

The definition of a function consists of a function header and a function body enclosed in braces. The function header contains the function name **isPriority**, the type of value returned by the function **int** and the list of formal parameters enclosed in parenthesis. In this case, the function has a single parameter **c** of type **char**. If the function has more than one parameter, they are separated by commas.

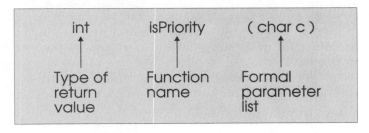

A Function at the Bottom Line

As you can see, the **isPriority** function returns the priority of the character passed to it, if that character is one of the operators. Let's now define the **isOperator** function which we call the **isPriority** function to check if the character is an operator:

```
int isOperator (char c)
{
    return (( c == '+' ||
        c == '-' ||
        c == '*' ||
        c == '/' ||
        c == '(' ||
        c == ')' ) ? 1 : 0);
}
```

Now we'll write a short program using these functions:

```cpp
#include <iostream.h>
#include <stdlib.h>
#define ERROR -1

int isOperator(char c)
{
...
}

int isPriority(char c)
{
...
}

void main()
{
   char a;
   while (cin >> a)
      cout << "Priority of " << a << " is " << isPriority(a) << '\n';
}
```

When executing the program, you can enter any of the operators we stated in the table above, any other character causes the program to terminate. Below is an example of the resulting output:

```
+
Priority of + is 2
-
Priority of - is 2
/
Priority of / is 3
*
Priority of * is 3
0
```

Declaring a Function

As you know, you can place the definitions of **isOperator** and **isPriority** after the **main()** function or in a separate file (but never within other function definitions). In this case, the compiler would have no information about the number and type of parameters and the return value type before you call **isPriority** which would prevent the program from compiling.

To resolve the problem, C++ provides a function declaration (rather than definition) mechanism. The difference between function declaration mechanism (prototyping) and a function definition, is that the former has no function body but provides the information about the number and type of arguments, and the type of value returned by the function.

A function declaration must precede the function call in the program:

```
#include <iostream.h>
#include <stdlib.h>
#define ERROR -1
```

```
int isOperator(char);   // Function declaration
int isPriority(char);   // Function declaration
```

```
int main()
{
...
}

int isOperator(char c)
{
...
}

int isPriority(char c)
{
...
}
```

As you can see from the declaration, the parameter list for the functions contain only the type and not the variable name, as the compiler only has to know the types passed and returned to be able to check the types.

With C it is common practice (though not good practice!) to declare functions with a blank parameter list. This allows the C compiler to accept any number or type of argument(s) even if they are wrong. This leads to all sorts of problems - especially run-time errors.

C++ doesn't allow this. Functions declared with a blank parameter list are just that - functions that don't have any arguments. If, later, the function is used with an argument, this causes a compiler error. Therefore, the following function declaration accepts no parameters and returns nothing:

```
void Increase();
```

This doesn't mean that the function does nothing, as obviously it can act upon global variables. Also, if this function is part of a class, then the function can use other members of the same class, and in fact this is exactly what happens with the **TreeNode** class we defined earlier:

```
void TreeNode :: Increase()
{
    count++;
}
```

A further utility of the forward declaration mechanism (that is, declaring a function before its definition) is that it relieves you of the need to take care of the internal structure of a function. You can program the function body later on, or try more than one implementation. What's really important is to know how you could reference the function, and what value is to be returned by the function.

Arguments and Parameters

The two words, argument and parameter, are interchangeable when talking about functions. However, for the following discussion, we will differentiate between the two. We will use parameter when we talk about the declaration or definition of the function, and argument when discussing the function call.

Generally, the type or number of parameters and the return type used in a function definition must match the declaration. In a function call, the type and number of arguments match those used in the function definition (declaration). Parameters and arguments are matched by position, rather than name and type. That is, the first argument in a function call is associated with the first parameter in the function definition, the second argument is associated with the second parameter, and so on. Matching by position is illustrated in the following figure.

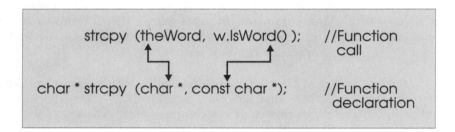

Matching Arguments to Parameters by Position

In a function call, you can use an expression as well as a function call, but the expression type or the return type must match the associated parameter type in the function call.

Strong Typing

C++ is strongly typed, which means that the argument type must match the parameter type in a function definition (declaration). The compiler checks parameters and arguments for type and reports an error if they mismatch.

> For a non-strongly typed programming language, the compiler doesn't check for type, and an invalid argument transfer in a function call might make the program behave abnormally.

Parameters and arguments can differ in certain cases, but the compiler must be able to convert arguments to the proper parameter type through default conversions. The following diagram recaps the default conversions used in C++ (as well as C).

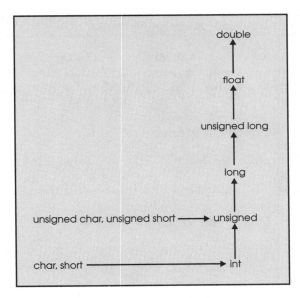

Default Type Conversions

If you need to specify a conversion explicitly, then you have two options. Firstly, you can use the familiar C style conversion, placing the type in parenthesis before the expression:

```
(type) expression
```

With C++, you can use a new functional form, where the value to be converted is enclosed in parentheses and the new type is specified before parentheses:

```
type (expression)
```

These two forms of syntax perform exactly the same job - it's completely up to you which one to use. From the standpoint of programming style, the functional form is more appropriate to C++, but sometimes it can lead to ambiguous code. There are some limitations to type casting, but we'll leave these until later.

Function Calls - What Happens Next?

A function call syntax is as follows:

```
expression (argument_list)
```

where **expression**, when evaluated, produces the function address. In a simple case, the expression is merely a function name. The **argument_list** is a list of actual arguments to be passed to the function. The list can be empty.

Here's how you carry out a function call:

1 Evaluate any expressions in the **argument_list**.

2 Initialize the parameters to the values of their associated arguments. If the argument types mismatch the parameter types, perform default or user-defined conversions.

3 Transfer control to the first statement in the function body.

Note that the sequence that arguments are evaluated in, just like in C, isn't specified, and is implementation-dependent. That's why you should never use expressions that depend on the argument evaluation order in the list of argument. For example, in the fragment:

```
int i = 1;
f(i++, i++);        // Poor programming style
```

function **f()** can be called for different implementations with the argument values (1,2), (2,1) or else (1,1) depending on the order of argument evaluation supported by the implementation.

Calling a Function by Pointer

As we said earlier, the *expression* before the parentheses must be evaluated to the function address. This means that a function can also be called by using a pointer to the function.

For example, the declaration:

```
int (* func_ptr) (int, int);
```

declares the identifier **func_ptr** as a pointer to the function with two parameters of type **int** and returns the value of type **int**. In this case, the function call can be as follows:

```
(* func_ptr) (i, j);
```

Here the address of function pointed to by **func_ptr** is obtained by using the dereference operator (*). Then, the function address is used for calling the function.

> You should never omit parentheses around the *func_ptr or else you'll declare the func_ptr function returning the pointer to int.

To assign a value to a pointer to function, use the function name without any parameter list in the assignment expression. For example, if we have the following declaration:

```
double (* func_ptr) (int, int), power (int, int);
```

we can then initialize **func_ptr** with:

```
func_ptr = power;
```

then the following two calls are equivalent:

```
(* func_ptr) (2, 5);
power (2, 5);
```

You may be wondering what this has to do with class methods, but as you will soon see, and may well have already guessed, functions are a fundamental part of classes. You need to understand ordinary functions well to get to grips with class methods.

Writing a Simple Calculator Program

Let's return to the problem we set ourselves at the beginning of the chapter. As with all problems, we must first state what the problem is.

Stating the Problem

We are going to design a program to perform four arithmetic operations on integers (add, subtract, multiply, and divide) and allow parentheses to be used to change the order of precedence. Thus, the program must be capable of evaluating, for example, the following expression in a valid order:

2 * 5 - 3 / (2 + 6) =

We will use the = operator to indicate to the program that the calculated result must de displayed. We won't bother checking the expression to ensure that it has been entered correctly to simplify the program. Therefore, you should take care when entering the expression that you match parentheses and operands to operators.

Let's look at the expression. The program will get operands and operators one at a time. You can performs multiplication (**2** * **5**) immediately after entering the – operator. You won't be able to perform subtraction until the end of the expression, that is, when the = operator is encountered. Thus you need a place in which to hold:

> The result of multiplication and other intermediate operations.

> Operators (until conditions are right for performing the operation).

For this, you can use data organization such as stack. You can imagine a stack to be much like a canteen plate warmer, where the last plate on the stack is the first one to be removed (we've even drawn you a plate warmer in case you don't know what one looks like!):

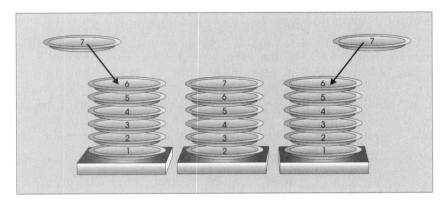

Canteen Plate Warmer!

We'll store the operands and operators from our program in this way. In other words, we will use 'Last In First Out' (LIFO) rather than the more familiar 'First In First Out' (FIFO).

As you may have realized, the operators and the operands that are entered are of different types, so that one stack won't be enough. Instead, we'll use two stacks: one for the operands which will store the integer values entered, and another to store the character type operators. We will actually use classes for these stacks, named **OperandStack** and **OperatorStack**.

To solve the problem, we'll read the next token in the expression and determine its type. If it is a number (that is, an operand), we'll place it on the operand stack.

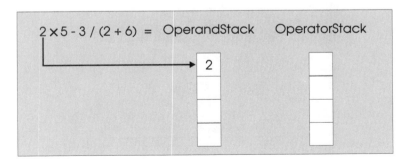

Placing an Operand on the Stack

Getting Your Priorities Right

If it is an operator (including an opening or a closing parenthesis), we determine the priority of the input operator. We have already discussed this function earlier in the chapter.

If the input operator priority is zero, or greater than that of the operator on top of the operator stack, the input operator will be put in the operator stack, because we don't know the priority of the next operator.

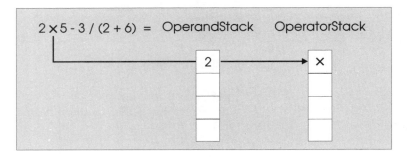

Placing an Operator on the Stack

Otherwise (that is, the input operator priority is lower or equal to the priority of the operator on top of the stack) we'll execute the operator on top of the stack using the two top elements of the operand stack as its operands. The executed operator is popped from the operator stack and the result is pushed to the top of the operand stack.

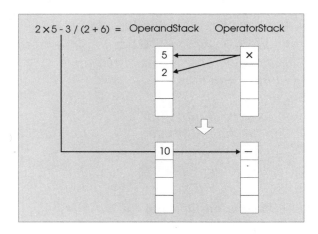

Performing a Calculation

The process is repeated until the input operator priority is greater than that of operator on top of the stack. Then the input operator is placed in the operator stack. Closing parentheses are not entered to the operator stack. When the input operator is a closing parenthesis, the top of stack is checked for a mating opening parenthesis, and, if there is a match, it is merely popped from the stack without any operation being performed.

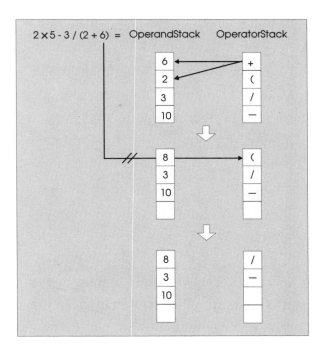

Performing the Parenthesized Calculation

Input tokens are supplied until the = operator occurs. We must then execute the remaining operators to empty the stack. The calculation result will be on the top of the operand stack. If the formula is syntactically valid, there must be no garbage in the stack. The following figure shows how the stacks change while evaluating the formula.

129

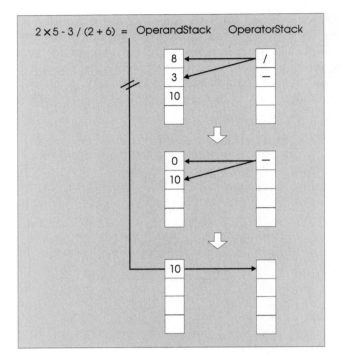

Performing the Remaining Operations

Defining Object Classes for a Simple Calculator Program

Now we must decide what classes we need for the solution to the problem. If we go back over the problem, we find that we use three nouns, a token, and the two stacks. Therefore we can use these as the classes for our program:

```
Token
OperandStack
OperatorStack
```

Now we must decide what is in these classes. If we start with **Token**, we know that the token can be either an operator or an operand. Since these are two different types, then we must separate them within the class. We could use a **union** for this, but as there is no limit on the memory, we'll use two separate members. We also need to know the type. For that we'll have a third member which will tell us the type of token. The **Token** class then has the following characteristics:

- **TokenType** is the type of a token (**NUMBER, OPERATOR, EQUALS**)
- **number** is a numeric operand
- **opsign** is an operation sign

```
class Token
{
public:
    int TokenType;
    long number;
    char opsign;
public:
    Token()
    {
        TokenType = 0;
        number = 0;
        opsign = 0;
    }

    Token & GetToken();
};
```

As you can see, we've added two class methods to our **Token** class: namely, a constructor and a method to obtain a token. The **GetToken()** method not only obtains the token from the keyboard, but determines the type of token by using the **isOperator()** function we used at the start of this chapter. The definition of the method is below, the **#define**, **#include**s and the **isOperator()** declaration are there solely to make sure the fragment compiles:

```
#define MAXLENGTH   20
#include <iostream.h>
#include <ctype.h>
#include <stdlib.h>

enum {NUMBER, OPERATOR, EQUALS};
int isOperator(char);

class Token
{...};

Token & Token :: GetToken()
{
```

```
    char c, s[MAXLENGTH];
    int i = 0;

    while ((c = cin.get()) == ' ');
    if (isdigit(c))
    {
        s[i] = c;
        while (isdigit(c=cin.get()))
            s[++i] = c;
            s[i+1] = '\0';
            number = atol(s);
            TokenType = NUMBER;
            cin.putback(c);
    }
    else if (isOperator(c))
    {
        opsign = c;
        TokenType = OPERATOR;
    }
    else if (c == '=')
    {
        TokenType = EQUALS;
    }
    else
        Err_rep(4);
    return *this;
}
```

There are a couple of lines in the **GetToken** function that you may not recognize:

```
    while ((c = cin.get()) == ' ');
```

and

```
        cin.putback(c);
```

These lines use some of the methods that are defined for the **IOSTREAM**'s input stream **cin**. The first **cin::get()** obtains a single character from the input buffer, while the second **cin::putback()** puts a character back on the input buffer. We need these to sort the numbers from the operators.

Push and Pop

For each stack, we must define a **Push** method that adds an element to the stack and a **Pop** method that removes an element from the stack. If we first consider the **OperandStack** as this is the shorter of the two classes, only

having the **push** and **pop** methods, plus a constructor. Again we have
included several **#define**s and a function declaration to make the fragment
more complete:

```
#define MAXLENGTH  20
#define OKEY    1
#define ERROR -1
#define MAXDEPTH 40
#include <iostream.h>
#include <ctype.h>
#include <stdlib.h>

enum {NUMBER, OPERATOR, EQUALS};
int isOperator(char);
void Err_rep(int errno, char * msgpart = 0, char * opt = 0, int top = 0);

class Token
...
class OperandStack
{
private:
   long stack[MAXDEPTH];
   int top;
public:
   OperandStack();
   int Push(long);
   long Pop();
};

// OperandStack class member function definition
OperandStack :: OperandStack()
{
   top = 0;
   for (int i = 0; i < MAXDEPTH; i++)
      stack[i] = 0L;
}

int OperandStack :: Push(long n)
{
   if (top < MAXDEPTH)
      stack[top++] = n;
   else
      Err_rep(1, "Operand");
   return OKEY;
}

long OperandStack :: Pop()
{
   if (top > 0)
      return stack[--top];
```

```
      else
         Err_rep(2, "Operand");
      return ERROR;
}
```

The **OperatorStack** class object contains an array of operation signs and a counter of elements in the stack (the stack top). As well as **push**, **pop** and a constructor, we'll define the priority compare operation for the input operator and the operator on top of the stack: **isHigherStack** and **isHigherOrEqual**, the **DoAction** operation to perform operator on top of the stack, and the **Clear** operation to perform operators remaining in the stack on termination of formula evaluation:

```
...
int isPriority(char);
...
class OperatorStack
{
private:
   char stack[MAXDEPTH+1];
   int top;
public:
   OperatorStack();
   int Push(char);
   char Pop();
   void Clear(OperandStack &);
   int isHigherStack(char);
   int isHigherOrEqual(char);
   int DoAction(OperandStack &);
};

// OperatorStack class member function definition
OperatorStack :: OperatorStack ()
{
   top = 0;
   stack[top] = '(';
   for (int i = 1; i < MAXDEPTH; i++)
      stack[i] = '\0';
}

int OperatorStack :: Push(char opsign)
{
   if (opsign == ')')
   {
      if (stack[top] == '(')
      {
         Pop();
         return OKEY;
      }
```

```
      else
         Err_rep(4);
   }

   if (top < MAXDEPTH)
      stack[++top] = opsign;
   else
      Err_rep (1,"Operator", stack, top);

   return OKEY;
}

char OperatorStack :: Pop()
{
   if (top > 0)
      return stack[--top];
   else
      Err_rep (2, "Operator");
   return ERROR;
}

int OperatorStack :: isHigherStack(char sign)
{
   return (isPriority (sign) > isPriority (stack[top]) ? 1 : 0);
}

int OperatorStack :: isHigherOrEqual(char sign)
{
   return (isPriority (stack[top]) >= isPriority (sign) ? 1 : 0);
}

int OperatorStack :: DoAction (OperandStack & opd)
{
   long op2;
   switch (stack[top])
   {
      case '+':
         opd.Push(opd.Pop() + opd.Pop());
         break;
      case '*':
         opd.Push(opd.Pop() * opd.Pop());
         break;
      case '-':
         op2 = opd.Pop();
         opd.Push(opd.Pop() - op2);
         break;
      case '/':
         if ((op2 = opd.Pop()) != 0)
            opd.Push(opd.Pop() / op2);
         else
            Err_rep(3);
```

```
          break;
      case '(':
      case ')':
          break;
   }
   Pop();
   return OKEY;
}

void OperatorStack :: Clear(OperandStack & opd)
{
   while (top)
      DoAction (opd);
}
```

Now we are at a stage where we can put together a working program.

Our Simple Calculator Program

Here is our complete calculator program. As before, all the hard work of the program has been done by the classes we use, making the main function small and understandable:

```
#define MAXLENGTH  20
#define ERROR -1
#define OKEY   1
#define MAXDEPTH 40
#include <iostream.h>
#include <ctype.h>
#include <stdlib.h>

enum {NUMBER, OPERATOR, EQUALS};
void Err_rep(int errno, char * msgpart = 0, char * opt = 0, int top = 0);
int isPriority(char);
int isOperator(char);

// Token class definition
class Token
{
...
};

// Token class member function definition
...

class OperandStack
{
...
};
```

```
// OperandStack class member function definition
...

// OperatorStack class definition
class OperatorStack
{
...
};

// OperatorStack class member function definition
...
```

```
// Simple calculator program

int isOperator(char c)
{
    return  (( c == '+' ||
        c == '-' ||
        c == '*' ||
        c == '/' ||
        c == '(' ||
        c == ')' ) ? 1 : 0);
}

int isPriority(char c)
{
    int ret;
    if (isOperator(c))
        switch(c)
        {
            case '(': ret = 0; break;
            case ')': ret = 1; break;
            case '+':
            case '-': ret = 2; break;
            case '*':
            case '/': ret = 3; break;
        }
    else
        return ERROR;
    return ret;
}

void Err_rep(int errno, char * msgpart, char * opt, int top)
{
    char * errmsg[] = {
        " stack overflow ",
        " stack empty ",
        " Divide by zero ",
        " wrong input ",
        " Never to be "
    };
```

```
   if (top)
      opt[top+1] = '\0';

   cout << msgpart;
   cout << errmsg[--errno];
   cout << opt << '\n';
   exit (ERROR);
}

int main()
{
   OperandStack opd;
   OperatorStack opt;
   Token token;

   while (token.GetToken().TokenType != EQUALS)
   {
      switch (token.TokenType)
      {
         case NUMBER:
            opd.Push(token.number);
            break;
         case OPERATOR:
            if (!((isPriority(token.opsign)==0) ||
(opt.isHigherStack(token.opsign))))
               while (opt.isHigherOrEqual(token.opsign))
                  opt.DoAction(opd);
            opt.Push(token.opsign);
            break;
         default:
            Err_rep(5);
            break;
      }
   }
// Clear stacks
   opt.Clear(opd);
   cout << opd.Pop() << '\n';
   return 1;
}
```

Examples of the program output are as follows:

```
2+3*(4+2)-5*(4/2*(6+3*5)+8)/50=
15

((15-5)/(1+4)+10)=
12

15*21-125/(20+5)=
310
```

Using Functions of the Same Name

You may have noticed that we defined two functions with the same name in each of the two classes **OperandStack** and **OperatorStack**:

- ▶ **Push** - for adding an element to a stack
- ▶ **Pop** - for removing an element from a stack.

In the **OperandStack**, we declared the functions as:

```
int Push(long);
long Pop();
```

and in the **OperatorStack**, we used:

```
int Push(char);
char Pop();
```

Using the same names for denoting similar operations on different classes is very convenient. But, what will the compiler do to select the right class function that you want to refer to?

Let's look at the **main()** function text. We need to specify which instance of the classes we want to call. We do this by placing the class instance name before the function name in the call, separating the two with a period. This is either **opd** for the **OperandStack** class object or **opt** for the **OperatorStack** class object as in:

```
opd.push(number);
opd.pop();
```

```
opt.push(c);
opt.pop();
```

This is not polymorphism, as the classes are not related, nor is it function overloading as the functions are distinguished by the class they belong to. It is simply a convenient way of using function names with classes. It is no different than having two **struct**s where both contain the same variable names. It is the instance of the object that tells the compiler which member is being talked about.

Passing Function Arguments by Reference

There is more than one way of passing arguments to a function. You will be familiar with passing by value, where a copy of the argument's value is passed, or by pointer where you pass a pointer to the argument. C++ allows a third option, using references. This way allows you to obtain the same result as with passing arguments by pointer but without having to dereference the pointer in the function body.

As you remember, we discussed how to declare a reference in Chapter 2. Let's have a quick recap of how to declare a reference:

```
char token  = '+';
char & sign = token;
```

Once you have initialized value of a reference, unlike a pointer you can't modify the address to which the reference is pointing. By assigning new values to a reference, you can modify the referenced memory location rather than its address. A reference is very much like an alternative name for a variable.

> The great thing about references is that there is no need to dereference them to use the value of the variable. This makes them ideal when using functions.

The Swap() Function

A good example of demonstrating the different ways of passing arguments to a function is a **swap** function which interchanges the value of arguments. The first example is invalid (passing arguments by value), since the function doesn't do its job. In the second and third examples, the function performs the job by using different ways of passing arguments (by value via pointer and by reference).

```
void swap (int a, int b)
{
   int temp = a;
   a = b;
   b = temp;
}
```

As you will probably know, this function would swap the values of the variables **a** and **b**. However, as these are local to the function, the function would actually fail in its required task. You know that you can correct this by using pointers:

```
// Program for illustration of call by value (with pointers)

#include <iostream.h>

void swap (int * a, int * b)
{
    int temp = *a;
    *a = *b;
    *b = temp;
}

void main()
{
    int x = 5, y = 7;
    swap (&x, &y);
    cout << x << " " << y << '\n';
}
```

The output would be:

7 5

The values of arguments are swapped. The only problem is that you need to use the address of operator **&** in the function call, and to deference the pointers in the function. It would be easy to forget to use either of these - hands up how many of you forget to use **&** when using **scanf()**?

With references, this is no longer a problem:

```
#include <iostream.h>

void swap (int & a, int & b)
{
    int temp = a;
    a = b;
    b = temp;
}

void main()
{
    int x = 5, y = 7;
    swap (x, y);
    cout << x << " " << y << '\n';
}
```

The output is:

```
7 5
```

The values of arguments are again swapped.

Reference Advantages and Disadvantages

The advantage of using a reference is that the function is easier to write, allowing you to alter **x** and **y** in this case from within the **swap()** function simply using **a** and **b**. The function call is simpler too - you don't have to remember to use **&**.

Strange though it may seem, the first disadvantage is that you might get unwanted side-effects. With C you would expect that a function call like **swap(x,y)** wouldn't swap the values of **x** and **y** as this is using call by value, while if you want to swap the values you would use **swap(&x,&y)**. Now with references **swap(x,y)** could be either passing by reference or by value. Obviously, if you have written the function yourself, then you will know what the result is, but if the function is part of a library of which you don't have the source, then the result could be quite unexpected.

> To put it in a more technical way, references violate data security!

The second disadvantage manifests itself when the argument type is not identical to the formal parameter type in a function call. In this case, the compiler will convert the type by creating an intermediate variable. You can see this from the following example of the **swap** function:

```cpp
#include <iostream.h>

void swap(int & a, int & b)
{
   int temp = a;
   a = b;
   b = temp;
}

void main ()
{
   int x = 5;
   unsigned int z = 7;
   swap (x, z);
   cout << x << " " << z << '\n';
}
```

When the **swap (x, z)** function is called, the following type conversion is performed for **z**:

```
int tempo = (int) z;
int & b = tempo;
```

The execution of **swap(x, z)** results in interchanging the position of the values of argument **x** and temporary variable **tempo**. The temporary variable is local to the **swap** function body and will be removed on exit from the function while the value of **z** remains the same. Execution results in the following being output:

```
7  7
```

This kind of error is difficult to trace. However, some compilers are kind to us and will issue a warning whenever a temporary variable is produced. So if a function which uses a reference returns unexpected answers, an obvious place to start debugging is with the warnings, or by checking the variable types used in the call.

Returning a Reference

You have seen how a reference can be used as a parameter type for a function. This is not its only use. You can specify the return type of a function to be a reference. Normally the returned value of a function is an R-value, that is, it can be used as the value to be assigned to another variable, or as part of an expression. If a function returns a reference, then the returned value is an L-value, and as such the function call can appear as a left-hand operand in an assignment statement.

Let's examine the following program:

```
#include <iostream.h>

char & blank(char *);
char * message = "C++ language";

void main ()
{
    cout << message << '\n';
    blank(message) = '\t';
    cout << message << '\n';
}
```

```
char & blank(char * s)
{
   for (int i = 0; (s[i] != ' ') && (s[i] != '\0'); i++);
   return s[i];
}
```

As you can see, we have defined the blank function to return a character reference:

```
char & blank(char *);
```

The function body finds the first occurrence of a space and returns a reference to this using

```
return s[i];
```

Therefore, the function call **blank(message)** is equivalent to using **s[i]** instead. However, the variable **s** is local to the function, but happens to be a pointer back to the original string. So, the line:

```
blank(message) = '\t';
```

is the same as writing (if message = "C++ language"):

```
message[3] = '\t';
```

The output from the program is as follows:

```
C++ language
C++        language
```

> When defining functions to return a pointer or reference, you should keep in mind the following rule:
>
> You should never return a pointer or a reference to a local variable.

For example:

```
int & func()
{
   int loc;
...
   return loc; // Error: local variable name can not be returned
}
```

The reason for this caveat is that space allocated to the variable is cleared when the function is exited, so the reference or pointer will be referring to a nonexistent variable. Therefore, you should always return a pointer or reference to a passed argument (if that argument was passed by pointer or reference). Therefore the following is incorrect:

```
int & func(int arg)
{
   return arg;
}
```

while the following two are correct:

```
int & func(int *arg)
{
   return *arg;
}
```

```
int & func(int & arg)
{
   return arg;
}
```

Using Default Parameter Values

Let's look at the definition of **Err_rep** function in the simple calculator program.

```
void Err_rep(int errno, char * msgpart, char * opt, int top)
{
   char * errmsg[] = {
      " stack overflow ",
      " stack empty ",
      " Divide by zero ",
      " wrong input ",
      " Never to be "
   };

   if (top)
      opt[top+1] = '\0';

   cout << msgpart;
   cout << errmsg[--errno];
   cout << opt << '\n';
   exit (ERROR);
}
```

The `Err_rep` function is used to generate error messages caused by conditions which come about by the entered expression. For example, for an entered character other than digits or the operators +, −, /, *, (,   ), and =, the wrong input message will be issued. If the number of operators is greater than that of operands specified, the Operand stack empty message will be issued. If the number of elements put in the stack exceeds that specified by **MAXDEPTH**, the stack overflow message will be issued. Below are examples of messages produced by the simple calculator program:

```
2+3*(4+2)-%*(4/2*(6+3*5)+8)/50=
wrong input

12 +(=
Operand stack empty

2+(3*(4+2))=
Operator stack overflow (+(*
```

> Note that to obtain the last message, you should specify the value of **3** in the **#define MAXDEPTH** directive in order to decrease the depth of the stack.

You may have noticed that the error message strings set in the function are not complete. The complete message is generated from the other arguments passed to the function.

The first parameter is an integer representing the message number, the second parameter specifies what stack (operand or operator) the error occurred with, if any. The third parameter passes the pointer to operator stack, and the fourth parameter passes the pointer to top of the stack. The message is then generated using this information.

Thus, to generate the last message, we would use the line:

```
Err_rep (1, "Operator", stack, top);
```

But, to generate the first, we have two options:

```
Err_rep (4, NULL, NULL, 0);
```

or just simply:

```
Err_rep(4);
```

You may well wonder how this final call is possible? Up to this point we have said that the number and types of arguments in a function call must match the number and types of parameters in a function definition. Let's look at the declaration of **Err_rep** at the beginning of the program:

```
void Err_rep (int errno, char * msgpart = 0, char * opt = 0, int top = 0);
```

As you can see, the second, third, and fourth parameters are assigned initial values of zero. These values are referred to as argument default values. This means that for those parameters, if values are missing from the argument list of the function call, then the default value is used instead. The default argument values can be specified either in a function declaration (as in our example), or in a function definition. But, this must occur before the function call is used, otherwise the compiler will report an error.

When specifying default values, you must do so from the last parameter and work forwards. In other words, the following declaration is invalid:

```
void Err_rep (int errno, char * msgpart = 0, char * opt = 0, int top);
```

A similar rule applies when calling the function: you can only omit trailing arguments, and leading arguments that don't have default values must be specified in the call. Therefore, all the following calls are incorrect:

```
Err_rep();
Err_rep(1,3);
Err_rep(1,"Operator",3);
```

There is another rule of default argument definition. Since there can be more than one declaration of a function, every subsequent declaration can add default values for the preceding arguments, but can't redefine the earlier specified default argument value in the declaration. This facility is very useful when calling a function repeatedly with particular arguments, and only occasionally using different values. It is also useful in stopping errors caused by not passing enough arguments to library functions.

Summary

We have covered a lot of ground in this chapter! We covered the basics of functions, recapping on the capabilities of C.

We then went on to develop a small calculator program which uses both normal C functions and also class functions or methods. We used a couple of stacks in which to store the mathematical expression, and also implemented precedence of the operators, including parentheses.

We also discussed using references to pass arguments to and from functions. We also looked at the useful feature of declaring default values for function parameters.

In the next chapter we will discuss the access rights to class members in more detail.

CHAPTER 5

Accessing Classes

In object-oriented programming, the concept of access restriction (encapsulation) requires that the internal data of a class be protected against any occasional outside effect. This simplifies writing programs by relieving the programmer from having to know about the internal workings of the class he or she is using. On the other hand, the behavior of a class is determined by the members that are visible to you as a programmer. In each specific case, you need to find a tradeoff between granting or restricting access to the contents of the classes.

This chapter discusses encapsulation and access rights to the members of the class.

In this chapter we will cover:

- Program structure
- Friend functions
- The lifetime of objects
- Dynamic memory allocation and deallocation

Program Structure

Arrangement of Class Definitions

You've already met fully-developed object-oriented programs when we discussed the word occurrence counting program from Chapter 1 and the simple calculator program from Chapter 4.

Let's look more closely at the structure of one of these programs. The figure below is a representation of the word counting program:

Word Class	declaration
	method definition
TreeNode Class	declaration
	method definition
WordTree Class	declaration
	method definition
GetWord	definition
Main Definition	

Program Structure

This arrangement of classes **Word**, **TreeNode**, and **WordTree** is no mere chance, as the **TreeNode** class uses the **Word** class as a data member. Accordingly, you should declare **Word** as a class name earlier than you normally would when using it to specify an instance of that type. As the **WordTree** class uses the **TreeNode** class, the **TreeNode** definition precedes that of the **WordTree**.

Any name introduced to denote a function, type, class member or other element can be used in the program after it has been declared. That is why the place of declaration is very important, since the scope can differ depending on where it has been placed in the program. The scope of a name is that part of the program in which you can use the name to access an element.

Local Scope

A block is a compound statement or a list of statements enclosed in braces. Any function body is a block. In the function body, any list of statements enclosed in braces is also a block.

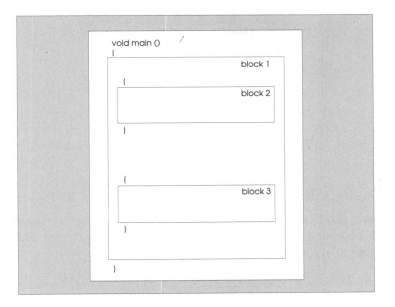

Blocks of Code

A name declared within a block is visible within that block (including all the blocks that are nested). Therefore, if we declare a variable **var1** in block 1, then that variable can be used in blocks 2 and 3 as well - unless, of course, we declare a variable **var1** in either of the blocks 2 or 3. In this case, the new declaration hides the variable from block 1.

Global Scope

Those names that have global scope are declared outside of any block. The scope of the name runs from where it's declared until the end of the program. Local names can hide a global name, but if required, the scope resolution operator `::` can be used to access the hidden name. For example, look at the following:

```cpp
#include <iostream.h>

int var1 = 1;

void main()
{
    int var1 = 2;
    cout << ::var1 << endl << var1;
}
```

The output from this is:

```
1
2
```

because the `::` overrides the local name, exposing the global name for our use.

Access to Private and Public Class Members

There is a third option when it comes to the visibility of names, and it is to do with classes. Private members of a class are local to the class, while public members have the same scope as the class itself.

For example, look at the definition of functions **Pop** or **Push** of the **OperandStack** class from the calculator program:

```cpp
// OperandStack class definition
class OperandStack
{
private:
    long stack[MAXDEPTH];
    int top;
public:
    OperandStack();
    int Push(long);
    long Pop();
};
```

```
int OperandStack :: Push(long n)
{
   if (top < MAXDEPTH)
      stack[top++] = n;
   else
      Err_rep(1, "Operand");
   return OKEY;
}

long OperandStack :: Pop()
{
   if (top > 0)
      return stack[--top];
   else
      Err_rep(2, "Operand");
   return ERROR;
}
```

You can use the names of the private data members **stack** and **top** without difficulty. Private members of a class are just that, private to the class, and can only be used within methods of that class. Members are by default private, but generally, the keyword **private** is used to emphasize this.

The only members of a class which are accessible have to be declared as public. The scope of these members are then bound by the scope of the instance of the class - that is, from where the instance is declared until the end of the program or block (just as with other types).

Methods of Accessing Public Members

There are various ways to access the public members of an instance, depending on how that instance is declared. As we have discussed before, you can use either **.**, **->**, ***.** or ***->** .

You may have noticed that we have used the scope resolution operator again - this time in the binary form to link the method definition to the class.

There may be times when a name hides the class name in a block. This can be remedied by using the keyword **class** when you need to declare an instance of the class. For example,

```
#include <iostream.h>

class Word
{
...
```

```
        }
```

```
void main()
{
    int Word = 12;   // Word is variable of int
    class Word w = "Word class object";
    cout << Word << '\n';
    cout << w.IsWord() << '\n';
}
```

The program produces the following:

```
12
Word class object
```

By qualifying that the second occurrence of the **Word** is the class, the compiler generates an instance of that class. Without **class**, several errors would occur at compilation. For example, our compiler generates the following:

```
testscop.cpp(4) : error C2146: syntax error : missing ';' before identifier
'w'
testscop.cpp(4) : error C2065: 'w' : undeclared identifier
testscop.cpp(4) : error C2446: '=' : no conversion from 'char [18]'to'int '
```

Nested Classes

In our examples, we placed the definitions of classes at a global level, that is, before all other functions. That is why their names have the global scope and you can freely use them for declaring objects of these classes.

However, the definition of one class can locate within that of another class. This new class definition is referred to as nested class definition. The name of nested class is local to its enclosing class, and is in the scope of the enclosing class.

Member functions of the nested class have no special rights of access to the enclosing class members, and obey the ordinary access rules. The reverse is also true, that is, the enclosing class member functions have no special rights of access to these of the nested class, and obey the ordinary access rules.

For example, look at the following definition:

```
// Word class definition
class Word
{
private:
   int wordLen;
   class String
   {
   private:
      char theString[20];
   public:
      setString(char * s)
      {
      ...
      }
   };
public:
   Word(char * w)
   {
      setString(w);
   };
};
```

Unfortunately, this code wouldn't work, mainly because the function call in the **Word** constructor is calling a class member, and there is no instance of the class to work with. Remember, a class definition is just defining a user type, not an instance of that type. Therefore, we would have to change the constructor:

```
// Word class definition
class Word
{
private:
   int wordLen;
   class String
   {
   private:
      char theString[20];
   public:
      setString(char * s)
      {
      ...
      }
   };
public:
   Word(char * w)
   {
      String s;
      s.setString(w);
   };
};
```

This *would* work, and *would* compile. However, the rules of scope come into play, and the instance of the **String** class is only valid during the block it is contained in (that is, the constructor). The instance would be destroyed as soon as the execution passes from the constructor. The only way to make this work is to make an instance of the class as part of the **Word** class:

```
// Word class definition
class Word
{
private:
   int wordLen;
   class String
   {
   private:
      char theString[20];
   public:
      setString(char * s)
      {
      ...
      }
   };
   String s;
public:
   Word(char * w)
   {
      s.setString(w);
   };
};
```

To access the private members of the nested class, you must define public methods, and then if the instance of the class is private, you must define further members of the enclosing class to access the public methods of the nested class. Therefore, based on the following definition:

```
class Enclosing
{
   class Nested
   {
   };

private: Nested N1;
public: Nested N2;
};

Enclosing E1;
```

to access **N1**, you need to specify some public members of **Enclosing**. To access **N2**, you can either use the public members of **Enclosing** as with **N1**, or use a more direct notation, as in the following:

```
E1.N2.public_members
```

In either case, you only get access to the public members of **Nested**, and therefore you need to write public functions to access the private members.

Nested Classes and Public Members

Within the nested class, you can use the public members of the enclosing class, but only by either passing a pointer or a reference to an instance of the enclosing class to the member of the nested class that is going to use enclosing class member. Here is a final example that illustrates this:

```cpp
#include <string.h>
#include <iostream.h>

// Word class definition
class Word
{
private:
    int wordLen;
public:
    class String
    {
    private:
        char theString[20];
public:
    Word(char * w)
    {
        s.setString(*this, w);
    };

    void showWord()
    {
        s.showString();
    }

    void setLenth(int len)
    {
        wordLen = len;
    }

    void printLen()
    {
        cout << wordLen << endl;
    }
    public:
```

```
        void setString(Word & tw, char * s)
        {
           strcpy(theString, s);
           tw.setLenth(strlen(s));
        }

        void showString()
        {
           cout << theString << endl;
        }
     };
     String s;
};

void main()
{
   Word w("astring");
   w.showWord();
   w.s.showString();
   w.printLen();
   w.setLenth(10);
   w.printLen();
}
```

The output from the program is as follows:

```
astring
astring
7
10
```

It would be fairly difficult to find a reason to use nested classes in real practice.

Local Classes

A class can be defined within a function definition. This class is referred to as local. The name of local class is local to its enclosing scope.

A function with the local class has no special right of access to class members and obey the ordinary access rules. There are a couple rules that are special to local classes:

1   Member functions of a local class must be defined within the class definition.

2   A local class can have no static data members.

Here is an example of local class definition:

```
void function()
{
    class Local
    {
    private:
      int i;
    public:
      Local() { i = 0; };
      Local (int y) { i = y; };
    };

    Local occurrence(273);
}

Local wrong;   // Illegal: Local class name now out of the scope
```

Friend Functions and Classes as a Bridge Between Classes

Let's have another close look at the **DoAction** function of the simple calculator program. This function is a member function of the **OperatorStack** class and therefore it can access the private data members of its own class. Think about the objective of the **DoAction** function: it performs an operation based upon which operator is on top of the operator stack using the top two operands on the operand stack. In other words, it needs access to the data member of another class, the **OperandStack**. In this case, we solved the problem of accessing members of another class by passing the **opd** object of **OperandStack** class as an argument of the **DoAction** function.

```
int OperatorStack :: DoAction (OperandStack & opd)
{
...
}
```

In C++, however, there is another way of relating different classes, that of declaring a function or a class the friend of another class.

Class Mates: The Friend Keyword

To declare a function the friend of a class, you should use the **friend** keyword in the function declaration which is within the class declaration. Before we demonstrate this with an example of the **DoAction** function, we'll remind you about one more property of member functions in a class. Every member function of a class always has one implicit parameter passed: the pointer **this** to the instance of the class. That's why in the definition of **DoAction** function (which is the member function of the **OperatorStack** class) you can refer to the data members **stack** and **top** of the current instance. If a function operates on instances of two independent classes, it should be one of the following:

▶ A member function of one of the classes, and a friend in the other.

▶ A global function that is declared a friend in both classes.

Global Friend Function

Let's consider the case of a global function:

```
class OperatorStack
{
...
    friend int DoAction(OperatorStack &, OperandStack &);
}

class OperandStack
{
...
    friend int DoAction(OperatorStack &, OperandStack &);
}

int DoAction (OperatorStack & opt, OperandStack & opd)
{
...
}
```

If a function has been declared a friend within a class, it's granted access to the class's private members. Being the friend of the **OperatorStack** and the **OperandStack** classes, our **DoAction** function can access the private data of both classes. However, the **DoAction** function has no implicit arguments now as it's no longer a member function of any class. You should explicitly pass pointers, or (as above) references to the instances of both classes. Then the class definition for the **DoAction** global function takes the following form:

```
int DoAction (OperatorStack & opt, OperandStack & opd)
{
    long op2;
    switch (opt.stack[opt.top])
    {
...
    }
    opt.Pop();
    return OKEY;
}
```

Now, when we use the **DoAction** function we must pass the two stacks that the function requires to perform the allotted task:

```
int main()
{
    OperandStack opd;
    OperatorStack opt;
...
    DoAction(opt, opd);
}
```

However, there is one problem we have overlooked. The **Clear** method of the **OperatorStack** function calls the **DoAction** function, so the original call **DoAction(opd);** is no longer valid. There are two possible ways to overcome this problem:

1   We could move the **Clear** function from the class definition, and as it uses the **top** member of the **OperatorStack** class, also making it a friend of that class.

2   This is the more elegant way. Leave the **Clear** function as a member of the **OperatorStack** class, but then pass the instance of that class to the **DoAction** function. You can do this using the **this** pointer. However, in our example of the **DoAction** function, we have used references, so we need to dereference the pointer we want to pass:

```
void OperatorStack :: Clear(OperandStack & opd)
{
    while (top)
        DoAction (*this, opd);
}
```

Using a Class Method as a Friend to Another Class

Now let's make the **DoAction** function the member function of the **OperandStack** class (rather than the **OperatorStack** as in the initial version of the simple calculator program) and declare it the friend of the **OperatorStack** class. Being the member function of the **OperandStack**, the **DoAction** function will have now an implicit argument, an instance of the **OperandStack** class, and the function will again receive only one parameter, an instance of the **OperatorStack** class.

```
class OperandStack
{
...
    int DoAction (OperatorStack &);
};

class OperatorStack
{
...
    friend int OperandStack :: DoAction (OperatorStack &);
};

int OperandStack :: DoAction (OperatorStack & opt)
{
    long op2;
    switch (opt.stack[opt.top])
    {
    ...
    }
    opt.Pop();
    return OKEY;
}
```

And the **DoAction** call in the main function takes the following form:

```
int main()
{
    OperandStack opd;
    OperatorStack opt;
...
    opd.DoAction(opt);
...
}
```

By making the **DoAction** function the member function of the **OperandStack** class, we have simplified the function body, since there is no need to qualify the names of functions **Push** and **Pop** with the name of the instance of the **OperandStack** (which is implied). The benefits of using this are small, although generally it does lead to more efficiently compiled code.

The Clear Function

Before we move on, there's one thing we've missed - the **Clear** function. Again it needs to be changed, either moving it to the **OperandStack** class and making it a friend of the **OperatorStack** class, or by rewriting it as follows:

```
void OperatorStack :: Clear(OperandStack & opd)
{
    while (top)
        opd.DoAction (*this);
}
```

Friend functions can be considered as a bridge which links the private members of a class to the outside world of the program. As such they are dangerous, as they overide the encapsulation which is a fundamental part of objects. But, they do have their uses.

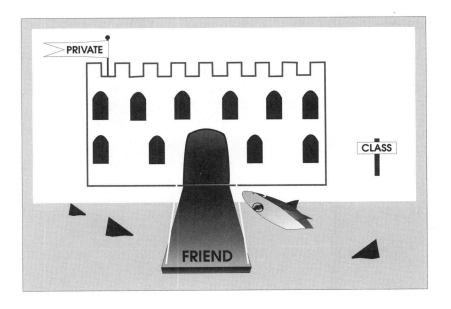

Friend to a Class

Friend Classes

You can define one class to be the friend of another class, thereby granting access rights to the private members of the second class. To declare a friend class, we do the following:

```
class date;

class time
{
private:
   long secs;
   friend class date;
};

class date
{
private:
   int month, day, year;
public:
   date(int m, int d, int y) { month = m; day = d; year = y;}
   long gettime (time & t) { return t.secs;}
};
```

The `gettime(time & t)` function is a member function of **date** class (which is the friend of **time** class and hence has access to **secs** data member).

To conclude this section, we should point out that friend functions or classes remove the protection given to private members of a class, and as such should not be used. You may think that not having the source code of a class would stop you from declaring a friend, but this is not the case. Unfortunately class inheritance gets around the problem of no source code, as we will see later.

Too Many Friends Deprive You of Your Private Life

Object Lifetime

Any object defined in a program, whether it be a built-in type or a class, has a beginning and an end, the same as any object or event in the real world. The object lifetime begins from its declaration or definition and the length depends on where you declared the object in the program. The object lifetime is in many ways similar to the scope of the declared object name, although there are some differences.

You can therefore create objects with local or global lifetimes, as well as objects whose lifetime is determined by the programmer (the so called dynamic objects). We can change the lifetime of objects by using specifiers, for instance, a static local variable remains 'alive' from the first time it is initialized in the block, until the program terminates. This is what we'll now move on to.

The Static Specifier

Generally, a block (or function) is reused several times during the execution of the program. Whenever the block is entered, local objects are created to be destroyed on exit from the block. Suppose we want to count how many times we entered a function without this count being accessed globally.

To solve the problem, you should add the **static** keyword to a local object declaration. This causes the variable to be stored permanently in memory (until the program ends). However, the scope of name remains local (within a block).

To demonstrate this, lets define a function which counts the number of times the function is used:

```
void function()
{
    static int counter = 0;
    counter++;
}
```

The first time the function is used, the variable **counter** is initialized to zero then incremented. On subsequent calls, the initialization is not performed, as the variable is already there, and the increment is still done. To check this we could write the following **main** function:

```
void main()
{
    for(int i= 0; i < 10; i++) function();
    cout << counter;    // Error, counter is not in scope
}
```

Unfortunately, the last line doesn't work because the name **counter** is local to the function. The lifetime of the instance is from the first call of the function to the termination of the program, but the name used to access it is repeatedly created and destroyed. If we want to access the static variable, then we must pass a pointer or reference to it back to the rest of the program.

We can remove the initialization for the static local variable **counter**, and just declare it:

```
void function()
{
    static int counter;
    counter++;
}
```

This is because the compiler provides for initializing static variables and objects.

> **A word of caution. Different compilers and systems (for example, Unix Vs Windows) may initialize the variables and objects in different ways, giving you unexpected results. It is therefore good programming practice to initialize variables manually, in the way you want them.**

Static Data Member

The **static** specifier can be used for declaring members of a class, both data members and member functions. In this case, no matter how many objects of the class are declared in the program (if any), there will be only one instance of the static class member common for all objects of the class.

This property of static data members can be very useful. For instance, if you have a database application where you dynamically allocate memory for instances of a class **Record**, then you can use a static member to keep a count of the number of records read in:

```
class Record
{
    static long record_count;
...
};

long Record::record_count = 0;
```

Then in the class constructor, you can increment this counter, and decrement it in the destructor:

```
Record::Record()
{
    record_count++;
...
}

Record::~Record()
{
    record_count--;
...
}
```

Each instance of the **Record** class accesses just one instance of the **record_count** variable.

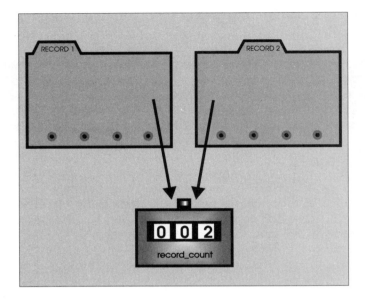

Static Data Member

Therefore, instances of a class containing a static member don't have exclusive rights to that member, unlike other members of the class. Moreover, the static member is accessible even when no instance of the object has been declared, providing of course, that the static member is public. So based on our **Record** class, this is the program:

```cpp
#include <iostream.h>

class Record
{
public:
   static int record_count;
   Record(){record_count++;};
   ~Record(){record_count--;};
};

int Record::record_count = 0;

void main()
{
   cout << Record::record_count << endl;
```

```
   Record rec1;

   cout << Record::record_count << endl;

   if(1)
   {
      Record rec2, rec3;

      cout << Record::record_count << endl;
   }

   cout << Record::record_count << endl;
}
```

and this is its output:

```
0
1
3
1
```

This is only possible because **record_count** is public. Static members of a class obey the normal rules of accessing class members, with a caveat that they can be initialized like global objects in the scope of a file. This means that the static data member declared private can be accessed only by member functions of the class. Since the static class member has no relation to a specific instance, you can use the class name rather than the object name to access it.

```
   cout << Record::record_count << endl;
```

However, you can also refer to the static member via the selection operator:

```
   cout << rec1.record_count << endl;
```

As there is only one instance of the member, it doesn't really matter which method you use.

Static Member Functions

A member function of a class can also be declared **static**. Static methods are closely related to static data members. There is only one copy of the function code which is shared by all the instances of the class. Although for most class methods there is only one copy of the function code, there are differences between static and non-static methods.

Unlike non-static member functions, the static member function of a class has no implicit **this** pointer. Therefore, if you want to access anything other than other static members of the class, you must explicitly pass either a reference or a pointer to the class instance. Then you can use the . and -> operators to access the members.

Also, you can't have two methods with the same name, nor can you have parameter lists that only differ in the **static** specifier. To illustrate this, the following two lines are mutually exclusive in a class declaration:

```
void function();
static void function();
```

However, function overloading will allow some overloaded function to be **static**, while others are not. This, for example, is perfectly valid.

```
void function();
static void function(int);
```

Finally, a local class can't have static members, either data or methods.

Why Use Static Members?

What are the benefits of using static members?

Apart from providing the common data feature for all objects that allows you to know how many objects were created or how many accesses were made to a function, static members are used:

- To decrease the number of names with global scope
- To make evident that a member belongs to a class
- To reduce storage requirements.

How Constructors Are Used

Let's rewrite the word counting program, introducing a static variable into the **Word** constructor to count the number of time the constructor **Word(Word & w)** is called.

```
Word :: Word(Word & w)
{
    static int counter = 0;
    cout<<"We have entered the constructor "<<++counter<<" times"<<endl;
    wordLen = w.IsWordLen();
```

```
    theWord = (char *) new char [wordLen + 1];
    strcpy(theWord, w.IsWord());
}
```

Running the program results in the following output:

```
static object^Z
We have entered the constructor 1 times
We have entered the constructor 2 times
We have entered the constructor 3 times
We have entered the constructor 4 times
We have entered the constructor 5 times
object : 1
static : 1
```

You may wonder why we accessed the constructor five times when we only input two words? To find out the reasons behind this, let's first discuss the situations in a program where the constructor is needed:

▶ When the object is declared with an explicit initial value, for example:

```
Word w1 (" It is Word object")
```

The above uses the **Word(char *)** constructor, and the **Word(Word &)** constructor is called for declaration:

```
Word w2 (w1);
```

▶ When the object is declared without explicit initial value but the class definition has the default constructor (this is the case when declaring **Word w;**).

▶ When the member function returns the value of a class object.

▶ When the member function is passed a class object as an argument.

▶ When an object is created as a result of type cast during expression evaluation.

▶ When an object is created by the **new** operator with the explicit initial value.

▶ When an object is created by the **new** operator without explicit initial value but the class has the default constructor.

▶ When the constructor is used explicitly in the expression.

Calling Word (Word &) Constructor

Ignoring other possibilities for now, let's find out when the **Word(Word &)** constructor with the static counter is called. We'll examine the **main** function as this is where most of the action takes place. It begins with the following declaration:

```
int main()
{
    Word w;
```

This is of no interest to us as the default constructor **Word()** will be called here.

```
    WordTree * tree = (WordTree *) new WordTree;
    for ( ; ; )
    {
        w = GetWord();
```

The **Word(Word &)** constructor is called here for the first time when the **GetWord** function returns the instance **w** of **Word** class as function value.

```
        if (!w.IsEmpty())
            tree->root = tree->Add(w, tree->root);
```

This line calls the **Add** function of the **WordTree** class:

```
TreeNode * WordTree :: Add(Word & w, TreeNode * p)
{
    if (p == 0)
        p = (TreeNode *) new TreeNode(w);
    ...
```

This in turn creates an instance of the **TreeNode** class, using its constructor:

```
TreeNode :: TreeNode(Word & w)
{
    word = new Word(w);
    ...
```

which creates an instance of the **Word** class. This, as you can see, creates an instance of the **Word** class, initializing it with the passed argument **w**, which is a **Word** instance itself. This is the second call of the **Word(Word &)** constructor.

The same two calls of the constructor occur for the second entered word, and the final call results from the final call of the **GetWord** function which terminates the program due to a *Ctrl+Z* being input.

How It Works

This highlights one of the problems with constructors - they can be called more often than you may have first thought. If you want to use the constructor as we have already done (to count the number of objects in memory), then this will work. But, you must increment the counter in every constructor, and decrement it in the destructor, otherwise you may find you have less (or more) instances than the counter tells you!

Dynamic Memory Allocation and Deallocation

You can create class or built-in type instances by using the **new** operator to allocate memory dynamically. In this case, memory is considered allocated to an object until it is explicitly deallocated by the **delete** operator.

Try It Out - Dynamic Allocation

Notice that automatic deallocation of the pointer to the memory allocated by the **new** operator doesn't involve deallocation of the dynamic memory obtained. Let's, for example, use our **Word** class:

```
...
Word * globpoi;
void main()
{
    {
        Word * wpoi = new Word ("This is a string");
        globpoi = wpoi;
    }
    cout << globpoi->IsWord() << '\n';
}
```

Since the pointer **wpoi** is local, it is allocated memory on entry to the block and deallocated on exit from the block.

The global pointer **globpoi** is used here to demonstrate that the string **"This is a string"** still exists in memory on exit from the block, while the **wpoi** pointer for the string is no longer exists.

Try It Out!

If we now add a line to the program to remove the allocated memory with the **delete** operator before terminating the block then you may or may not get the right output:

```
...
Word * globpoi;
void main()
{
   {
      Word * wpoi = new Word ("Clear storage ");
      globpoi = wpoi;
      delete wpoi;
   }
   cout << globpoi->IsWord() << '\n';
}
```

How It Works

Once you have **delete**d the dynamically allocated memory, then any reference to that block of memory will produce undefined results. Once memory no longer belongs to a program, the computer is completely at liberty to do with it as it pleases, so the data could still be there, or overwritten by some other process executing on the machine. Basically, once you have **delete**d an instance, then you can't use it.

Using the new Operator

You may have noticed already from the code that allocating memory with **new** is a lot different than what you may be used to with **malloc**. The **new** operator doesn't need to know the size of the type it is allocating space for, it can work this out for itself. The **new** operator also returns a pointer to the memory that doesn't require casting. If the predefined implementations of operators **new** and **delete** aren't appropriate for some reason, you can correct this in one of two ways:

1   Overload the operator function **new()**, that is, declare and define your own instance of the **new** function.

2   In the class being defined, declare the member operator function **new** to allocate memory for a class object and initialize it.

Either way, you will have to write a new version of **new** for every class that requires it. Of course, there is no reason why you shouldn't use the predefined **new** operator within your version.

If we are going to use the built-in version of the **new** operator, then we can use it with the following syntax:

```
new type (initial_value)
```

For example, we could write:

```
int * pointer = new int(5);
```

which causes the pointer **pointer** to point to an integer with the initial value of 5. This is very similar to what we did for an instance of **Word** in the **TreeNode(Word & w)** constructor:

```
new Word(w)
```

The similarity isn't there by accident - under C++ even the built-in types have constructors, so it is possible to initialize a variable at declaration in two ways. Either like this (as we are all familiar with):

```
int Integer = 0;
```

or like this:

```
int Integer(0);
```

You can't always initialize the memory obtained by the **new** operator. If you use **new** with an array of data types, as we do in the **Word** constructor:

```
new char [Len+1]
```

then you can't specify an initial value. This also holds true for classes, although with classes, you do have the opportunity to write a member function to do the initialization of the array for you.

```cpp
#include <iostream.h>

class Class
{
public:
    int number;

    static void initArray(Class * c, int i)
    {
        for(int count = 0; count < i; count++)c[count].number = count;
    }
};
```

```
void main()
{
    Class * c = new Class[10];
    Class::initArray(c, 10);

    for(int count=0; count<10; count++) cout << c[count].number << endl;
    delete c;
}
```

Here is a classic example of using a static method for a class. As the call to the method is not particular to an instance of the class, we can pass a pointer to the array instead. That way we have access to all the instances of the class in the array, providing we pass that information as well.

There is one other possibility which we mentioned earlier, and that is to define a new *new* operator for the class. We will cover this in chapter 12.

So far, with all our programs, we have assumed that the **new** operator will give us the memory that we want. This is bad practice, and not something which should be encouraged. To check to see if we did get the memory we should check the returned value, comparing it with **NULL**. If they are equal, then we don't have the memory and should report this fact to the user. However, we are getting ahead of ourselves, as handling of error situations such as the **new** operator execution failure, will be discussed in Chapter 12.

Using the delete Operator

The **delete** operator can destroy an object that has been created by the **new** operator. The pointer returned by the **new** operator is used as an operand for the **delete** operator.

delete can only be used only with memory which has been allocated with **new** and vice versa. Some compilers will allow you to mix **new** and **delete** with **malloc** and **free**, even without a warning, but the results are unpredictable. The reason for this is fairly obvious - look at the following program:

```
#include <iostream.h>
#include <stdlib.h>

class Class
{
public:
```

```
   Class (){cout << "constructor" << endl;};
   ~Class (){cout << "destructor" << endl;};
};

void main()
{
   Class * pointer = new Class;
   free(pointer);
}
```

Running the program results in the following output:

```
constructor
```

If we now change the program to use **delete** rather than **free**:

```
#include <iostream.h>
#include <stdlib.h>

class Class
{
public:
   Class (){cout << "constructor" << endl;};
   ~Class (){cout << "destructor" << endl;};
};

void main()
{
   Class * pointer = new Class;
   delete pointer;
}
```
we get the following:

```
constructor
destructor
```

As you can see, with classes, the **delete** operator ensures that the destructor of the class is called, whereas **free**, although releasing the memory back to the system, does the necessary tidying up required for classes.

Conversely, if we create a dynamic instance of a class using **malloc** instead of **new**:

```
#include <iostream.h>
#include <stdlib.h>
class Class
{
public:
   Class (){cout << "constructor" << endl;};
   ~Class (){cout << "destructor" << endl;};
};
void main()
{
   Class * pointer = (Class *)malloc(sizeof(Class));
   delete pointer;
}
```

this is the result:

```
destructor
```

That is, **malloc** allocates properly the storage for the class, but doesn't call the constructor.

Just as with **new, delete** does have some limitations that need to be overcome. This is done in the same way as with **new** by overloading the **delete** operator, either globally or in the class definition.

We'll cover this more fully, later.

Summary

In this chapter we have recapped on what you already know about the scope of variables within a program. We have shown how C++ has extended the rules, allowing you to declare instances of types, whether built-in or user-defined, whenever they are needed.

We have also shown how the scope of members within a class are affected by the access restrictions placed on a class. These restrictions can be overcome with the use of **friend** functions and classes.

In relation to the scope of instances of different types, we have shown how we can use the **new** and **delete** operators to dynamically declaring memory for the instances. We have shown some of the restrictions inherent in using these operators and the problem with using the standard C **malloc** and **free** functions. We have also touched upon the possibility of overloading these operators for our classes.

In the next chapter we will cover some nuances when using constructors and the rules for overloaded functions and operators.

CHAPTER 6

More About Member Functions

This and the following chapter describes more advanced uses of member functions, covering both constructors, which are used in creating an object and initializing it in different ways, destructors, which are used to tidy up an object that's being destroyed, function & operator overloading and friend functions.

We shall continue to explain these topics by referring to the member functions of our program example from Chapter 1 and also by developing some other classes.

We will cover:

- Default constructors
- Initializing the object consisting the members of other classes
- Copy constructors
- Constructors as type conversion operator

Constructors and Destructors

A well-designed class can be treated as though it were a black box. All details of its internal representation are hidden - particularly its data members which hold the object's state. This encapsulation means that you'll need to provide a mechanism which will facilitate the correct initialization of the object's state. Also, for non-trivial classes of objects, you'll need to provide a method to cleanly destroy objects when they are no longer needed.

Constructors

A constructor is a member function of a class which obeys the rules of function declaration and definition, but has the class as its scope. Like any ordinary C++ function, a constructor can be overloaded - that is, you can declare more than one constructor, but each must take different parameters. (Note that constructors can never be **const** functions).

> Overloading is frequently used for constructors. This provides different ways for you to create an object of that class.

For example, the **Word** class contains three kinds of constructors. Thus, the class allows you to design an object of the **Word** class in three ways:

- Without specifying parameters (the default constructor).

- By specifying a character string as a parameter.

- By specifying a reference to another object of the **Word** class as a parameter (the copy constructor).

```
class Word {
  private:
    char * theWord;
    int wordLen;
  public:
// Constructors
    Word();
    Word(char *);
    Word(Word &);
...
};
```

You no doubt remember the way of creating an object of the **Word** class from a character string (we discussed it earlier). The remaining two constructors are called the special constructors: the default constructor **Word()** and the copy constructor **Word(Word&)**. We'll discuss these in more detail later.

Defining a Constructor

A constructor is defined in exactly the same way as any other class member function, except that it does not have any return type - not even void. Unlike other class member functions, a constructor can be called implicitly.

this Pointer and Object Creation

Every object is associated with an implicit **this** pointer, which is passed as a hidden argument in all calls to member functions. **this** is set to point to an object **after** the object has been allocated memory but **before** the constructor is called. The point to be emphasized is that the constructor itself doesn't allocate memory for the object - it only performs the operations included in the function body, that is, the constructor body which will normally be an initialization of the object's data members.

> **The object's state is undefined when inside a constructor.**

Access Rules for Constructors

The access rules applied to private and public member functions are also applied to constructors. If a constructor is defined in the private section it will be inaccessible outside of the class itself. That is to say, only other instances of that class and friends of the class will be able to create instances of that particular class using that particular constructor. Private constructors are generally used to disable a particular constructor - typically the default or copy constructor.

For example:

```
class Stack
{
  private:
    Stack(int);
  ...
};
Stack S(500); // Error, the constructor is inaccessible
```

Default Constructor

It's often convenient to define a constructor which takes no parameters. Such a constructor is referred to as a default constructor, and will know for itself what properties must be endowed to an object. In the above-defined **Word** class, there *is* a default constructor:

```
Word :: Word()
{
  theWord = NULL;          // Create dummy word
  wordLen = 0;
}
```

Therefore, if you want to define a **Word** class object, it would suffice to specify its name.

```
Word w;
```

To create this object, the default constructor **Word()** is implicitly called. That is, the object created stores a zero-length string (but any word can be placed there later on). We'll demonstrate how you can do this in the subsequent sections.

There is another way of defining a default constructor. When you specify the values of default arguments in a constructor, you also define the default constructor.

```
Word :: Word(char * s = " ") // Create word from character string
{
  int Len;
  Len = strlen(s);
  theWord = (char *) new char [Len + 1];
  strcpy(theWord, s);
  wordLen = Len;
}
```

You can use this constructor in either of two cases:

1 To create a **Word** object from a character string.

```
Word w1("Yes");
```

This syntax ensures that the just defined constructor is called and the **w1** object points to the character string **"Yes"** of 3 bytes in length.

2 To create an object without specifying any parameters, in which case the object will contain a zero-length string.

```
Word w2;
```

The object has been defined without parameters. In this case, the object created by default will point to the string of only one blank.

Definition and Use of Default Constructors

Thus a constructor without any parameters or with parameters whose values have all got default values is referred to as a default constructor.

If you are going to use a default constructor to initialize objects of a class, the class definition must contain only one constructor. In our case, this must be *either* **Word()** *or* **Word(char * s = " ")**. Otherwise it would be impossible for the compiler to decide which of those two constructors should be used for an object.

```
Word w;
```

Important: If you don't provide a default constructor or a copy constructor, then the compiler will provide a default one. For any non-trivial class, you should provide both, or at least disable them by placing them in the private section of the class definition.

Destructors

In C++ a function which destroys an object is called a destructor. The destructor name is the name of the class, preceded by a ~ (tilde). A destructor, abbreviated to **dtor**, takes no parameters and, like the constructor, has no return value (not even void).

```
// Word class definition
class Word {
  private:
    char * theWord;
    int wordLen;
  public:
    Word();
    Word(char *);
    Word(Word &);
    ~Word();
```

```
    //...
};
// Destructor
Word :: ~Word()
{
  if (theWord != NULL)    // Before deleting, be sure
    delete theWord;   // the word exists
}
```

The destructor is called automatically in either of these two cases:

1   When the object declared goes out of its scope

2   When the object created by the new operator is deleted by the delete operator.

Using Destructors

A destructor is used to tidy up the object. Normally, this means that any memory allocated by the constructor will be de-allocated here, any files that were opened by the constructor will be closed here, and so on. If you don't provide a destructor then the compiler will generate a default one, but for all non-trivial classes you should provide one. The destructor should be placed in the public section of the class definition.

Try It Out - Initialization and Assignment of Objects

When writing a program you may frequently need to have two similar objects. If you find you do need two this is how you can write them:

```
Word  w1("String");
Word  w2  =  w1;
```

We declare object **w2**, then we initialize the value **w1**.

How It Works

Let's see what's going on and how the assignment works.

```
class Word {
  private:
    char * theWord;
    int wordLen;
  public:
```

```
// Constructors
   Word();
   Word(char *);
   ~Word();
   ...
};
```

None of the constructors defined in the class will be called to initialize object **w2**. The object **w2** is allocated the required space and the contents of **w1** is memberwise copied there. This results in two objects having absolutely the same contents. This can be represented schematically as in the following figure:

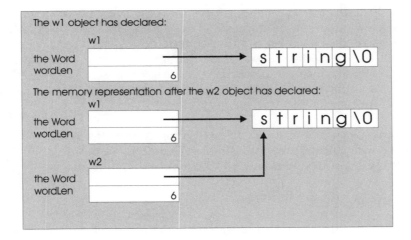

Memberwise Copying by Default

Since the **w2** object has mechanically copied the **w1** contents into it, without any constructor called, **theWord** pointer (of object **w2**) points to the same dynamic memory area as **theWord** pointer of object **w1**.

Objects and Scope

Let's take a look at what happens when **w1** and **w2** go out of their scope.

As we mentioned in the preceding section, the destructors for **w2** and **w1** are called in the reverse order to that of object declaration. Firstly, the destructor for **w2** is executed (see the figure overleaf):

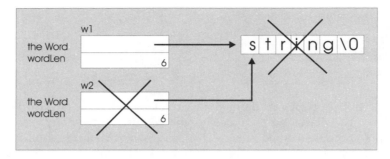

Destructor Action for w2 Object

Once the destructor **w2.~Word()** has been executed, the dynamic area with the "**string**" string is deallocated. However, the **w1** object is still containing the **theWord** data member which points to the already free location. Should you call the destructor for **w1**, it would also attempt to deallocate the already released memory block. In this case, the result of program execution would be unpredictable, since the language doesn't provide for applying the **delete** operator to the free memory block.

It's therefore proven that for objects with pointers, the result of memberwise copying will generally be undesirable! Therefore, we need another way of initializing an object with another object of the same class.

Copy Constructor

C++ enables you to control copying at **initialization** with a special constructor which has the following form:

```
Word  ::  Word(const  Word  &);
```

If the constructor is defined in the class, it will be called wherever one class object is initialized with another object of the same class. Let's look at the constructor of this kind for the **Word** class:

```
class Word {
  private:
    char * theWord;
    int wordLen;
  public:
    // constructors
```

```
   Word();
   Word(char *);
   Word(Word &);        //Copy constructor
   ~Word();
   char * IsWord();
   int IsWordLen();
...
};
Word :: Word(Word & w) // Create word from word (duplicate word)
{
  wordLen = w.IsWordLen();
  theWord = (char *) new char [wordLen + 1];
  strcpy(theWord, w.IsWord());
}
```

This constructor is referred to as a copy constructor and is called wherever one object is initialized with another object. In this case the dynamic string will be reallocated memory and the contents of objects will differ only in the pointers to the string (see the following figure).

```
Word w1("string");
Word w2 = w1;
```

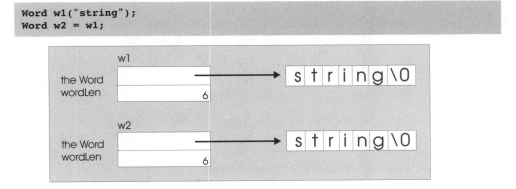

Copy Constructor Action

Thus there would be no attempt to twice deallocate the same memory block when the objects go out of their scope.

There are two other places where the copy constructor is called:

1　When an object is passed as a parameter of the function.

2　When an object is passed as a return value.

In both cases, a temporary object is created for which the copy constructor **X(X&)** will be executed. These temporary objects will be destroyed, and the destructor called, on exit from the function, that is, when the object goes out of scope.

Copy by Assignment

When you need to assign one object to another object of the same class, use the **=** operator. As you no doubt remember, there is a operator overload mechanism in C++ which lets you deal with the user-defined objects as easily and simply as with objects of predefined types.

Practically every operator can be overloaded to be further used with the objects of newly derived classes. Moreover, you should overload an operator (that is, write a function to support the desired actions) in order that it can be used for user-defined objects. If you don't provide the following operators then the C++ compiler will provide defaults: assignment (**=**), subscripting (**[]**) and address (**&**). For any non-trivial class the provision of a default assignment operator can cause problems (in the same way as with the copy constructor) as the default performs a simple memberwise copy.

```
Word w1("String");
Word w2;
W2 = w1;
```

Once the assignment is performed, the **w2** object will contain a precise memberwise replica of **w1**. (We have already discussed the disadvantage of applying memberwise assignment to the classes resulting from construction of a dynamic block for storing the data.)

When to Use a Copy Constructor

It's clear that the copy constructor **Word(Word&)** has nothing to do with the operator **w2 = w1;**. The copy constructor is only used for initializing an object. To have the operator executed properly, you should overload the assignment operator.

Now, our class takes the following form:

```
// Word class definition
class Word {
  private:
    char * theWord;
    int wordLen;
  public:
    Word();
```

```
   Word(char *);
   Word(Word &);
   ~Word();
   char * IsWord();
   int IsWordLen();
// Assignment one word to another
   Word & operator = (Word &);
 ...
};
```

As you know, to assign one object to another (if they both have a dynamic allocated memory) you should first access the required space and then copy the string into it. Let's try to write the assignment operator that resembles the copy constructor:

```
// Assignment operator
Word & Word :: operator = (Word & w)
{
  wordLen = w.wordLen;
  theWord = (char *) new char[wordLen + 1];
  strcpy(theWord, w.theWord);
  return * this;
}
...
Word w1("String");
Word w2("newString");
w1 = w2;
```

You may wonder what would happen if you apply the assignment operator - see the following figure:

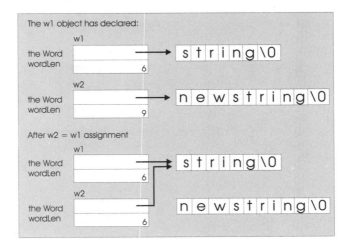

Assignment Operator Action

With the assignment complete, **w2** (as does **w1**) will contain the pointing character string **string**. The **newString** that has been pointed to earlier by a member of object **w2** will remain 'suspended', since there is no longer any pointer to this string. That pointer is replaced with one to **string** but the memory area, allocated to **newString**, remains allocated.

Thus, before you replace the string address for an object involved in assignment, you should deallocate the memory area pointed to by **theWord** of **w2**. This done, you can perform further actions involved in object assignment. Let's modify the function:

```
// Assignment operator
Word & Word :: operator = (Word & w)
{
  if (this != &w) {
    int Len = w.IsWordLen();
    if (theWord != NULL)
      delete theWord;
    theWord = (char *) new char [Len + 1];
    strcpy(theWord, w.IsWord());
    wordLen = Len;
  }
  return * this;
}
```

This would solve the problem of 'suspended' dynamic memory areas. If the pointer to be assigned the new string address is non-null, the memory area at the specified address is first deallocated. This would produce another problem though.

```
Word w("String");
w = w;
```

If the objects located to the left and right of the assignment operator are identical, memory deallocation would be impossible without data loss. Have a look at the figure opposite:

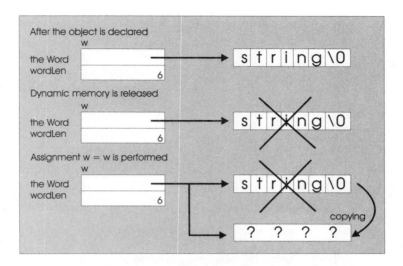

Assignment Operator with the Same Operands

Since our function releases the memory area at the old address before the assignment of the pointer, the operator would result in **theWord** data member pointing to the memory area obtained by copy from the already released memory. However, the memory could have been used in the period between deallocation and copy. Therefore, there is no guarantee that it contains the required data.

From what we've just said it appears that you should check for identical objects standing on the left and right-hand sides of the operator before you deallocate memory. To do this write the following:

```
if (this == &w)
return;
```

and then perform the remaining object copying work.

> You should always check for degeneration whenever you overload the assignment operator.

The assignment function now appears as follows:

```
// Assignment operator
Word & Word :: operator = (Word & w)
{
  if (this != &w) {
    int Len = w.IsWordLen();
    if (theWord != NULL)
      delete theWord;
    theWord = (char *) new char [Len + 1];
    strcpy(theWord, w.IsWord());
    wordLen = Len;
  }
  return * this;
}
```

This assignment function meets all our requirements.

> Let's emphasize once more that the = operator is used both for assignment and initialization. (Remember that these are different actions.)

However, the user-defined operator (operator =) is never applied to non-initialized objects. Regardless of whether the class has an operator = function or not, in the following case:

```
Word w1("String");
Word w2 = w1;
```

either the copy constructor **Word(Word&)**, is defined in the class, or the predefined memberwise assignment operator, but the user-defined operator = will never be called.

Constructor of Class with Other Class Members

You can use an object of one class as a data member of another class. This must be taken into account when you create or copy these class objects.

If you declare a class A with an object of class B as its data member, you must have the class B declared or defined by this time.

Here's an example:

```
// Declaration of class A
class A {
    int a;
  public:
    A(int);
};

// Declaration of class B with A class object
class B {
    int b;
    A clA;
  public:
    B(A & x, int c);
...
};
```

And here's another example:

```
// Declaration of class A
class A {
    int a;
  public:
    A(int);
};

// Declaration of class B with A class object
class B {
    int b;
    A clA;
  public:
    B(A &x, int c);
...
};
```

As you might guess, to create an object of class B, you should call two constructors: one defined in class B, and the other defined in class A, since class B contains an object of class A. You might then ask yourself a couple of questions:

1   In what order are the constructors called?

2   How can an argument be passed to the constructor of class A?

195

The answer to the first question is straightforward. The constructor for a class member is performed before the constructor for the class that contains it. In our case, the constructor of class A is called first and then the constructor of class B is called.

If a class contains several data members that act as objects of another class, the constructors are called in the same order that the class data members were declared. The last constructor called is the enclosing class constructor.

```
class X {};
class Y {};
class Z {
  int a;
  X b;
  Y c;
...
};
```

The constructor of class X is called first, then follows the constructor of class Y, and finally the constructor of encapsulating class Z is called.

The Initialization List

Arguments for the constructor can be given in the initialization list for the constructor of the enclosing class. The initialization list is a list of comma-delimited pairs, consisting of a member name followed by a parenthesized argument. The initialization list can only appear in the constructor definition and is separated by a colon from the signature. For example:

```
B :: B(A &x, intc): b(h), clA(V)
{
...
}
```

Each member can appear only once in the initialization list and passes a value to the named data member.

The procedure of constructor execution is divided into two parts:

1 Initialization (that is, initialization defined in the initialization list)

2 Assignment (the body of a constructor is executed)

If the body of a constructor is null (as in the case of constructor for class B), no assignment is performed for creating an object.

Alternatively, if the initialization list is absent and class members are assigned, their initial values in the body of the constructor initialization step is absent.

Creating Objects of Built-in Types

You can use the initialization list to create not only objects with objects of another class but objects of solely built-in types. For example:

```
class X {
    int a;
    char b;
  public:
    X(int, char);
};

X :: X(int v, char w) : a(v), b(w)
{
}
```

In this constructor, everything is performed in the initialization step without any assignment.

There is another way of getting the same result:

```
X :: X(int v, char w) : a(v), b(w)
{
  a = v;
  b = w;
}
```

In this case, the initialization step is not available and the assignment performs what is needed to set the values of properties for an object.

How to Give Initial Values: Initialization or Assignment?

For the most part, it doesn't matter whether the initial values are given by initialization or assignment (although initialization is more efficient).
However, for a class containing a data member with the **const**modifier or a reference type data member, the values of properties can only be set by the

initialization list at initialization time. For example:

```
class Example {
    int i;
    const int j;   // Constant
    int &ref;   // Reference
  public:
    Example(int value);
};
```

If the constructor appears as follows:

```
Example :: Example(int value)
{
  i = value;   // OK
  j = value;   // Error
  ref = value; // Error
}
```

an error message will be issued in response to the assignments **j=value** and **ref=value**. To set the values for the members **j** and **ref**, you should only use the initialization list:

```
Example :: Example(int val) : j(val), ref(val)
{
  i = val;
}
```

The argument in the initialization list can be a simple value or a complex expression including a function call.

Objects as Class Members and a Copy Constructor

In this section we'll deal with copying objects whose members are objects of another class.

Let's imagine there's a class A and a definition of class B, one member of which is an object of class A.

```
B object1;    // Definition
B object2 = object1; // Define object2 and copy object1 there
```

When the class object is copying, there are a number of different possibilities:

1   Neither the enclosing class (class B) nor the member class (class A) define the copy constructor X(**constX &**).

2   The enclosing class (class B) does not define the copy constructor, but the member class (class A) specifies the constructor.

3   Both the enclosing and the member classes specify the copy constructor.

In the first case, memberwise copy is performed for both classes since neither class specifies the constructor of the form X(**const**X &).

In the second case, memberwise assignment is performed to initialize an object of class B with an object of the same class. However, to initialize the member named **clA**, the copy constructor for class A (**A :: A(constA &)**) will be called. For example:

```
A myobA(10);
B myobB(myobA);
...
extern example(B wb);
example(myobB);
```

Here the constructor **A(A &)** is called to initialize the member named **clA** in the object **myobB** and the member **clA** of the local copy **wb**.

Memberwise initialization is generally used recursively for each class member which is an object of another class, unless the class specifies the copy constructor **X(X &)**. The copy constructor is preferable in this case.

Let's take a look at the third possibility. Suppose the enclosing class (class B) specifies a copy constructor. At this point the copy constructor defined in class B (**B :: B(B &)**) will be called to initialize a B class object with another object of the same class. In this case, the copy constructor won't be called automatically for initializing the member **clA** (**A :: A(A &)**). Therefore, it is completely up to the copy constructor for the enclosing class (**B :: B(B &)**) to correctly initialize **clA**.

Here are two alternatives for the constructor `B::B(B &)`:

```
B :: B(const B & x)
   {  bv = 0;
      clA = x.clA;
   }
```

Let's have a look at the following example:

```
B object(10);
B example = object;
```

Initializing Objects

To initialize the example object, the following is performed.

1   Example is an object of class B to be initialized by copy. There is the constructor `B :: (constB &)` defined for class B. (If the constructor is not available, memberwise copy is performed).

2   Check whether an initialization list is available. The list is **not** available.

3   Check whether other class objects are among the members of class B. Yes, there is an object of class A named `clA`.

4   Check whether class A has a constructor taking no arguments. Yes, class A defines the constructor `A :: A(int= 0)`. If the constructor is not available, an error message is issued.

5   Constructor `A(int= 0)` is called to initialize the variable example `clA`.

6   Constructor `B :: B(const& B)` is called to perform the assignment `clA = x.clA`. In this statement the assignment rather than the initialization is performed. (For more detail on this refer to section *Initialization and Assignment of Objects* in this chapter). Since there is no overloading defined for the assignment in class A, the assignment we deal with is the pre-defined assignment, that is, memberwise assignment. In other words, the copy constructor of class A (`A :: A(constA &)`) is not called.

If you want to call a copy constructor for a class object member from the copy constructor for the enclosing class (**B :: B(constB &)**), you should use an alternative constructor with an initialization list.

```
B :: B (const B & x) : clA(x.clA)
  {
    bv = 0;
  }
```

In this case, the copy constructor for class A is called first, then the class object member is initialized, and finally the copy constructor for the enclosing class (**B :: B(constB &)**) is called.

To be more precise, the copy constructor for the enclosing class (class B) will be called immediately. However, its execution is divided into two steps: initialization and assignment. During initialization the copy constructor for the member which is an object of class A is called. During assignment the body of constructor **B(B &)** is performed.

This is another demonstration of the differences between setting the class member to its initial value at initialization and assignment (that is, when the constructor is being executed). (As you no doubt remember, we have discussed the case of class members with the **const** modifier and of reference type.)

In other words, to provide for calling a copy constructor for a member which is an object of another class from the copy constructor of the enclosing class, you should use an initialization list.

Let's summarize:

▶ If the enclosing class hasn't defined the copy constructor **X(constX &)**, memberwise initialization is performed for every member.

▶ If a member which is an object of another class has the copy constructor defined for the class, the copy constructor of the appropriate class is called to initialize the member.

▶ If the enclosing class has a constructor of the form **X(X&)** specified, this constructor is called. However, this constructor is responsible for initializing its members (which are objects of another class).

Converting Objects of Different Classes

So that different class objects can interact, the class objects must have some properties which allow one class object to be converted to another class object.

You can do this in C++ by applying type casting. This operation can be applied both explicitly and implicitly. You have already met standard conversions provided for the built-in data types. In addition to the standard conversions, C++ provides a mechanism for defining user-defined conversions. Type conversion for a class object is performed by constructors or special conversion functions.

Any class can define a collection of conversions to be applied to instances of that class. For example, let's define a class **Complex** which provides a constructor that takes a type **int**. That is, it provides a method of constructing an instance of the **Complex** class from an **int**. This means that we can use an **int** wherever we could use a **Complex** object, and the compiler will apply the conversion we supplied in the constructor.

```
Complex comp(5);
comp + 5;
```

If provision is made for B-to-A conversion, you could call any function waiting for an A type parameter either with the A or B type argument. Similarly, user-defined conversions can be applied in any expressions.

Rules for Using Conversion Functions

The rules for using conversion functions can generally be stated as follows:

1 Only unambiguous user-defined conversions can be applied.

2 User-defined conversions obey the rules of scope.

3 Access is checked after ambiguity has been resolved.

User-defined conversions can specify two directions for type casting:

1 From any type to that of the class where conversion has been defined (constructors).

2 From the type of class where conversion has been defined to any type (cast function).

Type Casting

Constructor as a Cast Function

As you remember, the **Word** class discussed has the **Word(char*);** constructor:

```
class Word {
  private:
    char * theWord;
    int wordLen;
  public:
    Word();
    Word(char *);
    Word(Word &);
    ~Word();
  ...
};

Word :: Word()
{
  theWord = NULL;            // Create dummy word
  wordLen = 0;
}

Word :: Word(char * s) // Create word from character string
{
  int Len;
  Len = strlen(s);
  theWord = (char *) new char [Len + 1];
  strcpy(theWord, s);
  wordLen = Len;
}
```

and creates a **Word** class object from the character string **(char *)**. That is, an object of one type is constructed from an object of another type with the constructor. Thus, for example, we could write:

```
Word w1;
char *line = "It is a string";
w1 = Word(line);
```

The latter statement is performed as follows: the **Word(char *)** constructor is called to create a temporary object which will later be memberwise copied onto the **w1** object.

Let's take a good look at the right-hand side of the assignment. **Word** is either a class or else a type. **Line** is the name of an object of the character **string** type - that is, **line** is an expression and the syntax:

```
type(expression)
```

is nothing but the functional form of representing a type cast operator. Thus **Word(line)** is an explicit call of the **(char   *)** casting to the **Word** type.

Now we add the constructor of the form **Word(int)** to the **Word** class to create an object which reserves storage for an n-byte word.

```
Word :: Word(int a){
  wordLen = a;
  theWord = (char *) new char [a + 1];
  theWord[0] = NULL;
}
```

Then we might write the following:

```
Word w1;
w1 = Word(10);
```

Word(10) is also a functional form of representing an **int**-to-**Word** conversion operator.

> A set of constructors with a single argument defines a set of conversions from the type of constructor's argument to that of the class where the constructor has been defined.

Implicit/Explicit Calling

Such constructors can perform conversions automatically and be either called explicitly as in the above example or implicitly:

```
Word w1;
char * line = "It is a string";
w1 = line;   // Implicit from (char *)
             // to Word conversion
```

or

```
Word w1;
w1 = 10;     // Implicit conversion
             // from int to Word
```

If necessary, you can also apply standard conversions to the constructor argument, but they must be performed before the constructor is called. For example:

```
Word w1;
w1 = 74.938;
```

Firstly, the constant 74.938 is converted to **int** (by standard conversion, with the decimal part dropped) and then the **Word(int)** constructor is called to create a **Word** object from the **int**, that is, **int**-to-**Word** conversion takes place.

> Just a reminder that C++ can convert an argument of one numeric type to another numeric type at function call time disregarding the loss of the significant digits.

User-Defined Conversions

A user-defined conversion operation is only called when other conversions are impossible. Note that the constructor with one or more default arguments and one obligatory argument is also interpreted as a type cast operator. The rules for calling these constructors will be discussed in subsequent sections. For the time being, we can state that if the **Word** class is defined with two constructors of the form:

```
Word(char *);
```

and

```
Word(char *, int = 120);
```

then an error message will be issued for the string

```
Word w1 = "It is a string";
```

at compile time. This is due to the fact that both constructors specify **char*** to **Word** conversion and the compiler is unable to uniquely choose the user-defined conversion to be performed.

As we've already said, any constructor with a single argument specifies conversion from argument type to class type. The **Word** class can define the constructor of the form:

```
Word(Token&);
```

thereby specifying conversion from user-defined type Token to Word, that is, from one user-defined type to another.

Type Cast Operator as Class Member

In the previous section we saw how constructors can be used to provide conversion from a type to an object of our class, **Word**. In this section we'll show how conversion from our class **Word** to another type can be produced.

In C++ there is a mechanism to do this through conversion or cast functions which have the form:

```
operator type().
```

For example, if we wanted to provide a conversion function to allow objects of our **Word** class to be cast to a **char*** the function would be declared in this way:

```
class Word {
...
        operator char* (); // Conversion function
...
};
```

Conversion functions can be used for two things that can never be done with constructors:

1   Specify conversion from class type to the base type.

2   Specify conversion from one class to another class without modifying the declarations of the latter.

Neither parameters nor a return type could be specified in a conversion function as the return type is the type to be converted to, and the only parameter is an implicit, hidden pointer to the object to be converted.

These functions allow the compiler to apply an implicit conversion from the object-type to another type, in this case from a **Word** type to a **char*** type,

```
Word w("Hello World");
char*pString=w; // compiler applies implicit conversion from Word to char*
```

and a user of the class to explicitly cast from the object type to another type.

```
Word w("Hello World");
char*pString = char*(w);
```

Summary

In this chapter you have begun to see how to create class objects using constructors, and how to get rid of them when you no longer need them, using destructors. You have also looked at initializing your class objects, and latterly we have begun to look at type casting.

In the next chapter we move on to another feature of object-oriented programming processes when we consider the whole question of overloading.

CHAPTER 7

Overloading

If someone said to you that they were overloaded with work, you'd probably listen with compassion and think 'there but for the grace of God go I'. Or you might laugh at them and call them a sucker. On the other hand, if someone said to you that they were overloaded with money, spondooliks, cash, and wad, you'd probably neither listen with compassion nor laugh very much (unless you too were a stasher of the green folding, then maybe you could compare tax rates).

Overloading is itself an ambiguous term, but in C++ it is very definitely in the latter camp of the above example, that of a positive, even recommended process. Overloading functions in C++ enables a function to have more than one meaning, and operator overloading is an extension of this function enhancement to encompass operators.

In this chapter we'll cover:

- ▶ Overloading functions
- ▶ Exact matching
- ▶ Standard conversions
- ▶ Ambiguity
- ▶ Overloading operators
- ▶ Type casting

Overloading Functions

We've already said that a C++ program can have more than one function with the same name, and this is what is meant by function overloading. It's generally used when you want to perform similar operations on data of different types. This feature is most frequently used for defining constructors when you need to initialize an object in different ways. Its also used for specifying operator functions to be performed on a class type object, or objects of other types.

When a program uses the name of a function belonging to the set of overloaded functions, the appropriate instance is chosen by comparing the type of actual parameters with that of formal parameters. For example:

```
int min(int, int);
double min(double, double);

min(1, 2);    // Call the function min(int, int)
min(2.4, 7.4);   // Call the function min(double, double)
```

Compiler Options and Overloading

If more than one function has been declared with the same name, the compiler won't always treat this set of functions as overloaded. The following options are possible:

1 If the return values and signatures (type and the number of parameters) coincide for more than one function, the second and any subsequent declaration will be treated as redeclaration.

```
double min(double a, double b);
double min(double c, double d); // Redeclaration
```

In this example, the second operand redeclares the first operand since the type and number of parameters match while the names of parameters in the signature are ignored.

Since for any X the types X and X& allow the matching set of initializing values, the functions whose parameter types differ in only this respect cannot be overloaded. For example:

```
int func(int);
int func(int&); // Error, function types are
                // nearly the same
```

2   If the signatures of several functions match but the return values differ, the second and any subsequent declaration will be considered invalid.

```
unsigned int min (unsigned, unsigned);
long min (unsigned, unsigned);        // Error
```

An error message is issued for the second statement, because the signatures of functions match and the return values are not considered when the compiler decides whether the function is overloaded. An alternative type name defined by the **typedef** operator makes no change since **typedef** is only an alternative name rather than a new type.

```
typedef unsigned int Word;
unsigned int min(unsigned, unsigned);
long min(Word, Word);               // Error
```

3   If signatures for several functions differ (that is, parameters specified for a function differ in type or number), the function will be considered overloaded, provided its instances were declared within the same scope. For example:

```
int min (int, int);
double min (double, double);
```

In the above a function is overloaded.

Naming Class Member Functions

Class member functions of which one is a static member and the other is non-static cannot be given the same name.

There are some additional features:

▶ Enumeration is a specific type. Although **enum** is equivalent to **int**, two functions with the same name one of which is has **enum** and the other **int** as an argument can be overloaded.

▶ Parameter types of which one is a pointer (*) and the other is an array [ ] are identical and hence cannot be overloaded:

```
int func (int *);
int func (int[]);        // Error
```

Char, **unsigned char**, and **signed char** are different types. You can use them to declare functions to be overloaded. For example, the code below performs overloading:

```
char func(char);
unsigned char func(unsigned char);
signed char func(signed char);
```

Similarly, the types **char** *, **unsigned char** *, and **signed char** * differ. Thus the following code:

```
char func(char *);
unsigned char func(unsigned char *);
signed char func(signed char *);
```

represents overloaded functions.

Function Overloading Resolution

There can be more than one instance of a function with the same name at function overloading. Therefore, the compiler must have an algorithm for selecting the appropriate function. To select the proper instance of a function, the compiler must compare every instance declaration for the type, with the number of actual arguments and formal parameters in the function call. This process can be referred to as argument matching or disambiguation. There are possible three situations:

- An exact match is found
- A match is achieved by applying conversion, built-in or user-defined
- A match with more than one defined instance of the function: ambiguity

Let's take a closer look at each of them.

Exact Matching

An exact match is reached when the actual argument type matches that of the formal parameters for one declared instance of a function to be overloaded. Suppose there is the following set of functions:

```
void func(int);
void func(long*);
```

Then the call

```
func (10);
```

matches the instance of function with the formal parameter of **int** type since the actual parameter 10 is **int** in the call.

In other words, if an actual argument has the same type as a formal parameter for one of the functions in the set to be overloaded, the call is resolved by exact matching.

For example:

```
void func(char);
void func(double);
```

Suppose the function call takes the form:

```
func ('a');
```

There is an exact match with the instance of **void func(char);** since the actual argument type is identical to that of the formal parameter.

There is also a special case of exact match. The actual argument of `char, unsigned char` or `short` type and constant `0` are treated as exactly matching the formal parameter of `int` type. The unsigned argument of `short` type matches that of `int` if the internal length of `int` exceeds that of the `short`, otherwise the `unsigned short` exactly matches the `unsigned int`. The actual argument of `float` type exactly matches the formal parameter of `double` type.

Let's look at the following example. Suppose you wish to overload the following set of functions:

```
void func(int);
void func(double);
```

The function call takes the form:

```
func ('a');
```

The actual parameter is of **char** type. The set of overloaded functions has no instance with the same formal parameter. As a result, the function instance with the **int** formal parameter (**void func(int)**) will be selected. The example below is also a demonstration of an exact match.

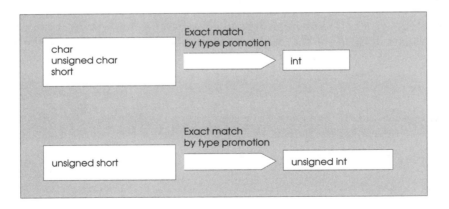

An Example of Exact Match

If a function call with the actual parameter of **char** is applied to a set of overloaded functions where one function has a **char** parameter and another function has an **int** formal parameter, the instance with the **char** formal parameter will be selected because no promotion is required for exact match.

The above is also true for the actual argument of float **type.**

If at least one instance with a parameter of **float** type is among the instances of the overloaded function, the instance will be selected. If no instance of the kind exists but there *is* an instance taking the parameter of type **double**, the instance will be selected and considered an exact match by promotion. Of two instances of the function, one of which takes a formal parameter of type **float** and the other type **double**, the function call causes the instance that takes the parameter of type **float** to be selected, because this kind of match requires no type promotion. Look at the following examples:

```
void func(char *);
void func(float);
...
func(3.14F);    // Exact match with func(float)
```

```
void func(char *);
void func(double);
...
func(3.14F);    // Exact match with func(double)
                // by type promotion
```

```
void func(float);
void func(double);
...
func(3.14F);    // Exact match with func(float)
                // without type promotion
```

Everything with regard to types **char** and **float** is only true for type promotion, that is, if an appropriate instance is selected by promotion to a higher type the match is considered exact. If a decrease to a lower type is required to match an instance, the match is considered non-exact. This match is reached by standard conversions.

In other words, the actual argument of type **int** can't exactly match a formal parameter of **char** or **short**. The same is true for a double actual argument which can't exactly match type **float**.

Function Overloading and Several Enums

Let's look at function overloading resolution for functions of which several have parameters of **enum** type.

Each name in an enumeration establishes a unique type. However, the type **enum** is equivalent to the type **int**, which implies that an actual parameter of **enum** type can exactly match either a function taking the formal parameter of the same type, or a function taking the formal parameter of **int** type. For example:

```
enum State {GOOD, BAD} drive;
enum Switch {OFF, ON};

void func(State);
void func(Switch);
void func(int);

  func(GOOD);       // Matches func(state)
  func(drive);      // Matches func(State)
  func(ON);         // Matches func(Switch)
  func(0);          // Matches func(int)
  func(1);          // Matches func(int)
```

In the above example, there is an exact matching instance for every function call. Now look at a set of overloaded functions with only two instances:

```
enum State {GOOD, BAD} drive;
enum Switch {OFF, ON};

void func(State);
void func(int);

  func(GOOD);       // Matches func(state)
  func(ON);         // Matches func(int)
  func(0);          // Matches func(int)
```

In this example, the first and third calls perform as expected: the actual parameter **GOOD** matches the formal parameter of type **State** and constant **0** is of type **int** thereby ensuring an exact matching instance for the call. The **func(ON)** call takes an actual parameter of **Switch** type. There is no function with this formal parameter in the set of overloaded functions, but **enum** is equivalent to **int**. It would therefore be reasonable to call an instance with the **int** formal parameter.

> You might well have noticed that exact match rather than a match by standard conversion occurs here. To be more precise, this is a second-level exact match.

The exact match rule is only true for the case of matching an actual parameter of **enum** type to a formal parameter of **int** type, that is, there could be no actual argument of **int** type exactly matching a formal parameter of **enum** type. In this case, standard conversions should be called.

If the set of overloaded functions includes a pair of functions of which one takes a reference or pointer to type **const**, and the other takes an ordinary reference or pointer, their functions should be distinguished. For example:

```
void func(int const *);
void func(int *);

const int x = 6;
int y;
const int *px = &x;
int *py = &y;

func(px);       // Matches func(int const *)
func(py);       // Matches func(int *)
func(0);        // Error: Ambiguity
```

The same is true for references and pointers to constant objects. These functions are distinguished at function overloading.

Match Achieved by Standard Conversions

If no exact match is found for the overloaded function call, an attempt is made to achieve a match by a standard or user-defined conversion. You should bear in mind that all conversions provided by C++ are equal in priority. User-defined conversions, standard conversions, and conversions involving the generation of a temporary variable are identical.

Let's look at some examples:

```
void func(double *);
void func(double);

func('a');          // Matches func(double)
```

Rules of Standard Conversion

By this call an instance with double parameter is selected by the rules of standard conversion. They read as follows:

1 An actual argument of any numeric type will match that of any other numeric type, including **unsigned**.

2 An actual argument of **enumeration** type will be converted to any numeric type.

3 Zero will match any numeric and **pointer** type.

4 An actual argument of **pointer** type can be converted to **void***type.

For example:

```
void func(double *);
void func(void *);
void func(char);
void func(char *);
int i;
double c;

func(i);              // matches func(char)
func(&i);             // matches func(void *)
func(c);              // matches func(char)
func(&c);             // matches func(double *)
func("string");       // matches func(char *)
func('a');            // matches func(char)
```

As we've already said, all conversions have identical priority. Therefore, conversion of a **char** to **unsigned char**, for example, takes no precedence over conversion of a **char** to a **double**. Whether or not the types are closely related is ignored. If more than one conversion can be applied to the same call, an ambiguity message is issued. For example:

```
void func(double );
void func(char);

func(748L);    // Error, ambiguous. Should it convert to double or char ?
```

Since there is no exact match, either of the two conversions can resolve the call: **long** to **char** or **long** to **double**. Both conversions are identical. To avoid this situation arising, you should use the explicit cast:

```
func(double(748L));    // for example
```

Also, user-defined conversions can be used to resolve the call of an overloaded function instance. For example:

```
void func(double *);
void func(char);
void func(char *);

class String {
     int sz;
     char *str;
   public:
     String(char *) { }
     operator char *() {}
};
String S("string");

func('a');    // Exact match func(char)
func(25);     // Standard conversion to func(char)
func(S);      // User-defined conversion to func(char *)
```

For the first call of **func('a')**, there is a matching instance **func(char)** in the overloaded function set - therefore, the call is resolved immediately.

The second call of **func(25)** takes the constant of type **int** as an argument. For this call there is no exactly matching instance, but type **int** is converted to **char** by standard conversions, and the match is achieved. The call is resolved to the **func(char)** instance.

The third call takes a variable of type **String** as an argument. There is no exact match for this call. However, the **String** class specifies conversion from **String** to **char** *. By this conversion an exact match is obtained, and an instance of **func(char** *) is called.

One Instance More

Though all conversions have the same priority, should the set of overloaded functions contain one instance more, for example, **void func(double)**, the result of the second call would be different:

```
void func(double *);
void func(char);
void func(char *);
void func(double);

class String {
      int sz;
      char *str;
   public:
      String(char *) { }
      operator char *() {}
};
String S("string");

func('a');    // Exact match func(char)
func(25);    // Error: Ambiguous
func(S);     // User-defined conversion to func(char *)
```

The first and the third calls are resolved in the same way as in the above example. However, the second call **func(25)** causes an error message to be issued. Since the actual parameter in the call can be converted both to **char** and **double**, the two conversions are equally applicable.

What If No Match? What If No Conversion?

If there is neither exact match nor conversion during the search for the exact match for an overloaded function, the function call will be resolved by a combination of user-defined and standard conversions.

In such a case an exact match can be achieved by applying standard conversions to the result of a user-defined conversions to produce the desired type. This combination of conversions, however, prevents you from using the second-level user conversions. Only one user-defined conversion is allowed to be applied in combination with standard conversions. For example:

```
void func(void *);
void func(double);

class String {
      int sz;
      char *str;
```

```
    public:
        String(char *) { }
        operator int() {}
};
String S("string");

func(S);    // User-defined String to int plus
            // standard conversion int to double
func(5);    // Standard conversion int to double
```

An exact match between the second call of **func(double)** instance is reached by standard conversion of actual argument from **int** to **double**.

The first call has no exactly matching instance and there are no conversions to immediately resolve the call. However, the **String** class defines conversion from **String** to **int(String:: operator int())**, and the conversion result can be then apply standard conversion from **int** to **double**. In this case the call of function such as **func(S)** will be resolved by calling **func(double)**.

Here is another example of such a case:

```
void func(int);
void func(float *);

class A {
...
    public:
        operator int();
};
class B {
...
    public:
        operator A();
};

B obj;

func(obj);    // Error, no appropriate conversion
```

This call will cause an error message to be issued. Seemingly, the **obj** of type **B** can be applied conversion (**operator A()**), defined in class **B**, and then converted to type **A**. Class **A** specifies conversion from type **A** to **int(A::operator int())** and it would be possible to select the **func(int)** instance to resolve the call. However, only one user-defined conversion level is allowed. An error message is issued:

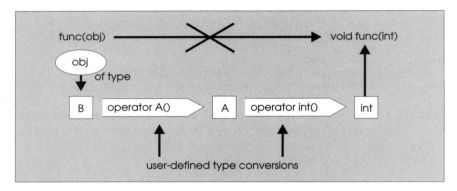

Two User-Defined Conversions Are Not Allowed

The Last Word

Thus if there is no exact match, or no conversions to make a match, or no combination of a single user-defined and a single standard conversion leading to unambiguous method selection, a search for match terminates and an error message is issued.

More Than One Function Matches - Ambiguity

Ambiguity arises in the following situations:

- When the compiler has no unique way of selecting between two conversions

- Different standard conversions produce different instances of overloaded functions

- More than one user-defined conversion is specified to reach the same objective.

Examples Where Error Messages Will Appear

An error message is issued in response to the following call because conversions are required for an exact match.

```
void func(long);
void func(double);

func('a');        // Error: ambiguity
```

However, all conversions are equivalent because type **char** can be converted to **long** and **double**. Therefore, there is no unique way of finding an exact match with the instance of overloaded functions, and an error message is issued:

```
class String;

void func(String);
void func(int);

class Letter {
     char ch;
   public:
...
     operator String();
...
};

class String {
     int sz;
     Letter *str;
   public:
     String();
     String(Letter);
};

main() {
Letter L;

func(L);    // Error: no match
}
```

In response to the **func** call, an error message is also issued since the function with the actual argument of **Letter** type has no matching instance in the overloaded function set. Therefore, conversions will be applied. To match exactly to a **func(String)** instance, you should convert from **Letter** to **String**. However, the declared classes define two conversions from **Letter** to **String**. The first is performed by the **String** constructor (**String(Letter)**), the second is performed by the converting function of the Letter class (**operator String()**). These conversions are equivalent and the compiler can't select the one to be used among them. An error message is issued. (Note that the use of casting doesn't resolve the ambiguity.)

In fact, the syntax

```
funct ((String)L);        // Ambiguity
```

produces the same result because the compiler can't judge which conversion should be called.

Explicitly Calling a Converting Function

To resolve the problem, you should explicitly call a converting function. For example:

```
func (L.operator  String());
```

If two conversions are equiprobable (with one leading to the desired result and the other requiring second-level standard conversions), no ambiguity arises. The compiler will select the conversion that leads directly to a unique resolution of the call. For example:

```
void func(char *);
void func(double);

class String {
     int sz;
     char *str;
  public:
...
     operator char *() { return str; }
     operator int() { return sz; }
};
String S;

func(S);
```

There is no matching instance in the set of overloaded functions to resolve the call of **func** with the actual parameter of type **String**. However, the **String** class specifies two conversions:

> **String** to **char***
>
> **String** to **int**

The first conversion (**String** to **char***) causes the call to be resolved by selection of the **func(char*)** instance. The conversion from **String** to **int** requires a standard conversion from **int** to **double** to resolve the **func(S)** function call to an instance with the formal parameter of **double** type. Therefore, the first conversion is selected to resolve the **func(S)** class. Irrespective of the fact that both conversions can be applied to the argument (all conversions are equiprobable), no ambiguity arises.

Overloading Functions with Multiple Arguments

If the set of overloaded functions includes instances with multiple arguments, a call of the instance is resolved by applying the matching rules for each argument in succession. When overloaded, the instance for which there was a match (either by exact matching or conversion) is selected.

The Best Match Rule

If there is more than one function instance with matching arguments, the so called 'best match' rule is applied. According to this rule, for the instance to be selected there must be an exact match for the maximum number of parameters, or else an exact match is achieved by lesser number of steps.

```
void func(long *, int);
void func(int, int);

func(5, 'c');        // Matches func(int, int)
```

The instance of **func(int, int)** will be selected for the call because there is an exact match for all arguments. Let's look at another example:

```
void func(int, char, double *);
void func(int, long, double);

double a = 5.0, *pd;
pd = &a;
func(6, 'a', pd);    // func(int, char, double *)
```

In this example, the first and the third arguments in both instances achieve an exact match. Therefore, the second argument will be involved in the process of selection. The second argument in the call exactly matches the formal parameter of the first instance. To achieve a match with the second parameter of the second instance, standard conversion is to be applied. The **func(6, 'a', pd)** call is uniquely resolved to the first instance in the set.

```
void func(int, double, long *);
void func(int, long, void *);

double a = 5.0, *pd;
pd = &a;
func(6, 'a', pd);    // func(int, long, void *)
```

In this example, both instances exactly match the first argument - therefore none is given precedence. To achieve a match with the second argument, standard conversions are applied to both instances. Conversion from **char** to **double** takes the same precedence as **char** to **long**, therefore none of the functions takes precedence by the second argument. The third actual argument of **double** * type can't be converted to **long*** by applying standard conversions, because such a conversion doesn't exist. Therefore, the first instance has no match with the third argument. As you might already know, the pointer to any type can be converted to **void** * type by a standard conversion. Therefore, by the third argument, the second instance takes precedence. Therfore, it is called.

If none of the instances takes precedence for any argument, an ambiguity message is issued:

```
void func(long, double);
void func(float, char);
int i, j;
func(i, j);    // Ambiguity
```

To find a match for both the first and the second arguments, standard conversions must be applied to the two instances. Standard conversions are identical. An error message is issued.

A call is also treated as ambiguous when one instance is given precedence for one argument and the other for another argument.

```
void func(int, char);
void func(long, double);
main()
{
   func('a', 78.67);    // Ambiguity
}
```

In this example, the first argument in the call exactly matches the formal parameter of **func(int, char)**, but standard conversions are to be applied to achieve a match with this instance for the second argument. Actually, standard conversions are to be applied to the first argument and an exact match must exist for the second argument to achieve a match with the second instance.

In this case, the first instance takes precedence by the first argument, and the second instance takes precedence by the second argument. To achieve an exact match with either of the instances, the same number of steps must be performed. Therefore, neither of them takes precedence over another and an error message is produced.

To resolve ambiguity, you should generally use explicit casting.

A Brief Round-Up

Before we move on to the subject of overloading operators, let's have a brief lie down and summarize what we've learned.

A special mechanism of constructors and destructors allows automatic initialization and release of class objects. You can overload constructors, and thereby define different ways of object initialization. (You can make them inline to improve the performance.)

Like constructors, you can overload any member function or global function. A call for this function is resolved by matching rules that are based on standard or user-defined conversions and allow you to choose a unique function instance.

Overloading Operators

A well-designed class requires that you define its behavior and properties when you create objects in different ways (constructors) or destroy them (destructors), when you convert one class object to another class object, and so on. Also, the class should be capable of participating in various expressions such as comparison or assignment of objects. In certain conditions, you need to define how objects should perform with regards to addition, subtraction or multiplication. In other words, you should define the behavior of a class object to perform specific actions on the class object, that is *in order to perform various operations.*

You can perform the same actions using different functions. For example, you can define the `greater()` function to compare objects of a class and call the function wherever comparison is to be performed. However, the same action is traditionally performed by the `>` operator.

However, operator overloading is when you you use a function which acts as an operator and has a short name coinciding with a C++ operator.

To define an operator overload, you can use the following syntax:

```
return-type  operator @ (argument-list)
```

where **@** is a sign of the operator which is to be overloaded.

You specify the meaning of operator **@** by defining a function named **@**.

Try It Out - Operator Overloading

Let's define the class of complex numbers by using the operator overloading mechanism.

```cpp
#include <math.h>
#define  FALSE  0
#define  TRUE   1
class Complex {
  private:
    double real;
    double image;
  public:
    Complex(double r)              { real = r; image = 0; }
    Complex(double r, double i)    { real = r; image = i; }
    ~Complex(void)                 { }
    int operator ==(Complex &);
    int operator >(Complex &);
    int operator <(Complex &);
};
int Complex :: operator ==(Complex & c)
{
  return ((sqrt(real * real + image * image) ==
          sqrt(c.real * c.real + c.image * c.image)) ?
          TRUE : FALSE);
}
int Complex :: operator >(Complex & c) {
  return ((sqrt(real * real + image * image) >
          sqrt(c.real * c.real + c.image * c.image)) ?
          TRUE : FALSE);
}
int Complex :: operator <(Complex & c)
{
  return ((sqrt(real * real + image * image) <
          sqrt(c.real * c.real + c.image * c.image)) ?
          TRUE : FALSE);
}
#include <iostream.h>
void main()
```

Try It Out!

```
{
  Complex c1(10.34, 77.2),
          c2(20.45, 77.2);
  if (c1 > c2)
    cout << "c1  isGreater c2\n";
  else
    cout << " c1 isLess c2\n";
}
```

In the **main** function, the comparison of two complex numbers is written in a natural and habitual way. Note that using an operator is only a short syntax form for an explicit call of an operator function, that is, the operator function may be called in the same way as any other function. For example:

```
void func(Complex & l, Complex & k)
{
  l > k;
// Short syntax for
// operator function call
  l.operator>(k);
// Full syntax for an
// operator function call
}
```

The above two syntactical forms are equivalent, but for better programming style, the first form is preferable. Thus the operator keyword is used to overload built-in operators in C++. If a function is to be overloaded, specific function instance depends on the type and number of arguments. Similarly, the operator may assume an additional meaning depending on the operands. The language provides the following operators for overloading:

Operators for Overloading						
+	-	*	/	%	^	&
|	~	!	,	=	==	!=
<	>	<=	>=	++	- -	
<<	>>	&&	||	+=	-=	
*=	/=	%=	^=	&=	|=	
<<=	>>=	[ ]	( )	->	->*	
new	delete					

From the above list you can see that almost every operators can be overloaded. The only exceptions are the following:

Operators You Can't Overload				
.	.*	?:	::	sizeof

Operator Overloading Rules

We discussed some operator overloading rules in Chapter 3. Let's recap on them and formulate additional rules concerning other aspects of operator overloading.

1 The language does not support defining new lexical characters for operators in addition to those supplied in the language. For example, you are not allowed to use a **@** that has been defined in PASCAL as an 'address of' operator. This limitation stems from the fact that the new operator precedence, hence the order of complex expression evaluation, is unknown to the compiler. Thus, for example,

```
@a + b * 2;
```

may be interpreted as

```
(@a) + (b * 2);
```

or as

```
@(a + b * 2);
```

There is no simple way for the developer to tell the compiler what the precedence of a new operator would be.

2 Operator overloading is not supported for built-in data types. For example, you cannot redefine integer addition:

```
int operator+ (int, int);
```

3 You are not allowed to define an additional operator for built-in types. For example, you cannot define addition of arrays. For this, you must first define a class, implementing the notion of an array, and then the addition operator within it.

4   You can't redefine the precedence of operators. For example:

```
x = y | z;
```

Irrespective of data types, the bitwise addition operator precedence is higher than that of assignment.

5   You can't change the syntax of operator in an expression.

If a certain operator has been defined in the programming language as unary (that is, ~), it can't overload it as binary. If the prefix form is used for operator notation, it can't be redefined into postfix. For example, if you use the following syntax for negation:

```
void operator! ();
```

you can write !a, but not a!.

The following operators can be defined only as unary:

```
++    --    !    ~
```

The following operators can be both unary and binary:

```
+    -    &    *
```

6   Since only those operators for which at least one argument is a user-defined data type can be overloaded, the operator function must be defined either as a member function of this type or as an global function friendly to this type. For example:

```
class String {
...
  public:
...
    String operator+ (String &);
};
```

or

```
class String {
...
  public:
...
    friend String operator+ (String &, String &);
};
```

If the **operator+** function has been defined both as a member function of **String** class and as an external function friendly to the **String** class, the following code would be ambiguous:

```
String a("hello");
String b("goodbye");
String c = a + b; // Ambiguity
```

7   For a unary operator to be overloaded, it must have no arguments for a class member operator function or only one argument (reference to object) for an external operator function. Actually, when a unary operator is overloaded as a member function, it is passed an implicit argument, the this pointer to the current object.

> Thus for any unary @ operator, the syntax @obj will be interpreted as the obj.operator@() for a class member, or as the operator @(obj) for a global function.
>
> The exception to this is when a unary operator could be postfix or prefix, for example, increment (++) or decrement (--), in which a dummy int argument is used to distinguish between them.

Under C++ the operator **++** member function with one argument defines the prefix **++** operator for a class object, while the operator **--** member function with two arguments defines the postfix operator. For a postfix operator, the second argument must be declared **int** and take the value **0** at function call.

For example:

```cpp
#include <iostream.h>
class X {
        int ax;
   public:
      X(int a) { ax = a; }
      X operator++();      // prefix ++a
      X operator++(int);   // postfix a++
      friend ostream & operator << (ostream &, X &);
};

X X :: operator++()
{
   ax = ax + 1;
   return ax;
}
X X :: operator++(int)    // postfix a++
{
   int temp = ax;
   ax = ax + 1;
   return   temp;
}

ostream & operator << (ostream & out, X & a)
{
   out << a.ax;
   return out;
}

int main () {
   X a(5);
   cout << "postfix " << a++ << '\n';
   cout << "prefix " << ++a << '\n';
   return 0;
}
```

8 A binary function to be overloaded must have only one argument (reference to object) for a class member or two arguments (references to objects) for a global function.

When a binary function is to be overloaded as a member function it's passed one implicit argument (the first argument), namely, the **this** pointer to the current object.

Thus, for any binary operator **@**, the syntax **obj1@obj2** may be either interpreted as **obj1.operator@(obj2)** for the operator defined as a class member or as operator **@(obj1, obj2)** for the operator defined as a global function.

233

The binary arithmetic operators

```
+    –    *    /
```

must return a class object for which they act.

Here's an example:

```cpp
#include <iostream.h>
#include <string.h>
class String {
   private:
      char * theString;
      int stringLen;
   public:
...
      String (int );
      String (char *);
      String & operator +(String &);
      void print () { cout << theString << "\n"; }
//   String concatenation
...
};
// Define "string concatenation" operator
String& String :: operator +(String & so)
{
   int len;
   len = this->stringLen + strlen(so.theString);
   String *temp = new String(len);
   strcpy(temp->theString, this->theString);
   strcat(temp->theString, so.theString);
   temp->stringLen = len;
   // Return concatenation result
   return *temp;
}
main()
{
   String a("moon");
   String g(" ");
   String b("rover");
   String c = a + g + b;
  c.print();
}
String :: String(int a)
{
```

```
  stringLen = a;
  theString = new char[a+1];
}

String :: String(char *s)
{
   stringLen = strlen(s);
   theString = new char[stringLen + 1];
   strcpy(theString, s);
}
```

Restrictions on Built-in Types

When the left operand in a binary operator to be overloaded is one of the built-in types rather than a user-defined type, the operator can't be overloaded as a member function. In this case, the operator must be defined as a global function where the first argument is one of the built-in types and the second argument is of the user-defined type.

Let, for example, **obj** be an object of class **A**. Then, for the **operator*** function defined as a member function of class **A**, the syntax **obj * 5** will be interpreted as **obj.operator*(5)**.

The syntax **5 * obj** is invalid since the constant **5** is an object of **int** type and the **operator*** function has been defined as a member function of class **A** rather than a global function with the first argument of **int** type:

```
A & operator * (int, A &);
```

9   The following operators must be overloaded only as class members:

```
=          [ ]          ( )          ->
```

Equivalent Operators and Overloading

Let's expand the **Complex** class by adding the capability of adding, subtracting, multiplying, dividing and assigning complex numbers.

```
#include <iostream.h>
#include <stdlib.h>

class Complex {
   private:
      double real;
```

```
        double image;
    public:
        Complex() {real = 0.0; image = 0.0;}
        Complex(double r) {real = r; image = 0;}
        Complex(double r, double i) {real = r; image = i;}
        ~Complex(void) { }
        int operator ==(Complex &);
        int operator >(Complex &);
        int operator <(Complex &);
        Complex & operator =(Complex &);
        Complex operator +(Complex &);
        Complex operator - (Complex &);
        Complex operator *(Complex &);
        Complex operator /(Complex &);
        void print() { cout << real << " + "
            << image << "i" << "\n";}
};

// Now we'll define the introduced operators:

// Assignment
Complex & Complex :: operator =(Complex & c)
{
    this->real  = c.real;
    this->image = c.image;
    return *this;
}
// Addition
Complex Complex :: operator +(Complex & c)
{
    Complex temp;
    temp.real  = this->real + c.real;
    temp.image = this->image + c.image;
    return temp;
}
// Subtraction
Complex Complex :: operator -(Complex & c)
{
    Complex temp;
    temp.real  = this->real - c.real;
    temp.image = this->image - c.image;
    return temp;
}
// Multiplication
Complex Complex :: operator *(Complex & c)
{
    Complex temp;
    temp.real = (this->real * c.real) - (this->image * c.image);
    temp.image = (this->real * c.image) + (this->image * c.real) ;
    return temp;
}
```

```
// Division
Complex Complex :: operator /(Complex & c)
{
   Complex temp;
   if ((c.real * c.real + c.image * c.image) == 0) {
      cout << "Division by 0\n";
      exit(-1)return 0;
   }
   else {
      temp.real = (this->real * c.real + this->image *
         c.image) / (c.real * c.real + c.image *
         c.image);
      temp.image = (-(this->real * c.image) + (this->image *
         c.real) / (c.real * c.real) + (c.image *
         c.image));
   }
   return temp;
}
void main()
{
   Complex a(23.65, 77.0), b(56.12, 65.44);
   Complex c;
   c = a + b;
   cout << "c = ";
   c.print();
}
```

In C++ there are some equivalent syntax forms for operators. For example:

```
int i = 5, j = 0;
j = j + i;
```

are equivalent to

```
j += i;
```

However, this equivalent syntax form for two one-character operators represented as a single two-character operator is only provided for the built-in data types. For user-defined data types, such operator equivalency isn't provided. No matter how the one-character operators = and + are defined in the **Complex** class, it doesn't infer that the two-character operator += may be used on complex numbers.

```
Complex a(5.0, 1.25), b(10.0);
a = a + b;
// Valid
a += b;
// Invalid
```

So that you can use the two-character operators **+=**, **-=**, ***=** or **/=** for the **Complex** type data, you must explicitly define them for the **Complex** type.

```
class Complex {
   private:
      double real;
      double image;
   public:
```

...

```
      Complex & operator +=(Complex &);
      Complex & operator -=(Complex &);
      Complex & operator *=(Complex &);
      Complex & operator /=(Complex &);
};
```

...

```
Complex & Complex :: operator +=(Complex & c)
{
   this->real  += c.real;
   this->image += c.image;
   return *this;
}

Complex & Complex :: operator -=(Complex & c)
{
   this->real  -= c.real;
   this->image -= c.image;
   return *this;
}

Complex & Complex :: operator *=(Complex & c)
{
   this->real  = (this->real * c.real) - (this->image * c.image);
   this->image = (this->real * c.image) + (this->image * c.real) ;
   return *this;
}

Complex & Complex :: operator /=(Complex & c)
{
   if ((c.real * c.real + c.image * c.image) == 0) {
      cout << "Division by zero\n";
      exit(-1);
   }
   else {
   this->real = (this->real * c.real + this->image *
      c.image) / (c.real * c.real + c.image *
```

```
        c.image);
    this->image = (-(this->real * c.image) + (this->image *
        c.real) / (c.real * c.real) + c.image *
        c.image);
    }
    return *this;
}
```

`...`

Operator Overloading and Type Casting

The discussed version of the **Complex** class allows you to use complex numbers in arithmetic expressions. For example:

```
Complex a(5.25, 1.0), b(0.1, 5.0), c(1.0, 1.0);
c = a * c + b / c;
```

This causes arithmetic operators defined in the **Complex** class to be performed on complex numbers. However, for the implementation of complex numbers to be complete, you should make provision for arithmetics in the cases when one of the operands is a built-in type value, that is, a data item of type **double**, **long**, **int** and so on. You can then define the set of operators to be performed on complex and built-in data types. For example, such operators as

```
Complex Complex :: operator +(double);
Complex operator +(double, Complex &);
```

are used to add a complex number to a floating point number.

Defining Arithmetic Operators

Similarly, you can define all arithmetic operators to be performed on complex numbers or any built-in type data item. With all these operators defined, the **Complex** class would become too cumbersome.

An alternative to the large number of operators is a set of conversions, both standard and user-defined.

For the **Complex** class, the user type conversion has already been defined, namely, a constructor with a single argument of type **double** – **Complex(double)**. This constructor is used to convert a floating-point number into a complex number by defining the floating-point number as a complex number with an imaginary zero part. This allows the operators on complex and double-precision floating-point numbers to be executed.

```
Complex a(1.5, 2.25);
double d = 5.125;
a = a + d;
// d converted to type Complex
a = d * a;
```

Apart from this, the language defines a set of standard conversions allowing any numeric type to be converted to **double**. Alternatively, the **Complex** class provides for converting from **double** to **Complex**. Therefore, the presence of a **Complex(double)** constructor and the operators +, −, *, and / for two operands of **Complex** type is enough for executing arithmetic operations on complex numbers. For example:

```
Complex a(5.25, 1.125);
int i = 5;
a = a + i;
```

This statement is executed as follows:

1 Variable **i** is cast to double by standard conversions

2 User-defined conversion (constructor) is performed and the double variable is casted to **Complex**

3 Addition is performed on two values of **Complex** type.

The user can also specify a set of conversions from **Complex** to any built-in type. Below is an example of conversion from **Complex** to **double**:

```
Complex :: operator double(void)
{
  return real;
}
Complex a(5.0, 1.0);
double d = 2.5;
a + d;
```

In this case, the built-in addition is performed on two floating-point numbers. It's assumed here that the **Complex** class doesn't specify conversion from **double** to **Complex**, that is, the **Complex(double)** constructor isn't available. The presence of both **double** to **Complex** and **Complex** to double conversions in the **Complex** class produces ambiguity in mixed computations.

```
Complex a(5.25, 1.1);
double d = 0.525;
a * d;
// Error
```

Since none of the user-specified conversions has predominance over another, an ambiguity message will be issued.

References and Operator Overloading

You no doubt remember that a new built-in type 'reference' in C++ creates an alternative name for a variable. Besides, there is another use that is more important, that is, argument passing and value-return by reference.

Passing Arguments to a Function in C and C++

In conventional C, arguments are passed to a function by value if no extra effort is made. That is, the function manipulates only the local copy of the arguments and hence can't modify the original, and the stack space allocated for the local copy is released on exit from the function and all variables are lost.

In C++, to vary an argument, you must pass the pointers to real variables to the function, but the function itself should be created on the assumption that it will obtain variable addresses rather than variables themselves. In this way you will have accomplished what you set out to do and the calling function will be able to handle varied variables.

R-Values and L-Values

Similarly, a value returned by the return statement is always a value rather than a variable. This means that an R-value is returned. To prevent it from being lost, you must assign it explicitly to any variable, since it can never appear in the left part of the assignment operator.

The problem can't be remedied by using pointers since the variable address is also an R-value. Moreover, arguments are passed to a function through a stack. For large objects to be passed to a function, the cost of copying becomes unbearable (both in terms of time and space).

In such a case, you can also pass pointers. To provide for handling a variable passed to a function, you must first dereference it. This will make your programs slightly less readable.

These problems can be readily solved by using arguments and a returned value of reference type. Actually, a reference is always a dereferenced pointer which is also an L-value as well. That is, a function is passed a variable address, but from the syntax point of view the reference is handled in the same way as an ordinary variable.

Try It Out

Let's explain this using some examples. For an ordinary decimal arithmetic, you can write:

```
int a = 5;
a++;
// a = 6;
```

Introduce a simple **integer** class and watch the effect of passing a value copy to the function at overloading the **++** operator.

```cpp
#include <iostream.h>
class Integer {
            int ia;
        public:
            Integer(int r = 0) { ia = r;}
            friend Integer operator++(Integer);
            void print() { cout << "a = " << ia
                            << "\n"; }
        };
void main()
{
  Integer a(5);
  a++;
// a = 5
  a.print();
}
Integer operator ++(Integer a)
{
  a.ia++;
  return(a);
}
```

How It Works

The above code result is **a = 5**, that is, the value of variable **a** remained unchanged. The **operator++** function manipulated the local copy of the object and the manipulation results were lost after completion, since they were unassigned. The **operator++** function can seemingly be implemented by passing a pointer to variable to the function. For example:

```
void operator++(Integer * a)
{
   a->ia++;
}
```

In this case, the main program may take the following form:

```
#include <iostream.h>
class Integer {
        int ia;
     public:
        Integer(int r = 0) { ia = r;}
        friend void operator ++(Integer *);
        void print() { cout << "a = " << ia << "\n";}
};
main()
{
 Integer a(5);
 (&a)++;
 a.print();
}

void operator++(Integer *a)
{
  a->ia++;
}
```

You can't omit the parentheses in the `(&a)++` statement, since the operators `&` and `++` have the same priority and must be performed from right to left. Such a way of recording, however, is equivalent to the statement:

```
&a = &a + 1;
```

However, the address operator can't appear in the left part of the assignment operator (as we've already said), since it differs from the L-value.

Therefore, the compiler responds with an error message to the `(&a)++` statement. These problems can be remedied by using a reference to **Integer** class overloading the **++** operator.

```
#include <iostream.h>
class Integer {
        int ia;
     public:
        Integer(int r = 0) { ia = r;}
```

```
        friend void operator ++(Integer &);
        void print() { cout << "a = " << ia << "\n";}
};
main()
{
 Integer a(5);
 a++;
 a.print();
}
void operator++(Integer &a)
{
 a.ia++;
}
```

After completion of the run the following appears on the screen:

```
a = 6;
```

The **++** operator overloading function is passed the reference to **Integer**. Since the reference is a dereferenced pointer, you will handle the variable **a** itself, rather than its copy, hence all updates performed by the function for variable **a** will be saved after return from the function.

If a function is awaiting a reference, you can call it by passing a variable name to the function - therefore, you can write **++a**. Since the reference to variable is an L-value, the expanded code **a=a+1** will also be valid. Thus, as you may see, the reference type argument is necessary in such a case.

Unpredictable Results

Bear in mind that if there's no match between an actual argument and a formal parameter of the reference type, the results produced by the function may be unpredictable. You can attribute this to the fact that type conversion for the reference argument is performed through the temporary store - that is, the local copy of the argument is actually produced. Then, the function manipulates this copy and all manipulation results will be lost upon completion. Let's look at an example:

```
#include <iostream.h>

class Word {
      unsigned int ib;
   public:
      Word(unsigned int k) { ib = k; }
      void print() { cout << "b = " << ib << "\n"; }
   friend int acc(Word);
};

class Integer {
```

```
      int ia;
   public:
      Integer(int k) { ia = k; }
      Integer(Word b) { ia = acc(b); }
      void print() { cout << "a = " << ia << "\n";}
   friend void operator++(Integer &);
};

main() {
Word b(7);
++b;
b.print();
}

void operator++(Integer &a)
{
++a.ia;
}

int acc(Word d)
{
return(d.ib);
}
```

Here, the **++** operator has been defined for the **Integer** class, and conversion from **Word** to **Integer** has been defined for class objects. An attempt to perform an increment operator on the object of **Word** class revealed that there is no match between the arguments.

Word to Integer for a Class Object

Therefore, to perform conversion from **Word** to **Integer** for a class object, you should create an **Integer** class object in the temporary space and then call the operator **++** function for the object. Thus the result will be lost on return from the function and the code produces the following:

```
b = 7
```

Therefore, you should be very careful when passing arguments of type reference to a function. References allow you to use the expressions with ordinary arithmetic operators for large objects, so avoiding unnecessary copying.

Note that an argument of reference type must be declared with the **const** keyword when references are used to decrease object copying overhead rather than to change it. In this case, an attempt to change an argument will cause the compiler to issue an error message.

Try It Out - Defining Operators for Integer

For example, one of the operator overloading rules reads that the overloaded operators **+, -, *, /, %** mustn't change their operands. If you want to define these operators for **Integer**, this is the code:

```
class Integer {
  int ia;
    public:
  Integer(int);
  friend void operator++(Integer&);
  friend Integer operator+(const Integer&, const Integer&);
                };
Integer operator+(const Integer&a, const Integer&b)
{
  Integer c = a.ia + b.ia;
  return c;
}
```

How It Works

By coding **const Integer&**, you actually emphasize that the function arguments can't be changed. The use of **const** isn't obligatory, but it's good programming style, and facilitates the use of the method to be used on **const** objects of this class.

Returning a Reference to an Object

The above example passes references to the function, but returns the object value. There are some cases, however, which require a reference to an object to be returned, for example, when a subscripting operator (**[ ]**) is to be overloaded.

Try It Out

Let a subscripting operator be defined in the **Array** class:

```
class Array {
          int sz;
          int * is;
      public:
          Array(int);
          int & operator[](int);
      };
int & Array :: operator[](int index)
{
  return is[index];
}

Array a(10);
```

Since the expression **a[5]** may appear both in the left and right side of the assignment, we can write it as follows:

```
a[5] = a[5] + a[0];
```

In this case, the **operator[]** function can return neither pointer nor value since none of them is an L-value.

How It Works

As you can see from the example, a function must return a reference in some cases. This can improve efficiency by avoiding having to copy the object onto the stack.

Creating a Reference Returning Function

When you create a reference returning function, bear in mind that since the reference will be passed from a function, the return value referenced can't be an automatic variable. This is because as soon as the function exits, the automatic is destroyed, leaving a dangling reference. Also, since the operator is used more than once in the expression, the result must not be a static variable, as it will be overwritten on subsequent calls. Generally, it should be allocated dynamic memory. Therefore, it's sometimes more efficient to copy the return value to save time and space. Besides, return value copy is more easily programmed than dynamic storage allocation for an object.

Subscripting

Among other operators to be overloaded there is a subscript operator. It is usually used to specify the meaning of subscripts for class objects. The **operator[]** function must be a member function of a class for which it is defined.

A subscript **operator[]** is considered to be binary. If class **x** were specified, then **x[y]** is interpreted as **x.operator[](y)** (where **x** is an object of **x**). The second parameter, the subscript, can be any type.

For the class **String** objects let's check whether the subscript violates an upper or lower boundary. Remember that the subscript operator can appear either to the left or right of the assignment operator - therefore, it must return a reference to a class object.

```
#include <iostream.h>
class String {
              char * str;
              int sz;
          public:
              String(char *);
                    char & operator[](int);
...
              };
char & String :: operator[](int ind)
{
  if( ind < 0 )
    {
      cerr << "\n Array boundary violation\n";
      return str[0];
    }
  else
    if ( ind >= sz )
      {
      cerr << "\n Array boundary violation\n";
      return str[sz - 1];
      }
    else
      return (str[ind]);
}

// Now we can write the main function code:

main()
{
    String A("subscripting");
    char c = A[9];
    cout << "c = " << c << "\n";
    A[9] = 'p';
    cout << "A[9] = " << A[9] << "\n";
}
```

Let's have a closer look at the subscript operator overloading in conjunction with an array of objects:

```
#include <iostream.h>
#include <string.h>
class String {
      char * str;
      int sz;
  public:
      String();
      String(char *);
      char & operator[](int);
```

```
        String& operator = (String &);
...
};
char & String :: operator[](int ind)
{
 if( ind < 0 )
    {
       cerr << "\n Array boundary violation(<0)\n";
       return str[0];
    }
 else
      if ( ind >= sz )
       {
       cerr << "\n Array boundary violation(>n)\n";
       return str[ind];
       }
      else
       return (str[ind]);
}

// Now we can write the main function code:

int i = 0;
void main() {
   String A[10]; // *
   String B("string-B"), C("string-C");
   A[0] = B; // **
// Global subscript operator
   A[1] = C; // **
// Global subscript operator
   cout << "Print A[0] ";
   for (i = 0; A[0][i] != '\0'; i++) cout << A[0][i]; // ***
   cout << "\n";
   cout << "Print A[1] ";
   for (i = 0; A[1][i] != '\0'; i++) cout << A[1][i]; // ***
   cout << "\n";
}
String :: String()
{
   str = 0;
   sz = 0;
}
String :: String(char *s)
{
   int len = strlen(s);
   str = new char[len + 1];
   strcpy(str, s);
   sz = len;
}
String& String::operator = (String &s)
{
```

```
    if (this != &s)
      {
        int len = s.sz;
        if(str != 0)
           delete str;
        str = (char *)new char[len + 1];
        strcpy(str, s.str);
        sz = len;
      }
  return *this;
}
```

The asterisked line **String A[10]** is the declaration of an array consisting of 10 **String** type elements. In this case, brackets **[]** don't represent the subscript operator, but serve as a modifier to inform the compiler about a declared array.

Following the general rules of the language, **A** isn't an object, but rather a constant pointer to an object of **String** type. This implies that the statements marked with two asterisks (******) involve a pointer to **String** and an **int** value.

The Global Subscript Operator

The subscript operator we have just overloaded waits for an object of type **String** and the **int** value. Therefore, statements **A[0] = B;** and **A[1] = C;** use the global subscript operator. This operator calls the overloaded assignment operator, since the global subscript operator results in an object of **String** class.

If you want to use the overloaded subscript operator, insert another pair of brackets, (as we did in the statements marked with three asterisks [*******]), since the subscript operator has been overloaded for the class object, and can't be overloaded in any other way. The first subscript operator applied to the array name produces the object of the specified type. The second subscript operator performs the user-defined actions.

Member Selection Operator (->)

You can overload a member selector **->** in the same way as other operators. The selector is treated as a unary operator for its left operand. The left operand may be either a class object or a reference to the class object on which operator overloading is performed.

The function **operator->** must be a class member which returns either a class object or a pointer to a class. Then the pointer is automatically handled by the predefined selector operator (by pointer) **->**. If an operator function is to return a class object, there must be the **operator->()** user function defined for the class. The second user-defined operator will be applied to the result of the first operator. Finally, the predefined selector **->** will always be used. Therefore, at least one user-defined operator function in the class hierarchy must return the pointer to the class.

For the **->** operator overloaded for class X, the expression **x->m**, where **x** is an object of **x**, will be interpreted as **(x.operator->())->m**.

Generally, it would be reasonable to overload the **->** operator for a highly developed hierarchy of classes.

Recall the hierarchy of class objects in the word occurrence counting code of Chapter 1:

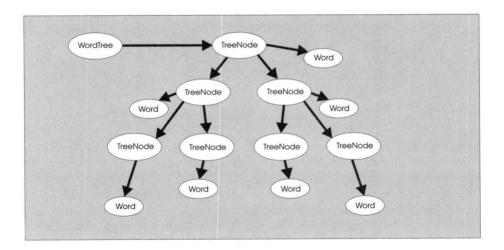

Highly Developed Hierarchy of Class Objects

The **WordTree** object contains a pointer to the tree root consisting of the **TreeNode** objects. Every node (**TreeNode** object) contains a pointer to the **Word** object. Suppose you wish to printout an unsorted **Word** object. For this you should use the overloaded selection operator (**->**). The **Word** class defines the **isWord** function to return the character string to be printed out. Besides, the **WordTree** object (which is actually a pointer to the word tree [a tree of **TreeNode** objects]) is always available. You'll achieve what you're aiming at if you specify overloading for the **->** operator - that is, by specifying the name of object in the top of hierarchy to the left of the **->** operator and the name of the target object member to the right of the operator.

To understand what the overloaded selection operators would return, look at the simplified hierarchy of objects:

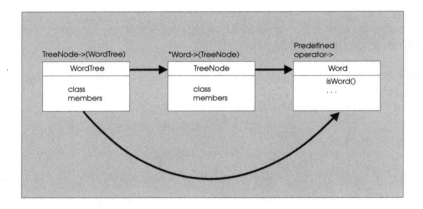

How to Overload Selection Operator for Class Hierarchy

The operator function defined for the **WordTree** class must receive either an object of the class or a reference to the class object as an argument. This operator function must return either an object or a reference to **TreeNode**. For the **TreeNode** class, the **->** operator must also be overloaded. In this case the operator function is also returned an object or a reference to the class it has been defined in, but returns a pointer to **Word**. You don't need to overload the **->** operator in the **Word** class (which is the last in the hierarchy). Here, the predefined selection operator is used to select the appropriate member.

Generally, the **->** overloading is used to hide the complexity of object selection mechanism for a sophisticated hierarchy of objects.

```
#include <iostream.h>
#include <string.h>
#include <ctype.h>

// Word class definition
class Word {
   private:
      char * theWord;
      int wordLen;
   public:
      Word();
      Word(char *);
      Word(Word &);
      ~Word();
      char * IsWord();
      int IsWordLen();
      int IsEmpty();
// Assignment one word to another
      Word & operator = (Word &);
// Compare two words
      int operator == (Word &);
      int operator < (Word &);
};

// Definition of Word class member functions
// Constructors


Word :: Word()
{
   theWord = NULL;    // Create dummy word
   wordLen = 0;
}

Word :: Word(char * s)    // Create word from character string
{
   int Len;
   Len = strlen(s);
   theWord = (char *) new char [Len + 1];
   strcpy(theWord, s);
   wordLen = Len;
}

Word :: Word(Word & w)    // Create word from word (duplicate word)
{
   wordLen = w.IsWordLen();
   theWord = (char *) new char [wordLen + 1];
   strcpy(theWord, w.IsWord());
}

// Destructor
```

```cpp
Word :: ~Word()
{
   if (theWord != NULL)
      delete theWord;
}

// Get pointer to word
char * Word :: IsWord()
{
   return theWord;
}

// Get the length of the word
int Word :: IsWordLen()
{
   return wordLen;
}

// Does word is empty
int Word :: IsEmpty()
{
  return (theWord[0] == '\0') ? 1 : 0;
}

// Assignment operator
Word & Word :: operator = (Word & w)
{
   if (this != &w) {
      int Len = w.IsWordLen();
      if (theWord != NULL)
        delete theWord;
      theWord = (char *) new char [Len + 1];
      strcpy(theWord, w.IsWord());
      wordLen = Len;
   }
   return * this;
}

// Relation operators
int Word :: operator == (Word & w)
{
   if ((strcmp(theWord, w.IsWord()) == 0) &&
        (wordLen == w.IsWordLen()))
      return 1;
   return 0;
}

int Word :: operator < (Word & w)
{
   if (strcmp(theWord, w.IsWord()) < 0)
```

```
            return 1;
        return 0;
    }

    // TreeNode class definition

    class TreeNode {
        private:
            Word * word;        // Pointer to word
            int count;          // Word count
        public:
            TreeNode * left;    // Pointer to left subtree
            TreeNode * right;   // Pointer to right subtree
        public:
            TreeNode();         // Constructors
            TreeNode(Word &);
            ~TreeNode();        // Destructor
            void Increase();    // Increase count of word
            Word * IsWord();    // Get a pointer to word
            int IsCount();      // Get a word count
            Word * operator-> ();
    };

    Word * TreeNode :: operator->() {
            return word;
    }

    // Definition of TreeNode class member functions


    // Constructor to create dummy node
    TreeNode :: TreeNode()
    {
        word = NULL;
        count = 0;
        left = right = NULL;
    }
    // Constructor to create a node with word
    TreeNode :: TreeNode(Word & w)
    {
        word = new Word(w);
        count = 1;
        left = right = NULL;
    }

    // destructor
    TreeNode :: ~TreeNode()
    {
        if (word != 0)
            delete word;
    }
```

```
// Increase word count
void TreeNode :: Increase()
{
    count++;
}

// Get a pointer to word
Word * TreeNode :: IsWord()
{
    return word;
}

// Get a counter
int TreeNode :: IsCount()
{
    return count;
}


// WordTree class definition


class WordTree {
    public:
        TreeNode * root;
    public:
        WordTree();
        ~WordTree();
        TreeNode * IsRoot();
        TreeNode * Add(Word &, TreeNode *);
        void Print(TreeNode *);
        TreeNode & operator->();
    private:
        void Destroy(TreeNode *);
};
```

// Definition of WordTree class member functions

```
#include "stdlib.h"
TreeNode & WordTree :: operator->() {
TreeNode * p = root;
int n;
while (1) {
    n = rand() % 2;
    if (n == 0)
        { if (p->left != 0)
            p = p->left;
          else break;
        }
    else {
```

```
        if (p->right != 0)
            p = p->right;
        else break;
    }
}
return * p;
}
```

```
// Constructor
WordTree :: WordTree()
{
    root = 0;
}

// Destructor
WordTree :: ~WordTree()
{
    if (root != 0)
        Destroy(root);
}

// Add a word to the tree
TreeNode * WordTree :: Add(Word & w, TreeNode * p)
{
    if (p == 0)
        p = (TreeNode *) new TreeNode(w);
    else if (*(p->IsWord()) == w)
        p->Increase();
    else if (*(p->IsWord()) < w)
        p->right = Add(w, p->right);
    else
        p->left = Add(w, p->left);
    return p;
}

// Print a wordtree
void WordTree :: Print(TreeNode * p)
{
    if (p != 0) {
        Print(p->left);
        cout << p->IsWord()->IsWord() << " : " << p->IsCount() << '\n';
        Print(p->right);
    }
}
// Private member function to destroy
void WordTree :: Destroy(TreeNode * p)
{
    if (p != 0) {
        Destroy (p->left);
        Destroy (p->right);
        delete p;
```

```
      }
   }

   // Our program for word occurrence counting

   Word GetWord()
   {
     char buf[40];

     cin >> buf;
     Word w = buf;

     return w;
   }

   int main()
   {
      Word w;
      WordTree * tree = (WordTree *) new WordTree;
      for ( ; ; ) {

         w = GetWord();
         if (!w.IsEmpty())
            tree->root = tree->Add(w, tree->root);
         else
            break;
      }
      tree->Print(tree->root);
      WordTree tr = * tree;
      cout <<    tr->IsWord();

      delete tree;

      return 0;
   }
```

Friends or Members?

Overloaded operator functions, other than =, [], () and ->, can be either
class member functions or global friend functions. The choice is really just a
matter of taste.

If an operator alters the state of an object, it must be a member (this is a
good rule in terms of programming style). It would therefore be natural to
declare operators ++, - -, *=, +=, and so on, as class members, and binary
operators +, -, *, /, %, and so on, as friends. It's also reasonable that
arguments be specified with the **const** keyword.

Another criterion of selection is whether type conversions have been defined. If no type conversion is specified, any function may be defined a friend or vice versa.

On the other hand, the presence of type conversions or friend operator functions decreases the number of functions required to implement operations on class objects. In this case, a reasonable trade-off needs to be found.

Summary

This chapter has dealt with the general concept of overloading your C++ programs. You have learned that both functions and operators can be overloaded, and that far from being a problem (as its name perhaps suggests), overloading is a recommended process.

A special mechanism of constructors and destructors allows automatic initialization and release of class objects. You can overload constructors, and thereby define different ways of object initialization. (You can make them inline to improve the performance.)

Like constructors, you can overload any member function or global function. A call for this function is resolved by matching rules that are based on standard or user-defined conversions and allow to choose an unique function instance.

For more convenience in handling class objects, C++ provides the operator overloading mechanism which allow you to use predefined operator signs to operate on objects in a conventional way.

You can overload the same operator more than once no matter which class operands would be involved. In this case, matching rules are also used to resolve this operator call.

In the next chapter, we'll deal with inheritance.

CHAPTER 8

Class Derivation - Inheritance

This chapter discusses inheritance in C++. Inheritance is a mechanism by which a new class can be built from an existing one. A new class based on an existing one is said to be derived from the 'original' class. The new class created by derivation is referred to as a derived class and the class inherited by the new class is referred to as a base class.

This is what we can do with a derived class:

> Add new data members and methods

> Overload class member functions

> Alter access to class members.

In this chapter we'll cover:

> Class derivation

> New classes via inheritance

> Access to classes

> Constructors and destructors of derived classes.

Classes, and Hiring a Car

Before we launch into derivation, lets create an example which will help to elucidate the key elements of classes and derivation. The example is that of a car hire company which might have a number of classes, one for each car: compact, mid-size, and luxury. Obviously these have a number of common features, (they're all cars!). Inheritance places the common features of a car, four wheels, an engine, a gearbox, and so on, in a base class **Car**, and then inherits the classes compact, mid-size, and luxury, from the base class, adding only what makes those classes different from the base class, **Car**. For instance the luxury might add power steering and tinted glass to the base class, whilst the compact would add nothing.

Introduction to Class Derivation

C++ allows relations to be established between classes. This is achieved through the class inheritance mechanism by which the programmer can build new classes from the existing ones. The new class can inherit both data and functions of the class from which it was derived. A hierarchy of data types sharing the same data and functions is created.

Let's demonstrate class inheritance by taking the task of Chapter 1 as an example.

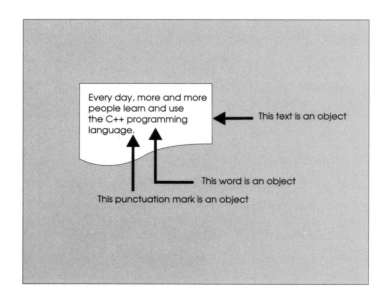

Text Fragment as an Example of the Simplest World of Objects

The previous figure shows a fragment of text from the C++ manual. This fragment is a simple example of the real world of objects which includes the object text which itself consists of a collection of other objects, namely words and punctuation marks.

Each object is defined by its class. What we need to do is define the following classes:

> A class identifying the whole text as a collection of words and punctuation marks

> A class identifying each word individually in the text

> A class identifying each punctuation mark.

Of more interest to us are classes that define the words and the punctuation marks. Let's define the classes, calling them **Word** and **Punctuation**.

Word Class Definition

```
// Class Word declaration without using of class derivation

#define MAXWORDSIZE        31

enum Boolean {

  False = 0,
  True

};

class Word {

  private:

    char theWord[MAXWORDSIZE];  // Word
    int wordLen;                // Word length

  public:

    // Constructors
    Word();
    Word(char *);
    Word(Word &);
    // Destructor
    ~Word();
```

```
    // Get word length
    int IsWordLen();
    // Word assignment
    Word & operator = (Word &);
    // Word comparisons
    Boolean operator == (Word &);
    Boolean operator > (Word &);
    Boolean operator < (Word &);
    // Word concatenation
    Word & operator + (Word &);

};
```

Punctuation Class Definition

```
// Class Punctuation declaration without using of
// class derivation

class Punctuation {

  private:

    char thePunct; // Punctuation sign

  public:

    // Constructors
    Punctuation();
    Punctuation(char);
    Punctuation(Punctuation &);
    // Destructor
    ~Punctuation();
    // Punctuation assignment
    Punctuation & operator = (Punctuation &);
    // Punctuation comparison
    Boolean operator == (Punctuation &);

};
```

As you see from the definitions of the **Word** and **Punctuation** classes, they have a great deal in common.

The **Word** class holds a word in the character array **theWord**. The **Punctuation** class holds a punctuation mark in the character variable **thePunct**. That is, both classes, **Word** and **Punctuation**, reserve memory space to hold the word and the punctuation mark. Moreover, the **Word** class defines the word assignment operator and the **Punctuation** class defines the punctuation mark assignment operator. The **Word** class has the word comparing operation and the **Punctuation** class has the punctuation mark comparing operation. Hence, both **Word** and **Punctuation** have similar data and functions. You may well wonder whether the data and functions common for both classes could be represented as a separate class.

Tokens

A word and a punctuation mark are minimum units of text that are of interest for us. The minimum unit of text is referred to as a token. Thus a text consists of a set of tokens where the token is either a word or a punctuation mark.

A word is a token, as is a punctuation mark. The notion of 'token' is the common feature relating the word to the punctuation mark. Let's represent a token as a class and call it **Token**.

What will the data and functions of the class **Token** be? We've already listed them when we talked about common data and functions of **Word** and **Punctuation**.

Let's define the **Token** class:

```
// Token class declaration
#define MAXTOKENSIZE          31

enum TokenClass {

  EmptyToken = 0,
  WordToken,
  PunctToken

};

enum Boolean {

  False = 0,
  True

};
```

```
class Token {

  protected:
    // Array for token
    char theToken[MAXTOKENSIZE];
    // Kind of token
    TokenClass tokClass;

  public:
    // Constructors
    Token();
    Token(char *);
    Token(Token &);
    // Destructor
    ~Token();
    // What kind of token is it
    TokenClass IsTokClass();
    // Token assignment
    Token & operator = (Token &);
    // Token comparison
    Boolean operator == (Token &);

};
```

Now, we can derive **Word** from **Token** by adding the word length, the greater than or less than operators for comparing words, and the word chaining operation to the **Token** class.

. . .

```
// Class Word declaration

class Word : public Token {

  private:

    int wordLen;  // Word length

  public:

    // Constructors
    Word();
    Word(char *);
    Word(Word &);
    // Destructor
    ~Word();
    // Get word length
```

```
    int IsWordLen();
    // Word assignment
    Word & operator = (Word &);
    // Word comparisons
    Boolean operator > (Word &);
    Boolean operator < (Word &);
    // Word concatenation
    Word & operator + (Word &);

};
```

Thus we have created the **Word** class which inherits all the features of the **Token** class but has additional features of its own. (Remember, the **Token** class used for deriving the new class is referred to as a base class. The class produced from the base class is referred to as a derived class.)

Use of Word Class Objects

```
// File test1.cpp
// class declarations and method definitions
#include "token.hpp"
#include "word.hpp"
```

```
// Using of objects of class Word
main()
{
  Word w("Week");  // First object of Word class
  Word w2("end");  // Second object of Word class
  // Third object of Word class
  Word w3 = w + w2;

  return 0;
}
```

Execution of the above code results in assigning the value **"Weekend"** to object **w3** of **Word**.

Creating a New Class by Inheritance

Definition of Class Derivation

Class derivation is a way of producing new classes from the existing ones. By deriving a new class from an old one, you ensure that the new class inherits data members and member functions of the old class.

Here is a common form of declaring a derived class:

```
class  derived_class_name :
    [public | private] base_class_name [...]
{
    class_member_declaration_list
};
```

The derived class declaration syntax resembles a normal class declaration excluding the derivation list in the declared class header:

```
    : [public | private] base_class_name [...]
```

The derivation list declares a class or classes to be used for deriving a new class. For example:

```
class Punctuation : public Token {
...
};
```

This example declares that the new class **Punctuation** is to be derived from **Token**.

The derivation list for **Punctuation** is shown in the following figure:

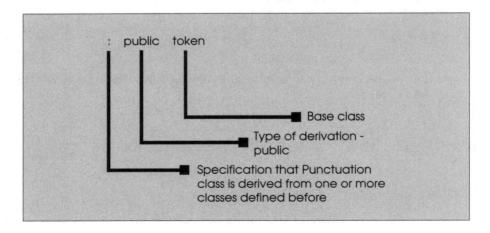

Class Derivation List

When declaring a derivation list you should follow these rules:

1 The derivation list can specify more than one base class.

2 The same base class can be specified only once in the list. For example, you can't declare the **Word** class as follows:

```
class Word : public Token, public Token {
...
};
```

The **Token** class is declared twice in the derivation list.

3 Any base class specified in the derivation list must either be declared before declaring the derived class or it must have a forward declaration specified.

A usual practice is to place the class definition in a separate file which has an extension **.H** or **.HPP** - for example, **TOKEN.HPP**. Thus, before defining the **Word** class, you should include the **Token** class definition placed in the separate file **TOKEN.HPP** next to the **#include** directive:

```
#include "token.hpp"
class Word : public Token {
...
};
```

If both the **Token** and **Word** definitions are specified in the same file (with the **Token** definition preceding that of the **Word**), you should specify a forward declaration for **Token**:

```
class Token;

// Definition of derived class Word
class Word : public Token {
...
};
// Definition of base class Token
class Token {
...
};
```

Derivation from a Single Base Class

There are two ways you can derive data and functions:

▶ From a single base class

▶ From more than one base class (multiple inheritance).

When you derive from the single base class, the derived class inherits data and functions of only one base class. For example, the classes **Word** and **Token** only inherit the members of **Token**. When more than one class is involved in derivation, the derived class inherits data and functions of more than one base class. Derivation from more than one base class will be discussed in the next chapter.

Public and Private Keywords

The keywords **public** and **private**, that can be placed in front of the base class name in the derivation list, specify access to the base class members inherited by the derived class.

For example:

```
class Punctuation : public Token
```

specifies a public derivation from **Token**.

This means that the derived class has access to all protected and public members of the parent class. Public inheritance is 'true' inheritance, and any user of the derived class has access to the public members of the base class.

The keyword **private** can be omitted, since any derivation is private by default. This means that the following

```
class Word : Token
```

specifies a private derivation from **Token**.

Private inheritance means that the derived class has access to the protected and public members of the parent class, but a user of the derived class has no access to any members of the parent class. For this reason it's inheritance as an implementation decision, rather than true design inheritance.

Our Base Class

We have selected **Token** as the base class for two derived classes **Word** and **Punctuation**. **Token** consists of data members and member functions. The data consists of a token and its category (word or punctuation mark), and the functions allow the token to be manipulated.

Let's define, for example, a member function for the token comparison **operator = =**. Two tokens are equal if their categories match, that is, a word can be compared with a word, and a punctuation mark with a punctuation mark, and the proper tokens match.

```
// Definition of member functions of class Token
// File token.hpp

#include <string.h>
#include <ctype.h>

...


// Constructors

Token :: Token()
{
  theToken[0] = '\0';
  tokClass = EmptyToken;
}

Token :: Token(char * s, TokenClass tc)
{
  strcpy(theToken, s);
  tokClass = tc;
}


Token :: Token(Token & tok)
{
  strcpy(theToken, tok.theToken);
  tokClass = tok.tokClass;
}

// Dummy destructor

Token :: ~Token()
{
}

// Get kind of a token

TokenClass Token :: IsTokClass()
```

```
{
  return tokClass;
}

// Token assignment

Token & Token :: operator = (Token & tok)
{
  strcpy(theToken, tok.theToken);
  tokClass = tok.tokClass;

  return *this;
}

// Two token are equal if
//   - their categories match, i.e. a word can be compared
//     with a word and a punctuation mark with a punctuation
//     mark
//   - the proper tokens match

Boolean Token :: operator == (Token & tok)
{
  if ((tokClass == tok.tokClass) &&
      (strcmp(theToken, tok.theToken) == 0))
    return True;
  else
    return False;
}

// Read token from input

istream & operator >> (istream & in, Token & tok)
{
  in >> tok.theToken;

  if (tok.theToken[0] == '\0')
    tok.tokClass = EmptyToken;
  else if (ispunct(tok.theToken[0]) != 0)
    tok.tokClass = PunctToken;
  else
    tok.tokClass = WordToken;

  return in;
}

// Write token to output

ostream & operator << (ostream & out, Token & tok)
{
  out << tok.theToken;

  return out;
}
```

Data Hiding

According to the data hiding rule for classes, all **Token** data is hidden from the **Token** user. This is made possible by the protected access specifier for C++ classes. Class members declared protected or private are only visible within the class scope, and are invisible outside the scope. All data members of the **Token** class can be used by member functions of the same class. A user wishing to access data in the **Token** class is restricted to only accessing **Token** functions. There is no other way of accessing the **Token** class data.

The **Token** class is an ordinary C++ class. You can create objects of the **Token** class and manipulate them by using functions of the class.

Let's define, for example, a token comparison operator. The first thing you need to do is to provide for keying tokens via a keyboard and displaying them on screen.

Now, we can modify the **Token** class definition by declaring two more functions in the **Token** class definition: one for reading a token from the screen, another for displaying the token on screen.

```
// Definition of member functions of class Token
// File token.hpp


...

#include <iostream.h>

...

class Token {

  protected:

    // Array for token
    char theToken[MAXTOKENSIZE];
    // Kind of token
    TokenClass tokClass;

  public:

    // Constructors
    Token();
    Token(char *, TokenClass);
```

```
    Token(Token &);
    // Destructor
    ~Token();
    // What kind of token is it
    TokenClass IsTokClass();
    // Token assignment
    Token & operator = (Token &);
    // Token comparison
    Boolean operator == (Token &);
    // Read token from input
    friend istream & operator >> (istream &, Token &);
    // Write token to output
    friend ostream & operator << (ostream &, Token &);

};
```

Operators **>>** and **<<** are not member functions of the **Token** class. They are declared friends to the **Token** class since they require the class objects **istream** and **ostream** as the first argument. Let's define these functions:

```
// Definition of member functions of class Token
// File token.hpp


...
```

```
// Read token from input
istream & operator >> (istream & in, Token & tok)
{
  in >> tok.theToken;

  if (tok.theToken[0] == '\0')
    tok.tokClass = EmptyToken;
  else if (ispunct(tok.theToken[0]) != 0)
    tok.tokClass = PunctToken;
  else
    tok.tokClass = WordToken;

  return in;
}

// Write token to output
ostream & operator << (ostream & out, Token & tok)
{
  out << tok.theToken;

  return out;
}
```

Now let's look at the code comparing two tokens.

```cpp
// Using of object of base class Token
// File test2.cpp

#include "token.hpp"

main()
{
  Token tok;   // First object of the Token class
  Token tok2;  // Second object of the Token class

  // Read the first token from screen into tok object
  cout << "\nEnter first token: ";
  cin >> tok;

  // Read the second token from screen into tok2 object
  cout << "\nEnter second token: ";
  cin >> tok2;

  // Compare the tokens
  if (tok == tok2)
cout << "\nTokens " << tok << " and " << tok2 << " are equal";
  else
cout << "\nTokens " << tok <<" and "<< tok2 << " are not equal";

  return 0;
}
```

Protected Access to Class Members

Up till now we've looked at two levels of access to class members: public and private. To recap, private members are only accessible within the class, that is, only class member functions and friend functions and classes can access them. Public members are accessible both inside and outside the class. Class members declared public can be used either by member functions of the same class, or by member functions of other classes and non-class member functions.

The **protected** keyword introduces a third level of access for class members. This keyword is used in the class from which a new class will be derived. The protected access means that the members declared protected are only accessible to the base class members, or to the class members derived from the base class.

Data members **theToken** and **tokClass** in the **Token** class have the **protected** specifier. They can be accessed by both the **Token** member functions and by the member functions of classes derived from **Token**. If you remember, the classes derived from **Token** are **Word** and **Punctuation**. Thus, data members **theToken** and **tokClass** will also be accessible in **Word** and **Punctuation**.

Derived Classes

We have chosen **Token** as our base class, (which represents the minimum unit of text, a token). From this we have derived the class **Word**. The **Word** class then adds members to those defined by the **Token** class.

Let's have another look at the declaration of the class **Word**:

```
class Word : public Token {

  private:

  int wordLen;  // Word length

  public:

  // Constructors
  Word();
  Word(char *);
  Word(Token &);
  Word(Word &);
   // Destructor
  ~Word();
  // Get word length
  int IsWordLen();
  // Word assignment
  Word & operator = (Word &);
  // Word comparisons
  Boolean operator > (Word &);
   Boolean operator < (Word &);
  // Word concatenation
  Word & operator + (Word &);
  // Read word from input
  friend istream & operator >> (istream &, Word &);

};
```

The derived class **Word** inherits the members of the base class **Word**: the data members **theToken** and **tokClass** as **Token** class members that are visible as protected, and all **Token** class functions since they are visible as public.

The **Word** class has its own members defined: the data item **wordLen** for holding the word length, and functions testing the words for 'greater than' or 'less than', for concatenating the words and calculating the word length.

Word Class Member Function Operator<

Take a look at the following code:

```
// Definition of member function operator < of
// class Word


class Word : public Token {
...
}
```

```
Boolean Word :: operator < (Word & w)
{
  if (strcmp(theToken, w.theToken) < 0)
    return True;
  else
    return False;
}
```

Word::operator< uses **theToken** data item (which is the **Token** class member). The following syntax

```
strcmp(theToken, w.theToken)
```

is valid since **theToken** is inherited by the **Word** class.

Try It Out - A Program to Compare Objects

Earlier, we compared the **Token** class objects. Now, let's write a program for comparing objects of the derived class **Word**. The actual words will be entered from the screen.

Before you can enter words from the screen, the **Word** class needs to be able to accept these words. For example, the **Token** class is capable of token input/output. The functions of token input/output are declared friendly to

Token. Thus they can access **theToken** and **tokClass** data items that define the token.

But can the derived class **Word** inherit this property from the **Token** class?

If a function (whether it is an outside function, or a member function of another class) is declared a friend to any class, it will have access to all class members either visible public or private and protected. The function **operator>>** has access to the **theToken** and **tokClass** data items of the base class **Token**. Therefore the global **operator>>** has access to the **Token** class members, but not to the members that the **Word** class adds, such as **wordLen**.

Accordingly, the following syntax

```
Word w;
cin >> w;
```

is valid.

However, a word is a token plus a word length. That is, the **Word** class contains a member of its own, the **wordLen** data item. The **operator>>** and **operator<<** functions have no access to **wordLen** of the **Word** class. Thus, if you use the **Token**-friendly **operator>>** function for reading a word, the **wordLen** will be assigned no value, that is, it will hold no word length.

There is something else of importance regarding input. The **Token**-friendly **operator>>** function reads a token. You know, however, that not every token input is a word. What you need is to make sure that the token read is a word. This is why you should define a special word read function for the **Word** class. As for displaying a word on screen, the **Token**-friendly **operator<<** function is fine.

The **Word** class is therefore somewhat different:

```
class Word : public Token {

  private:

   int wordLen;  // Word length

  public:

   // Constructors
   Word();
   Word(char *);
   Word(Token &);
   Word(Word &);
    // Destructor
   ~Word();
   // Get word length
   int IsWordLen();
   // Word assignment
   Word & operator = (Word &);
   // Word comparisons
   Boolean operator > (Word &);
    Boolean operator < (Word &);
   // Word concatenation
   Word & operator + (Word &);
   // Read word from input
   friend istream & operator >> (istream &, Word &);

};
```

Let's define the word read function:

```
// Definition of function operator for input of
// word

class Word : public Token {
...
}
```

```
// Read word from input

istream & operator >> (istream & in, Word & w)
{
  while (1) {

    in >> w.theToken;
```

```
    if (w.theToken[0] == '\0')
      break;
    else if (ispunct(w.theToken[0]) != 0)
      continue;
    else
      break;
  }

  w.tokClass = WordToken;
  w.wordLen = strlen(w.theToken);

  return in;
}
```

Now let's demonstrate the comparison of two words with the following program:

```
// Using of object of derived class Word
// File test3.cpp

#include "token.hpp"
#include "word.hpp"

main()
{
  Word w;    // First object of the Word class
  Word w2;   // Second object of the Word class

  // Read the first word into w object
  cout << "\nEnter first word: ";
  cin >> w; // The read operator that is a friend
        // to the Word class is used

  // Read the second word into w2 object
  cout << "\nEnter second word: ";
  cin >> w2;

  // Compare the objects w and w2
  // The function operator== inherited from Token class is used
  if (w == w2)
    cout << "\nWords " << w << " and " << w2 << " are equal";
  else
    cout << "\nWords " << w << " and " << w2 << " are not equal";

  return 0;
}
```

Overloading Base Class Members in Derived Class

The derived class can overload certain member functions of the base class, that is, it can define member functions of its own using the same **signature** as in the base class. The **Word** class redefines the **operator**= of the Token class. The **operator**= of the base class **Token** appears as follows:

```
// Assignment member function of class Token

class Word : public Token {
...
}
```

```
// Token assignment
Token & Token :: operator = (Token & tok)
{
  strcpy(theToken, tok.theToken);
  tokClass = tok.tokClass;

  return *this;
}
```

If there is no word assignment function defined in the **c** class, the following assignment statement

```
Word w("Weekend");
Word w2;
w2 = w;
```

will use the token assignment function, that is, the **operator**= function of the **Token** class. This assignment will result in the following values for **w2** data items:

```
theToken -   Weekend\0
tokClass -   WordToken
wordLen  -   ?
```

The **wordLen** data item is assigned no value. Therefore, to ensure a correct assignment of words, you should endow the **Word** class with its own assignment function, that is, with the **operator=** function.

Let's define the **operator=** function for the derived class:

```
// Assignment member function of class Word
```

```
class Word : public Token {
...
}
```

```
// Word assignment
Word & Word :: operator = (Word & w)
{
  // The base class operator= is used to assign values
  // to data item theToken and tokClass

  Token::operator =(w);
  wordLen = strlen(theToken);

  return *this;
}
```

Now, with the word assignment function defined in the **Word** class, one word will be correctly assigned to another word.

```
Word w ("world");
Word w2;
w2 = w; // Assignment is correct
```

The values assigned to object **w2** are as follows:

```
theToken    - world\0
tokClass    - WordToken
wordLen     - 5
```

Access to Derived Class Members

Since the derived class consists of an inherited portion and of its own portion, let's concentrate on access to the derived class members, both inherited and own.

Access to Inherited Members

Although the derived class inherits all members of the base class, it can't access every inherited member. The derived class can access the base class members in the public and protected sections. The derived class has no access to the base class members in the private section.

Members of the **Word** class can access the **theToken** and **tokClass** data members of the **Token** class as they are protected members, and can access all public member functions of the **Token** class (there are no protected member functions in the **Token** class, but if there were, they would be accessible as well).

```
// Definition of member function operator > of
// class Word


class Word : public Token {
...
}
```

```
Boolean Word :: operator > (Word & w)
{
  if (strcmp(theToken, w.theToken) > 0)
    return True;
  else
    return False;
}
```

Let's define another member function of the **Word** class, **operator>**. In the function body, we used the **theToken** item of the base class **Token**. The **operator>** function can reference **theToken**. In the **Token** class, this member is accessible as protected. Therefore **theToken** will also be accessible as protected in the **Word** class.

Here's more code which deals with **Word** comparison:

```
// Using of objects of derived class Word
// File test4.cpp

#include "token.hpp"
#include "word.hpp"

main()
{
  Word w;    // First object is a word
  Word w2;   // Second object is a word

  // Read the first word
  cout << "\nEnter first word: ";
  cin >> w;

  // Read the second word
  cout << "\nEnter second word: ";
  cin >> w2;

  // Compare the words
```

```
   if (w > w2)
     cout << "\nWord " << w << " is greater then word " << w2;
   else  if (w < w2)
     cout << "\nWord " << w << " is less then word " << w2;
   else
     cout << "\nWords " << w << " and " << w2 << " are equal";

   return 0;
}
```

In this example the following functions were used:

> Comparing words for greater than: the **operator>** function of **Word** class

> Comparing words for less than: the **operator<** function of **Word** class

> Reading words from the screen: the **operator>>** function (which is a friend of **Word** class)

> Writing words on the screen: the **operator<<** function (which is a friend of **Token** class).

Class Scope Operator

Let's go back to the **Word** assignment function, that is to the **operator   =** member function of the **Word** class. We'll introduce a new definition of the function:

```
// Assignment member function of class Word


class Word : public Token {
...
}
```

```
// Word assignment
Word & Word :: operator = (Word & w)
{
  // The base class operator= is used to assign the values
  // to data item theToken and tokClass

  Token::operator =(w);
  wordLen = strlen(Token::theToken);

  return *this;
}
```

Have a look at the following possible implementation for the **Word** class assignment operator:

```
// Word assignment
Word & Word :: operator = (Word & w)
{
  operator= (w);
  wordLen = strlen(theToken);

  return * this;
}
```

As any good C programmer will tell you, you've just written an infinite loop! The problem is the call to **operator=()**, which simply calls the **Word::operator=**, when what we actually wanted was for it to call the Token **operator=** function.

If you want to call the **Token** class's assignment function in the **Word** class's assignment function body, you must use the **Token** class name to qualify the function:

```
Token :: operator= (w);
```

Alternatively, and possibly more intuitively, you could have written:

```
Token(*this) = Token(w);
```

This assumes that you have provided a copy constructor for the **Token** class.

Rules for Accessing Inherited Members

Let's have some rules for accessing the inherited members of the base class in the derived class:

1 The derived class can access the inherited members of the base class which have protected and public accessibility.

2 The derived class can't access the base class members which have private accessibility.

3 There's no need to use the base class name to qualify the inherited members to be accessed, unless the derived class has overloaded the method and you explicitly want to call the base class method.

Type Casting Under Class Derivation

An instance of a derived class effectively 'contains' instances of the base classes. This means that an instance of the derived class, for example **Word**, can also be treated as an instance of the base class, in this case **Token**.

Let's define a Word class object:

```
Word w;
```

The following figure shows the arrangement of object **w** in memory.

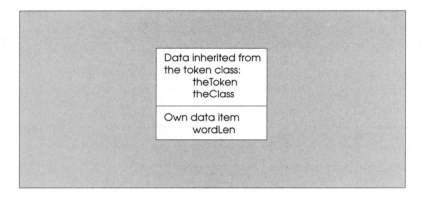

Arrangement of the Derived Class Object in Memory

Since the derived class contains the base portion, implicit type casting between the base and derived classes may occur. This implicit type casting may be as follows:

- A derived class object can be implicitly converted to a base class object

- A derived class reference can be implicitly converted to a base class reference

- A pointer to the derived class can be implicitly converted to a pointer to the base class.

Casting Object of Derived Class to Object of Base Class

Let's look at the case where there is conversion of a derived class object to a base class object.

The following is a function that prints the token with information about the **Token** class.

```
// Print token

#include "token.hpp"

void Print(Token tok)
{
  cout << tok << " - ";
  cout << ((tok.IsTokClass() == WordToken) ? "word" :
                                  "punctuation");
}
```

The **Print** function receives the **Token** class object as an argument. The object of both classes, **Word** and **Punctuation**, contains the **Token** class object. Thus the objects of **Word** and **Punctuation** classes can also be passed to the **Print** function.

```
Word w("Object");
Print (w);
Punctuation p('-');
Print (p);
```

The objects **w** and **p** are cast to **Token** class objects while being passed to the **Print** function.

Casting Reference to Derived Class to Reference to Base Class

You've already encountered an example of casting a reference to the derived class to a reference to the base class while defining the **Word** class member functions, or to be more precise, while defining the word assignment function. However, we didn't refer to it as such.

Let's have another look at the word assignment function definition:

```
// Assignment member function of class Word


class Word : public Token {
...
}
```

```
// Word assignment
Word & Word :: operator = (Word & w)
{
  // The base class operator= is used to assign values
  // to data item theToken and tokClass

  Token::operator =(w);
  wordLen = strlen(theToken);

  return *this;
}
```

Take a closer look at the expression used for calling the token assignment function for **Token** class:

```
Token :: operator= (w);
```

In the above expression the token assignment function is passed a reference to word. The word is an object of the derived class **Word**. Hence the **operator=** function of **Token** class is passed a reference to the derived class.

The **operator=** function is declared in the **Token** class as follows:

```
operator= (Token &);
```

This function is declared as a function to take a base class reference as argument. The token assignment function is passed a reference to a **Token**. The **Token** is held in the **Word**. Thus the procedure whereby you execute the operator

```
Token :: operator= (w);
```

is as follows:

1 The reference to **Word** class is converted to a reference to **Token** class.

2 The token assignment function is passed a reference to the base portion of **w** or reference to the base class.

Casting Pointer to Derived Class to Pointer to Base Class

Now it's time to introduce the class we mentioned at the beginning of the chapter which defines token text.

Let's represent token text as an array:

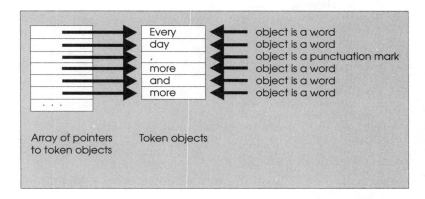

Token Text Object Represented Schematically

The token text object is an array of pointers where each pointer addresses a **Token** object. Since the token is either a word or a punctuation mark the pointer addresses either a **Word** object or a **Punctuation** mark object.

Let's define a class defining this representation of the token text object. The class will be named **TokenText**.

```
// Class TokenText definition
// File text.hpp

#define TEXTSIZE          1000

class TokenText {

  private:

    Token * tokens[TEXTSIZE]; // Array of tokens
    int count;                // Count of tokens in array
```

```
  public:

    // Constructor
    TokenText();
    // Destructor
    ~TokenText();
    // Insert new token into text
    void Insert(Token *, int);
    // Remove a token from text
    void Remove(int);
    // Get a token from text
    Token * GetToken(int);
    // Get count of tokens in text
    int GetCount();
    // Read tokens into text from display
    friend istream & operator >> (istream &, TokenText &);
    // Write tokens from text to display
    friend ostream & operator << (ostream &, TokenText &);

};
```

The **TokenText** class defines an array of pointers to **Token** class objects. Thus the pointed object can be an object of class derived from the **Token** class. This can be an instance of either the **Word** or **Punctuation** class.

The Insert Function

Let's now define a function that adds a new token to the token text, namely, the **Insert** function:

```
// Definition of member function Insert of class TokenText

class TokenText{
...
}
```

```
// Insert the token pointed by tok into position n

void TokenText :: Insert(Token * tok, int p)
{
  int pos;

  // We should be sure the token can be placed into text
  if (p < 0)
    pos = 0;
  else {

    if (p >= count)
```

```
      pos = count;
    else
      pos = p;
  }

  // If new token is inserted between text tokens
  // we should free space for it in text

  if (pos < count) {

    for (int i = pos, j = count - pos; i < count; i++)
      tokens[i + j] = tokens[i];

  }

  // And, finally, insert new token into text.
  // Increase token counter
  tokens[pos] = tok;
  count++;
}
```

Here's some more example code, which produces the token text:

```cpp
// Creation of token text
// File test5.cpp


#include "token.hpp"    // Declaration of class Token
#include "word.hpp"     // Declaration of class Word
#include "punct.hpp"    // Declaration of class Punctuation
#include "text.hpp"     // Declaration of class TokenText

main()
{
  // Token text object
  // Object 'text' have no tokens
  TokenText text;
  Word * w;             // Pointer to object of class Word
  // Pointer to object of class Punctuation
  Punctuation * p;

  // Adding tokens to text object
  w = (Word *) new Word("Every");
  text.Insert(w, text.GetCount());
  w = (Word *) new Word("day");
  text.Insert(w, text.GetCount());
  p = (Punctuation *) new Punctuation(',');
  text.Insert(p, text.GetCount());
  w = (Word *) new Word("more");
  text.Insert(w, text.GetCount());
```

```
w = (Word *) new Word("and");
text.Insert(w, text.GetCount());
w = (Word *) new Word("more");
text.Insert(w, text.GetCount());

// Output token text to screen
cout << text;

return 0;
}
```

Actually, the member function **Insert** is passed the location of another class object which is related to it. This is a powerful abstraction mechanism making the real object type indefinite. We'll discuss how the mechanism is controlled in subsequent chapters.

Constructors and Destructors of Derived Classes

Constructor of Derived Class

You may recall from the previous chapter that in order to allow an instance to be properly initialized we need to provide a constructor. Whilst some constructors take no parameters, or all are defaulted, others require parameters. For a class that isn't inherited we've already seen how these parameters are used to initialize an object:

```
MyWord::MyWord(char* pWord)
{
  lenWord = strlen(pWord);
  theWord = new char[lenWord + 1];
}
```

But what if, as is the case with the **Word** class after we've developed it, the constructor of the base class (**Token**) also requires parameters in order to correctly initialize itself? The answer is that the derived class passes the required parameters back to the base class. The syntax used is:

```
derived_class_name :: derived_class_constructor_name([arg_list])
              :  base_class_constructor([arg_list])
                 [,...]
{
   derived_class_constructor_body
}
```

The base class constructor is indicated in the derived class header. For example, **the Word(char *)** constructor header contains the constructor of base class **Token**:

```
Word:: Word (char * s)
       : Token (s, WordToken)
```

If the base class constructor is passed arguments, the arguments must be specified in the list of arguments of the derived class constructor:

```
Word(char * s): Token (s, WordToken)
```

The constructor of base class **Token** is passed arguments, namely the C++ string (that is why it has been specified in the argument list of the **Word** class constructor). Thus the argument list for the derived class constructor consists of arguments for the proper constructor of the derived class and arguments for the base class constructor.

In the example we are discussing, the **Word** class constructor is only passed arguments for the **Token** class constructor and has no arguments of its own.

If the base class has no constructor (or if the base class constructor requires no arguments), the base class constructor can be specified in the derived class constructor header.

Here is the **Word** class constructor for creating an empty word:

```
// Definition of constructor of class Word

class Word : public Token {
...
}
```

```
// Create a dummy word

Word :: Word() : Token()
{
  wordLen = 0;
}
```

This **Word** class constructor uses the constructor for creating an empty token of **Token** class:

```
// Definition of constructor of class Token

class Token {
...
}
```

```
// Create a dummy token

Token :: Token()
{
  theToken[0] = '\0';
  tokClass = EmptyToken;
}
```

Since the **Token** class constructor is passed no arguments, you can omit it from the header of the **Word()** constructor:

```
// Definition of constructor of class Word

class Word : public Token {
...
}
```

```
// Create a dummy word

Word :: Word()
{
  wordLen = 0;
}
```

Execution Order

When a derived class object is being created, the base class constructor is always executed first, that is before the derived class constructor. For example,

```
Word w ("Weekend");
```

The order of calling constructors when object **w** is created is as follows:

1   Constructor **Token(char *, TokenClass)** of **Token** class

2   Constructor **Word(char *)** of **Word** class.

Here is the **Token** class constructor:

```
// Definition of constructor of class Token

class Token {
...
}
```

```
// Create a token from character string

Token :: Token(char * s, TokenClass tc)
{
  strcpy(theToken, s);
  tokClass = tc;
}
```

The data items **c** and **tokClass** will be assigned values by the time the **Word** class constructor is called. Thus, the derived class constructor can use the values of inherited data items. The **wordLen** item is assigned a value depending on the value of the inherited item **theToken**:

```
wordLen = strlen(theToken);
```

Derived Class Destructor

When a derived class object is to be deleted, the derived class destructor is called before the base class destructor. To put it another way, destructors are called in the reverse order to that of constructors. For a **Word** class object, the **~Word()** destructor is invoked first and then the **~Token()**, if any exist.

Creating a New Class by Restricting Access to an Existing Class

As we've said, there are two kinds of inheritance in C++: public and private. The syntax for them is as follows:

```
class derived_class_name
   : [public  |  private] base_class_name
{  ...  };
```

With public inheritance, the derived class can access the inherited base class members declared public and protected. The derived class can define members of its own. Thus the public derivation can be treated as an existing class extension. The **Word** class is an extension of the **Token** class.

All the examples demonstrated up till now use the public derivation. Let's have a closer look at private derivation.

Private Inheritance

The base class and the derived class are relative rather than absolute notions. The derived class can be used as a base class for a new class derived from it, and so on.

Let's create a new class to define the notion of word counter that has already been used earlier. This class will be referred to as **WordCounter**. We'll use the **Word** class to create the **WordCounter** class.

```
// Declaration of class WordCounter
// File counter.hpp

class WordCounter : private Word {

  private:

    // Word counter
    int counter;

  public:

    // Constructor
    WordCounter(Word &);
    // Destructor
    ~WordCounter();
    // Increase word counter
    void Count(Word &);
    // Print word and counter
    friend ostream & operator << (ostream &, WordCounter &);

};
```

To create the **c** from the **Word** class, a private derivation is used.

With the private derivation, the inherited members of the base class having public or protected accessibility become the members of the derived class having private accessibility.

All members of the **WordCounter** class (both public and protected) inherited from the **Word** class became the members with the private accessibility. The following table shows the accessibility for the **WordCounter** class members.

Member	Data or Function	Derived or Own and Accessibility
theToken	data	derived/private
tokClass	data	derived/private
IsTokClass	function	derived/private
operator=	function	derived/private
operator==	function	derived/private
IsWordLen	function	derived/private
operator<	function	derived/private
operator>	function	derived/private
operator+	function	derived/private
counter	data	own/private
Count	function	own/public

The inherited members of **WordCounter** class are accessible within the scope of **WordCounter** and aren't accessible outside the class. The inherited members can be only accessed by member functions of **WordCounter** class.

Here is the **Count** function definition of **WordCounter** class:

```
// Declaration of class WordCounter
// File counter.hpp

class WordCounter : private Word {
...
}
```

```
// Definition of member functions of class WordCounter

// Constructor

WordCounter :: WordCounter(Word & w) : Word(w)
{
  counter = 0;
}

// Dummy destructor
```

```
WordCounter :: ~WordCounter()
{
}

// Increase word counter

void WordCounter :: Count(Word & w)
{
  // Increase word counter only if
  // words are mating
  if (operator ==(w) == True)
    counter++;
}

// Print word and counter
ostream & operator << (ostream & out, WordCounter & w)
{
  out << (Word &) w << " : " << w.counter;

  return out;
}
```

The **Count** member function uses the **operator==** member function inherited from the **Word** class.

Let's define the **WordCounter** class object:

```
Word w ("Object");
WordCounter wc(w);
```

Which actions can be performed on object wc of the **WordCounter** class? Can we get the word length held in object **wc**?

```
int l = wc.IsWordLen(); // is legal?
```

The answer to these questions is no, and the statement is illegal. The **IsWordLen** member function isn't accessible outside the **WordCounter** class, since it has been declared with the private specifier. That's why the **wc** object has no access to the **IsWordLen** member function. This object can only access members with public visibility, that is the **Count** member function.

The **WordCounter::Count** member function gets a reference to word, that is, the word object, as an argument. To obtain the word from the text, we use the **GetToken** function of the **TokenText** class. This function returns the pointer to token. Thus, before calling the **WordCounter::Count** member function, you should do the following:

1   Make sure that the next token in text is a word. For this, use the statement:

```
tp->IsTokClass() == WordToken
```

2   Convert the pointer to token that is returned by the **TokenText::GetToken** member function to the pointer to word:

```
(Word *) tp
```

The conversion is applicable if you have previously assured yourself that the pointer points to word

3   Apply the dereference operator to the converted pointer:

```
* ((Word *) tp)
```

This will get you the word object. This object, or to be more precise, the reference to the object, is passed to the **WordCounter::Count** member function.

The private derivation allows certain inherited members of the base class with public and protected access to leave the derived class members with public and protected access.

This is how you do it:

▶   In the protected section you should specify the members with protected access to be inherited from the base class and qualified with the base class name if you want them to remain protected in the derived class.

▶   In the public section of the derived class, you should specify the public members to be inherited from the base class and qualified with the base class name, if you want them to remain public in the derived class.

For member functions, it would be sufficient to specify only the function name without any argument list. For example:

```
class WordCounter :: private Word {
  private:
...
  public:
    Word :: IsWordLen;
...
};
```

The inherited **IsWordLen** member function with the public access will remain public in the **WordCounter** class.

You've learned that with private derivation the inherited members of the base class become the derived class members with private access. This implies that:

- A derived class object has no access to inherited members
- Base class members become inaccessible for subsequent derivations.

The private derivation serves for hiding certain base classes or members to prevent them from being used in subsequent derivations.

Summary

Let's emphasize the key points you should have learned from this chapter.

Inheritance is a mechanism for creating a new class from an old class. The old class can be modified by adding new members or by altering the objective or accessibility of individual members for creating a new class.

A class can be derived from the existing one as follows:

```
class   derived_class_name
    :  [public  |  private] base_class_name
{
    member   declarations
}
```

The **protected** keyword is another access specifier for class members.

The derived class can contain constructors. The derived class constructor must call the base class constructor for passing arguments in the following way:

```
derived_class_name (argument-list)
   :  base_class_name    (argument-list)
```

A derived class object can frequently be treated as a base class object.

References or pointers to derived class can be implicitly converted to references or pointers to a base class. You can declare a reference (or a pointer) to the base class and initialize it to the object (address) of the derived class.

CHAPTER
9

Virtual Functions and Polymorphism

This chapter discusses **polymorphism**, which in C++ is implemented through the use of **virtual functions**.

When you derive new classes from a base class, a hierarchy of related classes is created. The relationship between them is based on the fact that objects of any class in the hierarchy can be referred to via a pointer (or reference) to the base class.

Virtual functions can be accessed by a pointer to the base class in the hierarchy. The redefined functions to be selected are dynamically identified at run-time. This selection mechanism is based on the type of object pointed to by the pointer, and is called dynamic binding.

In this chapter we'll cover:

- Polymorphism
- Polymorphism at derivation
- Virtual functions
- Function binding
- Calling virtual functions.

Polymorphism

In the preceding chapter, you met the concept of class inheritance in C++. Class inheritance is a mechanism for building a hierarchy of interrelated classes. Class inheritance implies there is a base class defined that can be further used for deriving new classes, inheriting all properties of the base class, including its data and functions.

Try It Out - Creating a Hierarchy of Classes

Let's create a small hierarchy of classes as an example. We'll use the shapes of the following figure - a circle, a triangle, and a rectangle - as our objects:

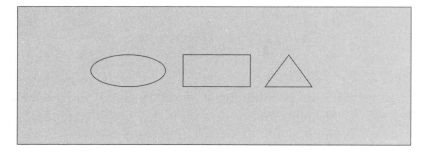

Two-dimensional Geometric Figures

We now need to identify the properties inherent to these objects. Let's first define the common properties inherent to all objects as a separate class.

The circle, rectangle, and triangle are two-dimensional geometric figures. What characterises any two-dimensional geometric figure is the concept of 'area'. Therefore, we'll associate the characteristic 'area of figure' with the concept of 'geometric figure'. Let's introduce the class **Figure**:

```
class Figure {
   public:
      Figure();        // Constructor
      ~Figure();       // Destructor
      double Area();   // Get an area

};
```

The 'area of figure' in the **Figure** class is defined by the **Area()** member function. The **Area()** function returns the area of the figure.

We can now derive the notions (classes) characterizing the circle, rectangle, and triangle from the base notion of a geometric figure. Each of these classes contains the features characterizing specific geometric figure:

▶ A circle is defined by its radius

▶ A rectangle is defined by its length and height

▶ A triangle is defined by its height and base.

> Since the area of specific figure is uniquely defined by its characteristics, the Area() function must be redefined for every derived class.

Let's introduce the **Circle** class to define the circle:

```
class Circle : public Figure {
   protected:
      double radius;   // Radius of a circle
   public:
      // Constructor
      Circle(double);
      // Destructor
      ~Circle();
      // Set a radius of circle
      void SetRadius(double);
      // Get a radius of circle
      double GetRadius();
      // Get an area of a circle
      double Area();

};
```

This is the **Rectangle** class:

```
class Rectangle : public Figure {
   protected:
      double length;   // Sides of a rectangle
      double width;
   public:
      // Constructor
      Rectangle(double, double);
```

```
    // Set sizes of a rectangle
    void SetSize(double, double);
    // Get a height
    double GetHeight();
    // Get a width
    double GetWidth();
    // Get an area
    double Area();

};
```

Finally, we can define the **Triangle** class:

```
class Triangle : public Figure {
   protected:
       double side;    // Sides of a triangle
       double side2;
       double angle;   // An angle between two sides
   public:
       // Constructor
       Triangle(double, double, double);
       // Destructor
       ~Triangle();
       // Set sizes of triangle
       void SetSize(double, double, double);
       // Get a sizes
       double GetSide();
       double GetSide2();
       double GetAngle();
       // Get an area
       double Area();

};
```

Thus we have derived several classes from a single base class (as you can see from the following figure):

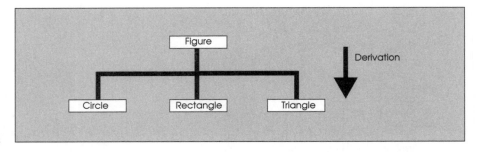

A Hierarchy of Classes Derived from the Base Class

How It Works

When several new classes are derived from the same base class, a hierarchy of derived classes is created which share the same data and functions. This is one key feature of derived classes (we discussed in the preceding chapter).

Polymorphism at Derivation

Now we are going to tackle another class derivation feature: the use of polymorphism at derivation.

The principle of polymorphism is the use of a unique name (function) throughout a type hierarchy to denote a single type action. Every type in the hierarchy implements the action in the way that is adequate for it. For example, every class in our 'two-dimensional geometric figures' hierarchy has an operation 'get figure area'. However, every derived class performs the operation in its own way.

> Polymorphism, in terms of its Greek origins, literally means 'having many shapes'.

Area Calculations for the Geometric Figures

The circle area is defined by its radius and is calculated by the following formula:

```
pi * radius * radius
```

The rectangle area is defined by its dimensions, and is calculated by the following formula:

```
width * height
```

The triangle area depends on two sides and the angle between them, and is calculated by the following formula:

```
(side1 * side2 + sin(angle))/2
```

Although the 'get geometric figure area' action has the name **Area()** in all classes (base and derived), different actions are performed.

For example, let's define the **Area()** function for the **Rectangle** class:

```
double Rectangle :: Area()
{
    return height * width;
}
```

Actions performed by the **Area()** function depend on the object (circle, rectangle or triangle) for which the function has been invoked.

Thus we have created the hierarchy of interrelated classes **Figure**, **Circle**, **Triangle**, and **Rectangle**. Since the classes forming the hierarchy are interrelated, we must provide for controlling common features of this family of classes.

Reviewing Implicit Conversions Between Derived and Base Classes

Because the base and derived classes are closely related (owing to the fact that the class derived from the base class contains the base part), there may be some implicit conversions between them. These implicit conversions are referred to as predefined standard conversions. We have already mentioned standard conversions in the preceding chapter, when discussing class derivation, but let's recap on them here:

▶ An object of the derived class is implicitly converted to an object of the base class. For example:

```
Circle c;        // Object of Circle class
Figure fig = c;  // Conversion from Circle to Figure
```

▶ A reference to a derived class is implicitly converted to a reference to a base class.

GetArea()

Let's define the global **GetArea()** to be used for calculating the area of any object in the **Figure** family:

```
double GetArea(Figure & obj)
{
    return obj.Area();
}
```

Here is an example of a call to **GetArea()** function:

```
Circle  c(3);
Rectangle r(2,4);
cout <<"Area of circle: " << GetArea(c);
// Reference to Circle is converted to reference to Figure
cout <<"Area of rectangle: " << GetArea(r);
// Reference to Rectangle is converted to reference to Figure
```

A pointer to a derived class is implicitly converted to a pointer to a base class. For example, let's declare the pointer to the **Figure** class as follows:

```
Figure * f;
```

The pointer **f** can point both to an object of the **Figure** class and an object of the classes **Circle**, **Triangle**, and **Rectangle**:

```
Circle c(5);
f = &c;   // Pointer to Circle (&c) is converted
       // to pointer to Figure
```

Note that the above conversions are performed without explicit specification of type conversion.

Try It Out - Generating a List of Geometric Figures as Objects

Suppose we want to create a list of geometric figures such as those shown in the following figure:

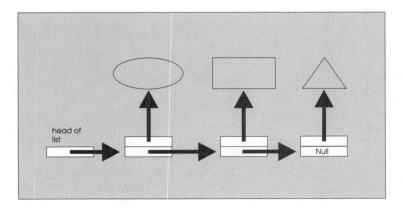

List of Geometric Figures

Firstly, we need to define a class to describe the structure of the previous figure:

```cpp
// Figure class defines general notion
// "plane geometric figure"
#include <iostream.h>
#include <math.h>

class Figure {
   public:
// Constructor
      Figure() {}          // Dummy constructor
// Destructor
      ~Figure() {}         // Dummy destructor
// Get a surface area
      virtual double Area();
};

// Figure class member functions definition

double Figure :: Area() {
   return 0;
}

// Circle class definition

class Circle : public Figure {
   protected:
      double radius;
   public:
      Circle (double);      // Constructor
      ~Circle() {}          // Dummy destructor
// Set a radius
      void SetRadius (double);
// Get a radius
      double GetRadius();
// Get a surface area
      virtual double Area();
};

// Circle class member function definition
// Constructor

Circle :: Circle (double r) {
   radius = r;
}

// Set a radius of a circle
void Circle :: SetRadius (double r) {
   radius = r;
}
```

```
// Get a radius of a circle
double Circle :: GetRadius () {
   return radius;
}

// Get a surface area of a circle
double Circle :: Area() {
   return 3.14159 * radius * radius;
}

// Triangle class definition
class Triangle : public Figure {
   protected:
      double side;
      double side2;
      double angle;
   public:
      Triangle(double, double, double);        // Constructor
      ~Triangle() {}             // Dummy destructor
// Set sizes of a triangle
   void SetSize (double, double, double);
// Get a size of a first side
   double GetSide();
// Get a size of a second side
   double GetSide2();
// Get a angle between two sides
   double GetAngle();
// Get a surface area
   virtual double Area();
};

// Constructor
Triangle :: Triangle(double s, double s2, double a) {
   side = s;
   side2 = s2;
   angle = a;
}

// Set sizes of a triangle
void Triangle :: SetSize(double s, double s2, double a) {
   side = s;
   side2 = s2;
   angle = a;
}

// Get a size of a first side
double Triangle:: GetSide() {
   return side;
}

// Get a size of a second side
```

```cpp
double Triangle :: GetSide2() {
   return side2;
}

// Get a angle between two sides
double Triangle :: GetAngle() {
   return angle;
}

// Get an area size of a triangle
double Triangle :: Area() {
   return side * side2 * sin(angle) / 2;
}

// Rectangle class definition
class Rectangle : public Figure {
   protected:
      double height;
      double width;
   public:
      // Constructor
      Rectangle(double, double);
      // Dummy destructor
      ~Rectangle() {}
      // Set sizes of a rectangle
      void SetSize(double, double);
      // Get a height of a rectangle
      double GetHeight();
      // Get a width of a rectangle
      double GetWidth();
      // Get an area size
      virtual double Area();
};

// Constructor
Rectangle :: Rectangle(double w, double h) {
   width = w;
   height = h;
}

// Set (change) sizes of a rectangle
void Rectangle :: SetSize(double w, double h) {
   width = w;
   height = h;
}

// Get a width of a rectangle
double Rectangle :: GetWidth() {
   return width;
}
```

```
// Get a height of a rectangle
double Rectangle :: GetHeight() {
   return height;
}

// Get an area size of a rectangle
double Rectangle :: Area() {
   return width * height;
}

// FigureList class definition
class FigureList {
   public:
      static FigureList * head;        // Head of list
   private:
// Pointer to a figure
      Figure * obj;
// Pointer to the next element of the list
      FigureList * next;
   public:
      FigureList(Figure *);        // Constructor
// Add a figure to a list
      FigureList * Add(Figure *, FigureList *);
// Destroy a list of figures
      void Destroy(FigureList *);
// Print area size of all figures in a list
      void Print(FigureList *);
 };

FigureList * FigureList:: head = 0;

// Constructor
FigureList :: FigureList(Figure * fp){
   obj = fp;
   next = 0;
   if (head == 0)
      head = this;
}

// Add a new figure to the list
FigureList * FigureList :: Add(Figure * f, FigureList * p) {
   if (p == 0)
      p = new FigureList(f);
   else
      p -> next = Add(f, p->next);
   return p;
}

// Destroy a list of figures
void FigureList :: Destroy (FigureList * p) {
   if (p != 0) {
```

```
            Destroy (p->next);
            delete p;
        }
    }

    // Print area size of all figures in the list
    void FigureList :: Print(FigureList * p) {
        Figure * fp;
        if (p != 0) {
            fp = p->obj;
            cout << fp->Area() << '\n';
            Print (p->next);
        }
    }

    double GetArea(Figure & obj) {
        return obj.Area();
    }

    int main ()
    {
        Circle c(4);
        cout << " Area of circle: " << GetArea(c) << '\n';
        FigureList flist(&c);
        Rectangle r(2.5, 3);
        cout << " Area of rectangle: " << GetArea(r) << '\n';
        flist.Add (&r, flist.head);
        Triangle t(5, 4.5, 1);
        cout << " Area of triangle: " << GetArea(t) << '\n';
        flist.Add (&t, flist.head);

        flist.Print (flist.head);
        flist.Destroy(flist.head);

        return 0;
    }
```

How It Works

The call of **Area()** function can be bonded to one of the function definitions in the classes **Circle**, **Triangle**, and **Rectangle** - see the figure opposite:

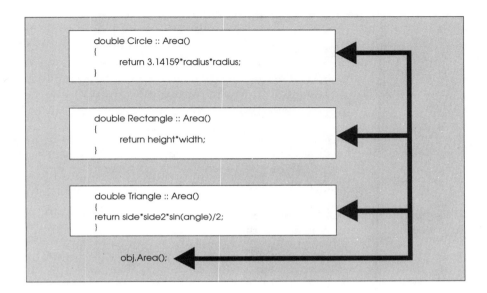

Bond Between a Function Call and the Function Definition

This relationship between data types determines a programming style that hides the real type of an object.

The global **GetArea()** function doesn't know which geometric figure it has passed. This function can be used to calculate the area of circle, triangle, or rectangle. The same is true for the **Print()** function, which is a member of **FigureList** class. The **Print()** function doesn't know what geometric figure is pointed at by the **fp** pointer.

Virtual Functions: The Bond Between Function Calls and Definitions

Why can the following statement be used for calculating the surface area of three different objects?

```
obj.Area() and fp->Area()
```

The bond between a function call and function definitions is based on the type of object upon which the function has been called to act, and is supported in C++ by the virtual function feature.

In the **Figure** class, the **Area()** function is declared as virtual.

```
class Figure {
   public:
      Figure();
      ~Figure();
      virtual double Area();
};
```

A virtual function is a function defined within a base class which can be redefined within any class derived from the base class. The instance of virtual function to be called by the function call expression depends on the object to be acted on by the called function.

Thus polymorphism is an object-oriented feature implemented in the C++ language and enables you to do the following:

▶ Use the same name of function (in our examples, the **Area()** function) to denote actions of the same type. However, the function is implemented differently depending on the type (class) of an object upon which the function will act.

▶ Use the same name (in our examples, **obj** and **fp**) to denote objects of different classes that have been derived from the same base class. Objects with this name will respond differently to a common set of operators.

Dynamic Binding Notion

Virtual functions are a special type of class member functions. The notion of virtual function closely relates to class inheritance. A class member function can be declared as virtual under the following conditions:

▶ A class with a virtual function is the base class in the derivation hierarchy.

▶ A function implementation depends on the class and will be different in each derived class.

To put it differently, a virtual function is a function defined in the base class, which can be redefined in any class derived from the base class.

A virtual function can be called via a pointer or a reference to the base class. Which virtual function instance is to be called by the function call depends on the class of object addressed by the pointer or reference. The question of which virtual function instance is to be called is resolved at program run time, rather than compilation or link time. This mechanism is referred to as dynamic binding or run-time type resolution.

Two Kinds of Function Binding

The C++ language supports two kinds of function binding:

1 Static function binding or operator/function overloading.

2 Dynamic binding or virtual functions.

Function binding implies that a function instance (function code) which is to be used in the function call is identified. The following figure shows the binding of a function call with a function definition.

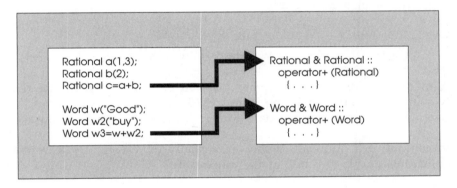

Function Binding

In this example, there are two function calls used (the operator is also a function):

▶ Adding two rational numbers

▶ Adding or concatenating words.

One function call uses the **operator+** function of the **Rational** class, another the **operator+** function of the **Word** class.

Static Function Binding

You can give the same name to two or more functions. However, the functions should differ either in the number or type of parameters. The C++ mechanism function overloading, which facilitates this, has been discussed in the preceding chapters.

The C++ language provides the user with a set of built-in data types. For example, there are data types for representing variable-length integers, real numbers of different precision, and so on. However, the range of number types supported by C++ may be insufficient for many applications, especially with regards math.

Extending the World - Adding Rational Numbers

Let's extend the world of C++ numbers by adding rational numbers.

A rational number is any number that can be represented by the ratio of two integers. Thus, for example, 1/2, 2/5, 3/10, and 2 are rational numbers while the *pi* number and square root of 2 are not rational numbers.

In computing, a rational number is normally represented by a decimal approximation. If you output the number 1/3

```
cout << 1/3;
```

the printed value will be **0.333333**. No matter how close this approximation is, it's not precise. If you type in the sum 1/3 + 1/3, the result produced will be **0.666666** while the result of printing the number 2/3 should be **0.666667**. This means that the expression

```
if ( (1/3 + 1/3) == 2/3)
```

produces an incorrect result. What we need is to represent rational numbers so that there is no loss of precision when math operations were performed upon them.

Since a rational number consists of a numerator and a denominator, you could represent the rational number as the following class:

```
class Rational {
   private:
      long n;    // Numerator
      long d;    // Denominator
};
```

However, the **Rational** class must be extended for the following reasons:

1 The rational number must be presented as an irreducible fraction. For example, 1/3 and 2/6 are equal while their numerators (1 and 2) and denominators (3 and 6) are not equal. Difficulties emerge when you compare these numbers. Therefore, there is a need for a function that can reduce a rational number to an irreducible fraction.

2 You must know how rational numbers are created, that is, the **Rational** class must contain one or more constructors.

3 You must know how arithmetic and logical operations are to be performed on rational numbers.

This can be done as follows:

```
// Definition of member function of class Relational
// File relational.hpp

class Rational {
...
}

// Constructors
Rational :: Rational(long num, long den)
{
   n = num;
   d = den;
// Reduce the rational number to irreducible fraction
   reduce();
}

// Constructor with one argument has additional meaning:
// it performs conversion operation a number to
// rational number in expressions

Rational :: Rational(long num)
{
   n = num;
   d = 1;
}

// Assignment of rational numbers

Rational & Rational :: operator = (Rational & r)
{
   n = r.n;
   d = r.d;

   return *this;
}
```

```
}

// Comparison of rational numbers

int Rational :: operator == (Rational & r)
{
// The following expression is valid because rational
// number is represented as irreducible fraction

   if ((n == r.n) && (d == r.d))
      return 1;
   else
      return 0;
}

int Rational :: operator != (Rational & r)
{
   return !operator ==(r);
}

int Rational :: operator > (Rational & r)
{
   long num = n * r.d;
   long num2 = r.n * d;
   if (num > num2)
      return 1;
   else
      return 0;
}

int Rational :: operator < (Rational & r)
{
   long num = n * r.d;
   long num2 = r.n * d;
   if (num < num2)
      return 1;
   else
      return 0;
}

// Addition of rational numbers
Rational & Rational :: operator + (Rational & r)
{
   n = n * r.d + d * r.n;
   d = d * r.d;
   reduce();
   return *this;
}

// Subtraction of rational numbers

Rational & Rational :: operator - (Rational & r)
{
```

```
   n = n * r.d - d * r.n;
   d = d * r.d;
   reduce();
   return *this;
}

// Multiplication of rational numbers

Rational & Rational :: operator * (Rational & r)
{
   n = n * r.n;
   d = d * r.d;
   reduce();
   return *this;
}

// Division of rational numbers

Rational & Rational :: operator / (Rational & r)
{
   n = n * r.d;
   d = d * r.n;
   reduce();
   return *this;
}

// Reducing a rational number to
// irreducible fraction

void Rational :: reduce()
{
   long num, num2, rem;
   int sign = 1;
   if (n < 0) {
      sign = -1;
      n = n * sign;
   }
   if (n > d) {
      num = n;
      num2 = d;
   }
   else {
      num = d;
      num2 = n;
   }
   do {
      rem = num % num2;
      num = num2;
      num2 = rem;
   } while (rem > 0);
```

```
   n = n / num;
   d = d / num;

   n = n * sign;
}

// Display rational number on screen

ostream & operator << (ostream & out, Rational & r)
{
   out << r.n << '/' << r.d;

   return out;
}
```

Adding and Creating Rational Numbers

Let's see how rational numbers can be created and added.

Here's the rational class constructor:

```
// Constructor

Rational :: Rational(long num, long den)
{
   n = num;
   d = den;
// Reduce the rational number
// to an irreducible fraction
   reduce();
}
```

Rational Number Adding Function

Thus, we have introduced a new object, a rational number, and defined a set of functions enabling you to use rational numbers in expressions.

For example, you can add rational numbers as follows:

```
#include <iostream.h>
#include "rational.hpp"
main()
{
   Rational a(1,5);   // Rational number 1/5
   Rational b(2);     // Rational number 2/1 or simply 2
// Addition of two rational numbers a and b
// Display the result
   Rational c = a + b;
   cout << c;   // 11/5 is displayed

   return 0;
}
```

Once you have overloaded the addition **operator+**, you can add rational numbers.

In the preceding chapter, we demonstrated how the addition operator can be overloaded for concatenation.

```
// Adding rational numbers
Rational & Rational :: operator+ (Rational &);
// Adding or concatenating  words
Word & Word :: operator+ (Word &);
```

Consequently, the same addition **operator** + function is given two different meanings. The **operator** + can be used both for adding rational numbers and for concatenating words. The instance of the **operator** + which will be used is identified by the types of its arguments at operator call time. This is illustrated in the following figure:

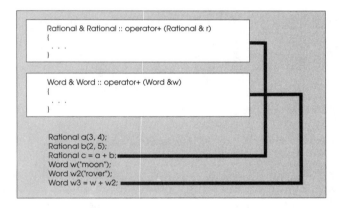

Binding the Function Call to the Function Definition at Overloading

Static Binding

The instance of the **operator+** which will be used (that is, binding) is identified at compilation, since both the operator definition and the types of arguments in its call points are known by this time. The compiler knows that this **operator+** call

```
a + b
```

involves two objects of the **Rational** type. Therefore, it binds this call with the definition of the **operator+** belonging to the **Rational** class. This mechanism is referred to as static binding.

Dynamic Function Binding

Let's go back to the list of geometric figures shown in the earlier graphic. A specific node in the list is unaware of which geometric figure or else which class object **Circle**, **Triangle** or **Rectangle** is pointed to by the **obj** pointer (see the following figure).

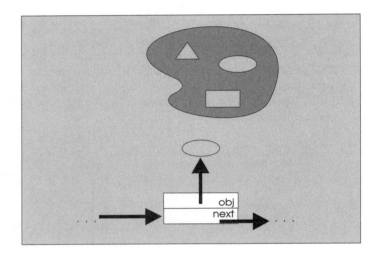

The Node of Geometric Figure List

That is why the call of figure area calculating function **Area()** in the body of the **FigureList::Print()** function can be bound with one of the function definitions in the classes **Circle**, **Triangle**, and **Rectangle**.

However, we don't know which class function will be called at this step of compilation. Since we don't know which **Area()** function definition is to be bound to the call, the executable file must store the definition table for the **Area()** function and provide for searching the table for the definition required to call the function. This mechanism is based on the type of object for which it is called and is referred to as dynamic binding.

Dynamic binding is supported by the virtual function mechanism. In the **Figure** class which is the base class for the **Circle**, **Triangle**, and **Rectangle** classes, the **Area()** function is defined as virtual.

Defining Virtual Functions

A function is defined as virtual by specifying the **virtual** keyword when the function is declared in the base class.

```
virtual  return-value-type    function-name
                 (parameter-declaration-listopt);
```

Only a member function of the class can be declared as **virtual**.

```
class Figure {
   public:
      Figure();
      virtual double Area();
};
```

The **Area()** function, which is a member of the **Figure** class, has been declared as **virtual** and therefore the following pertain:

- ▶ It's common to the whole hierarchy of classes based on the **Figure** class.

- ▶ The function definitions are different in the derived classes and are unknown at the **Figure** class declaration time.

- ▶ The **virtual** function declared in the base class of the derivation hierarchy is practically never used for the objects of the class, that is, it has no definition.

To emphasize the fact, we can use the following syntax:

```
virtual  return-value-type    function-name
                 (parameter-declaration-listopt)  =  0;
```

These virtual functions are referred to as pure virtual functions.

```
class Figure {
   public:
      Figure();
      virtual double Area() = 0;
};
```

The **Area()** function in the **Figure** class is declared as a pure virtual function. This means that the **Area()** function has no definition in the **Figure** class.

Abstract Classes and Pure Virtual Functions

A class with one or more pure virtual functions is referred to as an abstract class. An abstract class can be used only as a base class for the newly derived classes. You can't create objects of an abstract class.

For the **Area()** function declared as a pure virtual function in the **Figure** class, the following operators are invalid:

```
Figure fg;              // Invalid
Figure * fp = new Figure;   // Invalid
```

The **Figure** class underlies our hierarchy of geometric figures. It introduces the concept of geometric figure and defines common properties for the concept. Among these common properties is the **Area()** function which returns the area of the figure. The **Figure** class does not define any specific figure. It would be reasonable then to have the **Area()** function defined in the **Figure** as a pure virtual function.

> Note that a class with no public or protected constructors is also virtual, but this requires the default and copy constructors to be explicitly declared as private, otherwise the compiler provides public default and copy constructors.

Rules for Defining Virtual Functions

Let's set up the rules for defining virtual functions in the base and derived classes:

1 Defining a virtual function in the base class:
A virtual function initially declared in the base class must be either the pure virtual function or there must be a definition specified for the function.

2 Defining a virtual function in a derived class:
If you declared a pure virtual function in the base class, you should also define the function in the derived class or else the function would be redeclared as a pure virtual function. If there is no declaration for the virtual function in the derived class, the derived class would inherit the pure virtual function of the base class by default. In this case, the derived class would also be an abstract class and you could not instantiate objects of the derived class.

3 If the definition of a function in the derived class doesn't match its declaration as virtual, or it differs in the return value type, and the number and type of parameters, the function is not virtual for the derived class.

Try It Out - Adding Three-Dimensional Figures

Let's extend our view of geometric figures by adding three-dimensional figures to the family under consideration. For this, we'll have three-dimensional figures derived from two-dimensional figures. The hierarchy of geometric figures objects will appear as follows:

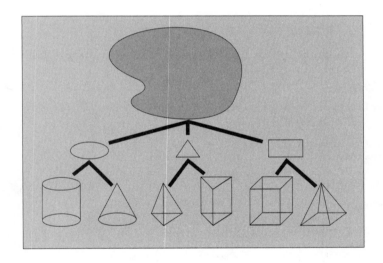

Hierarchy of 'Geometric Figure' Objects

Now is not the time to give you a full implementation of every class defining the objects of the previous figure. Let's realize just one branch of the hierarchy and define the classes represented in the figure overleaf:

327

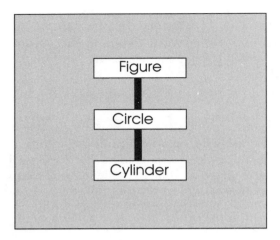

Hierarchy of Derived Classes with One Base Class

How It Works

```
// Declaration of class Figure
// File figure3D.hpp

#ifndef Figure_Class
#define Figure_Class

class Figure {

   public:

      // Constructor
      Figure() {}
      // A surface area of geometric figure
      virtual double Area() = 0;
      // A volume of geometric figure
      virtual double Volume() = 0;

};
...
#endif
```

Now the class object has a volume in addition to its surface area. **Area()** and **Volume()** are declared as pure virtual functions in the **Figure** class.

Notice how we have used a **#define** to stop multiple declarations from occurring in the source code.

Here is the **Circle** class:

```
// Declaration of class Circle
// File circle3d.hpp

#ifndef Circle_Class
#define Circle_Class

// Include declaration of class Figure
#include "figure3d.hpp"

class Circle : public Figure {

   protected:

      double radius;  // Radius of a circle

   public:

      // Constructor
      Circle(double);
      // Surface area of a circle
      virtual double Area();
      // Volume of a circle
      virtual double Volume();

};
...
#endif
```

The **radius** data item has been declared as **protected** in the **Circle** class. This is so that derived classes of the **Circle** class can access it.

```
// Definition of class Circle
// File circle3d.hpp


...


// Constructor

Circle :: Circle(double r)
{
   radius = r;
}

// Surface area of a circle
double Circle :: Area()
```

```
{
    return 3.14159 * radius * radius;
}

// Volume of a circle
double Circle :: Volume()
{
    return 0;
}
```

A circle is a plane figure and therefore has no volume. The **Volume()** function is defined as a zero-value returning function in the **Circle** class. We couldn't have the **Volume()** function declared as a pure virtual function in the **Circle** class since this would prevent us from creating objects of the **Circle** class.

> If a virtual function is redefined in the derived class, the virtual keyword can be omitted, that is, it becomes an ordinary definition of the class member function.

The **Circle** class redefines the virtual functions **Area()** and **Volume()** of the **Figure** class. Therefore you can omit the **virtual** keyword for the functions in the **Circle** class.

Here is the redefinition of the **Circle** class:

```
class Circle : public Figure {

    protected:

        double radius;  // Radius of a circle

    public:

        // Constructor
        Circle(double);
        // Surface area of a circle
        double Area();
        // Volume of a circle
        double Volume();

};
```

The Cylinder Class

The **Cylinder** class defines a three-dimensional geometric figure, the cylinder. The cylinder base is a circle. Therefore, the **Cylinder** class is derived from the **Circle** class.

```
// Declaration of class Cylinder
// File cylinder.hpp

#ifndef Cylinder_Class
#define Cylinder_Class

// Include declaration of class Circle
#include "circle3d.hpp"

class Cylinder : public Circle {

   private:

      double height;  // A height of a cylinder

   public:

      // Constructor
      Cylinder(double, double);
      // Surface area of a cylinder
      virtual double Area();
      // Volume of a cylinder
      virtual double Volume();

};
...
#endif
```

This is the **Cylinder** class constructor:

```
// Constructor

Cylinder :: Cylinder(double r, double h) : Circle(r)
{
   height = h;
}
```

Notice that the **Cylinder** class constructor contains the call for the **Circle** class constructor. The **Cylin**der class has been derived from the **Circle** class. That is why the **Cylin**der class constructor must explicitly call that of the **Circle** class to initialize the radius data item to be inherited.

This is the **Area()** virtual function of the **Cylinder** class.

```
// Surface area of a cylinder

double Cylinder :: Area()
{
   return 2 * Circle::Area() +
            2 * 3.14159 * radius * height;
}

// Volume of a cylinder

double Cylinder :: Volume()
{
   return Circle::Area() * height;
}
```

You will probably have noticed that the scope resolution operator comes before the **Area()** function call. With the operator not specified, the **Area()** function of the **Cylinder** class rather than the **Circle** class would be called.

Calling Virtual Functions

A virtual function is called by a reference or a pointer to the base class where it has been initially declared. The virtual function call is interpreted on the class of the object for which it has been called.

If you go back to the list of geometric figures, you'll see that it now includes both two and three-dimensional geometric figures. Therefore we slightly modified the **Print** function of the **FigureList** class: the function will print both the area and the volume of the figure.

```
void FigureList :: Print(FigureList * p) {
   Figure * fp;
   if (p != 0) {
      fp = p->obj;
      cout << Surface area: " << fp->Area()
         << " Volume: " << fp->Volume()
         << '\n';
      Print(p->next);
   }
}
```

In the **Print** function body, there are two calls specified for the **Area()** and **Volume()** virtual functions:

```
fp->Area()
```

and

```
fp->Volume()
```

The **Area()** and the **Volume()** functions are called through a pointer **fp** to the **Figure** base class. Which function is called depends on the class of object pointed to by the **fp** pointer.

```cpp
// Example of objects of classes Cone and Cylinder
// File fglist.cpp

#include <iostream.h>

#include "cylinder.hpp"
#include "flist.hpp"

int main ()
{
   // Create cylinder
   Cylinder cyl(4.5, 4);
   cout << "Area of cylinder: " << cyl.Area() << '\n';
   cout << "Volume of cylinder: " << cyl.Volume() << '\n';
   // Add cylinder into the list
   FigureList flist(&cyl);

   // Create circle
   Circle circle(5);
   cout << "Area of circle: " << circle.Area() << '\n';
   cout << "Volume of circle: " << circle.Volume() << '\n';
   flist.Add (&circle, flist.head);

   // Print area and volume of figures from the list
   cout << '\n';
   flist.Print (flist.head);

   // Delete the figure list
   flist.Destroy(flist.head);

   return 0;
}
```

The output produced by this program is as follows:

```
Area of cylinder: 240.332
Volume of cylinder: 254.469
Area of circle: 78.5397
Volume of circle: 0

Surface area: 240.332 volume: 254.469
Surface area: 78.5397 volume: 0
```

Virtual Functions Table

Every class having one or more virtual functions has an associated virtual dispatch table. This table stores the address of all virtual functions for the class. Every object of a class having virtual functions is provided with a pointer to the virtual table for the class. For example, the following figure shows the virtual table for an object of the **Circle** class:

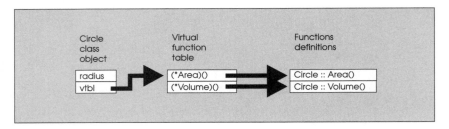

Virtual Table for the Circle Object

The virtual function calling scheme is as follows:

1 A pointer to the object's virtual table is retrieved.

2 The virtual table contains an entry (a pointer) with the desired virtual function.

3 The retrieved pointer is dereferenced and the function call completes.

Thus the virtual call

```
Circle c(2,5);
Figure * p;
p = &c;
p-> Area();   // Virtual call of Area() function
```

is transformed to the following call syntax with the use of the **Circle** virtual table:

```
*  (p->vtble [1])  ();
```

Note that this is implementation dependent, that is, different compilers may implement it in different ways.

The described procedure of binding the virtual function with its definition is performed dynamically at run-time.

The derived class contains a copy of the virtual table for the base class. If the derived class redefines virtual functions of the base class, then the entries for those functions in the virtual function table are modified to hold the address of the new functions. Thus the virtual table of the derived class contains:

▶ The virtual functions of the base class if the mating functions of the derived class were not redefined.

▶ The redefined virtual functions of the derived class.

In the **Cylinder** class that has been derived from the **Circle** class both the **Area()** and **Volume()** functions are redefined. Therefore, the virtual table of **Cylinder** contains only the **Cylinder** virtual functions.

When a Virtual Function Call is Resolved as Statically Nonvirtual

There are some cases when a virtual function call is nonvirtual, that is, the function call is resolved statically at compilation time, rather than dynamically at run-time.

1 The virtual function is not called by pointer or reference.

The class object is specified in the virtual function call syntax:

```
Cylinder c(3, 4.1);          // Cylinder class object
cout << "Surface area: " << c.Area()
   << "\nVolume: " << c.Volume();
```

In the above example, the calls of virtual functions **Area()** and **Volume()** are nonvirtual. The calls are performed via object **c** of the **Cylinder** class. In the function call points, the object class, **Cylinder**, is known. That is why the **Area()** and **Volume()** functions of the **Cylinder** class are called.

2 The virtual function is called by pointer or reference but not qualified by the class name.

```
Cylinder c(4, 3.3);          // Cylinder
Figure * p = &c;             // Pointer to class Figure
cout << "Surface area of cylinder base: "
   << p->Circle::Area()
   << "\nSurface area of cylinder: "
```

```
    << p->Area()
    << "\nVolume of cylinder: "
    << p->Volume();
```

In this example, there are two **Area()** virtual function calls specified. The first **Area()** function call, however, is not linked dynamically as we have explicitly qualified it with the name of the **Circle** class. This means that we are saying (regardless of anything else) we want the **Area()** function of the **Circle** class to be called - and so it is. The second call to **Area()** is resolved dynamically.

Here is another example of a statically linked call to a virtual function>.

Let's go back to the member function for cylinder volume evaluation:

```
double Cylinder :: Volume() {
    return Circle :: Area() * height;
}
```

The **Area()** function call is static. The **Area()** function of the **Circle** class will always be called in the **Volume()** body.

Scope of Virtual Functions

Suppose there is the **Figure** class declared as follows:

```
class Figure {
    public:
        Figure();
        virtual double Area() = 0;
    protected:
        virtual double Volume() = 0;
};
```

In the **Figure** class, the **Area()** virtual function is accessed as public while the **Volume()** virtual function is accessed as protected.

Public, Private, and Virtual Functions

What does public and protected access mean when applied to virtual functions?

A virtual function is called by pointer or reference to the base class. The **Area()** function of the **Figure** class has public access. Therefore, any virtual call of the function via the pointer or reference to the **Figure** class has the public access level. This would also be true for the **Area()** function in the derived classes, even though, for example, the **Area()** function is accessible as protected in the derived classes. Accordingly, the following function definition is legal:

```
double Area(Figure * p) {
   return p->Area();
}
```

If a virtual member function (for example, **Volume()** of **Figure** class) is accessible as protected, every virtual call of the function by pointer or reference to the **Figure** class will have the protected access level. Accordingly, you can't define the external function as follows:

```
double Volume(Figure * p) {
  return p->Volume();   // Error
}
```

Virtual calls of the **Volume()** function can be implemented, for example, via the pointer or reference to the **Circle** class. Thus the access level for a virtual function in the base class defines the access level for virtual functions in the derived classes.

From the above, we can conclude that virtual functions obey the same access rules as ordinary member functions, whether or not the virtual function call is resolved dynamically at run-time.

Advantages of Using Virtual Functions

Let's discuss the advantages of applying virtual functions.

Suppose there is no member function declared virtual in the **Figure** base class of the geometric figure hierarchy:

```
class Figure {

   public:

      Figure();
      double Area()     { return 0; }
      double Volume()   { return 0; }

};
```

Every class derived will have the **Area()** and **Volume()** functions of its own.

What would you do now to implement our list of geometric figures? You might choose, for example, the following **FigureList** class implementation option.

This is the **FigureList** class definition:

```
// FigureList class definition

class FigureList {

   public:

      Figure * obj;    // Pointer to a figure
      FigureClass cl;  // Kind of a figure
      // Pointer to the next element of the list
      FigureList * next;

   public:

      // Constructor
      FigureList(Figure *, FigureClass, FigureList *);
      ~FigureList();                // Destructor
      // Add a figure to a list
      FigureList * Add(Figure *, FigureClass, FigureList *);
      // What kind of a figure is stored in the element of
      // the list
      FigureClass ClassOf();
      // Destroy a list of figures
      void Destroy(FigureList *);
      // Print area size and volume of all figures in a list
      void Print(FigureList *);

};
```

As you can see, a new data item and a function have appeared in the **FigureList** class. The **cl** data item stores information about which figure is pointed to by which list entry. The **ClassOf()** member function returns the value of the **cl** data member.

Now the **FigureList** class constructor appears as follows:

```
enum FigureClass {

    CircleClass,
    TriangleClass,
    RectangleClass,
    CylinderClass,
    ConeClass,
...

};

Figure * fp;
FigureList * fl;
fp = new Cylinder(3, 5);
fl = new FigureList(fp, CylinderList, fl);
fp = new Cone(2, 4);
fl->Add(fp, ConeClass, fl);
```

and so on!

The **Print** function that prints out the area and volume for every figure in the list is also changed.

```
void FigureList :: Print(FigureList * p)
{
    Figure * fig;
    if (p != 0) {
        fig = p->obj;
        switch (p->ClassOf()) {
            case CylinderClass :
                cout << ((Cylinder *) fig)->Area() << '\t'
                        << ((Cylinder *) fig)->Volume();
                break;
            case ConeClass :
                cout << ((Cone *) fig)->Area() << '\t'
                        << ((Cone *) fig)->Volume();
                break;
...
        }
        cout << '\n';
        Print(p->next);
    }
}
```

The **Print** function definition has become more complicated. It now contains a switch with a set of options. We were forced to introduce the switch operator into the **Print** function definition because there is a pointer to the **Figure** base class stored in the list entry. With the **Area()** or

Volume() function called via the pointer, the call will always be interpreted as that of **Area()** or **Volume()** function belonging to the **Figure** class. Thus, for example, with the following syntax:

```
fig = p->obj;
cout << fig->Area() << '\t' << fig->Volume();
```

the **Area()** and **Volume()** functions of the **Figure** class are called. To have a function of the desired class called, such as **Cylinder**, you should cast the **fig** pointer to that of the **Cylinder** class pointer:

```
case Cylinder :
   cout << ((Cylinder *) fig)->Area() << '\t'
      << ((Cylinder *) fig)->Volume();
```

This conversion of the base class pointer to the derived class pointer is safe enough because we are certain that the list entry references the derived class object. However, we must store as many options as the object classes in the list.

Here are the conclusions derived from the example:

1 The responsibility for defining an object type lies with you rather than the compiler. The **FigureList** class is forced to keep the **cl** data member to define the object type.

2 The program that has been written in this style is tied up to the implementation details of the derivation hierarchy. Thus the code will change with the derivation hierarchy.

These problems can be eliminated by the virtual function or dynamic binding feature.

Virtual Destructors

Like an ordinary class member function, the destructor of class can be declared virtual. Then the destructor of every class derived from the one with the virtual destructor declared will also be virtual.

When should the destructor of a class be declared virtual? To answer the question, let's look at a short example. There are two classes, the base and the derived, created with the constructors that dynamically allocate memory.

The base class in the two-class hierarchy is the **Person** class. The **Person** class contains information about a person's identity such as name, age, and address.

```
class Person {
   protected:
      char * name;
      char * address;
      int age;
   public:
      Person(char *, int, char *);
      ~Person();
      virtual void Print();
};
```

In the **Person** class, the data item's name and address are represented by pointers so that they will be allocated memory dynamically at object creation time. Therefore, the **Person** class constructor is defined as follows:

```
Person :: Person(char * n, int a, char * s)
{
   age = a;
// Allocate memory for name
   int i = strlen(n);
   name = new char [i + 1];
   strcpy(name, n);
// Allocate memory for address
   int i = strlen(s);
   address = new char [i + 1];
   strcpy(address, n);
}
```

Thus the object of the **Person** class will have additional memory that has to be released when the object is deleted (either by the **delete** operator or when the object goes out of the scope). Since the name and address were allocated memory by the object's constructor, it should be released by the object's destructor.

This is the **Person** class destructor:

```
Person :: ~Person()
{
   delete name;
   delete address;
}
```

The second class derived from the **Person** class is the **Employee** class. The **Employee** class contains information about a person as belonging to the company staff.

```
class Employee : public {
   private:
// Date of employment
      char hire[11];
// Kind of activity
      char * status;
      float salary;
   public:
      Employee(char *, int, char *, char *, char *, float);
      ~Employee();
      virtual void Print();
};
```

In the **Employee** class the status data item is represented by the pointer. The status data item will be allocated memory dynamically at creating an object of the **Department** class. In a similar way as in the case of **Person** class, dynamic memory allocation/deallocation for the **Employee** class is carried out by the constructor and destructor respectively.

This is the **Employee** class constructor:

```
Employee :: Employee(char * n, int a, char * s,
          char * h, char * d, float y)
          : Person(n, a, s)
{
   strcpy(hire, h);
   int i = strlen(d);
   status = new char [i + 1];
   strcpy(status, d);
   salary = y;
}
```

The **Employee** class destructor deallocates memory that has been allocated by the constructor at object creation time:

```
Employee :: ~Employee()
{
   delete status;
}
```

Let's write a short test example using the **Employee** class objects.

```
// Example of personal list
```

...

```
main()
{
    int i;
    Person * personal[3];    // Personal list
    // Create a personal list
    personal[0] = new Employee("Scott Graham", 35,
            "15, 10th Street, Berkeley",
            "03/25/1989", "Editor",
            100000.00);
    personal[1] = new Employee("Michael Wood", 28,
            "100, 7th Street, Berkeley",
            "10/09/1993", "Copy editor",
            75000.00);
    personal[2] = new Employee("Chris Murray", 40,
            "2, 5th Avenue, Berkeley",
            "03/25/1989", "Corrector",
            50000.00);
    // Print the personal list
    for (i = 0; i < 3; i++)
        personal[i]->Print();
    // Delete the personal list
    for (i = 0; i < 3; i++)
        delete personal[i];
    return 0;
}
```

Look closely at the last statement in the code. Will the object **delete** operator of **Employee** class operate properly? The syntax

```
personal [i]
```

is a pointer to the **Person** class. By deleting an object via the pointer to the **Person** class, you'll cause the **Person** destructor rather than the **Employee** destructor to be applied. It is clear then that such a construction for **Employee** object deletion wouldn't be operational.

In this situation you should use a virtual destructor. You should declare the destructor virtual in the **Person** class. To do this, specify the **virtual** keyword before the destructor name.

```
class Person {
   protected:
      char * name;
      char * address;
      int age;
   public:
      Person(char *, int, char *);
      virtual   ~Person();
      virtual void Print();
};
```

The **Employee** class destructor will also be virtual. Accordingly, the destructor call

```
delete personal [i]
```

is virtual. The destructor instance to be called will be identified by the object class at run-time. Since the object we are deleting belongs to the **Employee** class, the destructor for this class is called.

> **If your class declares any virtual functions then it should also declare its destructor as virtual, even if the destructor has an empty body.**

The **EMPLOY.CPP**   program produces the following:

```
Scott Graham     35       15, 10th Street, Berkeley
03/25/1989       Editor   100000
Michael Wood     28       100, 7th Street, Berkeley
10/09/1993       Copy editor     74000
Chris Murray     40       2, 5th Avenue, Berkeley
03/25/1989       Corrector       50000
```

Summary

1 A function is declared virtual by specifying the **virtual** keyword in the function declaration:

```
virtual  return-value-type  function-name
                (parameter-declaration-list);
```

Only the class member function can be virtual.

2 A function is declared virtual when:

   ▶ The class where the virtual function has been initially declared is the base class in the derivation hierarchy.

   ▶ The function implementation depends on the class and may differ in the derived classes.

3 The virtual function is invoked by reference or pointer to base class the virtual function is first declared.

4 Virtual functions obey the same access rules as ordinary class member functions.

5 The virtual function in the base class may have no definition. This virtual function is referred to as a pure virtual function. To declare a pure virtual function use the following virtual function declaration syntax:

```
virtual   return-value-type  function-name
             (parameter-declaration-list)  =  0;
```

The class with the pure virtual functions declared is an abstract class. This class is referred to as an abstract since you can't create objects of the class.

6 The destructor of the class can also be virtual. To emphasize the fact, the virtual keyword is specified before the name of the destructor:

```
virtual  ~class-name();
```

A destructor of every class derived from the one with the virtual destructor declared is also virtual. If your class declares any virtual functions then it should also declare its destructor as virtual, even if the destructor has an empty body.

CHAPTER 10

More About Class Derivation

In this chapter we'll look further into the subject of class derivation. As you already know, the usefulness of classes can be increased by the mechanism of inheritance. This mechanism allows new classes to be created from existing classes.

There is more that you can do with derivation. C++ allows you to derive new classes from multiple classes, enabling you to access a fuller range of functionality. The process is made even more useful by the ability of base classes to be declared virtual, avoiding the problem of multiple duplication.

In this chapter we'll cover:

- Inheriting from multiple classes
- Accessing a derived class member
- The problems of ambiguity
- Virtual base classes
- Multiple inheritance.

Introduction to Multiple Inheritance

When one class, say for example, class **B**, is derived from another class, class **A**, it inherits all or part of the features of class **A**. Class **A** is referred to as a **base** class and class **B** is referred to as a **derived** class. In its turn, class **B** can be used as a base class for deriving one or more new classes. In C++ this can appear as follows:

```
class A  { ... };
class B: public A { ... };
class C: public A { ... };
class D: public B { ... };
class E: public B { ... };
class F: public C { ... };
class G: public C { ... };
```

Classes **B** and **C** are the classes derived from class **A**. Also, classes **B** and **C** are the base classes for classes **D**, **E F**, and **G** respectively. Class derivation results in a hierarchy of classes which can be represented as a tree - see the following figure:

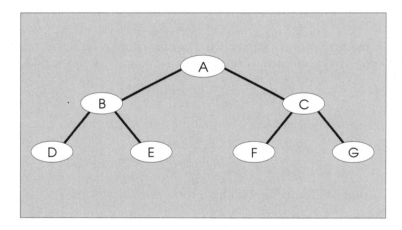

A Class Hierarchy With Derivation From One Class

The class hierarchy that we created is an example of derivation from a single class: every new class derived inherits the properties of only one base class. Class **C** is only derived from class **A** and class **F** inherits the properties of class **C** only. It is true that class **F** inherits the properties of class **A**, but it only has the properties of class **C**.

By deriving a new class from a single base class you can:

- Add new properties to the base class.
- Strip the base class of some of its properties.
- Redefine the properties of the base class.

The capabilities provided by the derivation mechanism are sufficient for creating new classes. There are, however, some applications where you should resort to another form of class derivation.

One example of just such an application is the development of a windows-oriented user interface. Each notion in Windows such as a window, a scrolling bar, a button, and so on, can be represented as a separate class. Suppose you want to have an object like a scrollable window in Windows. You define the scrollable window as a combination of both the window and scrolling bar properties.

We will demonstrate this with an example of C++ classes.

```
// Base class defining the window
class Window{
// window properties
  public:
    Window(Rect);
    ~Window();
// window interface
};

// Base class defining the scrolling bar
class ScrollBar{
// scrolling bar properties
  public:
    ScrollBar(Rect);
  ~ScrollBar();
// scrolling bar interface
};
```

Let's define the **ScrollableWindow** class using two classes - **Window** and **ScrollBar** - as a base:

```
class ScrollableWindow : public Window,
        public ScrollBar
{
// ... additional properties for scrollable window
```

```
  public:
    ScrollableWindow(Rect);
    ~ScrollableWindow();
// ... additional interface for scrollable window
};
```

Now we have created a new class from two classes. This form of class derivation is referred to as **multiple derivation**. We'll demonstrate multiple derivation with the following example:

```
class A { ... };
class B { ... };
class C { ... };
class D : public A, public C { ... };
class E : public C { ... };
class F : public D, public E { ... };
```

As a result, we obtain the class hierarchy as figured below:

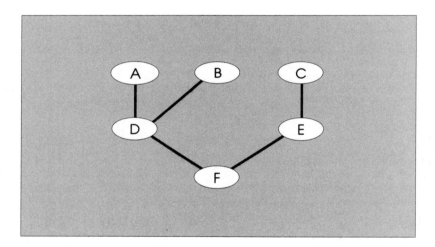

Class Hierarchy Produced by Multiple Derivation

Inheriting from Multiple Classes

C++ enables you to create a new class from more than one existing class through the inheritance mechanism. The derived class inherits the data members and member functions of several base classes.

Syntactically, you can represent this as follows:

```
class derived_class_name
         ┌ public    ┐
    :    │ private   │      base_class_name_1,
         └ protected ┘
         ┌ public    ┐
         │ private   │      base_class_name_2
         └ protected ┘
            [ , . . . ]
    {
    . . .
    };
```

The Inheritance Mechanism

A colon following the derived class name points to the beginning of a derivation list. The derivation list is a list of comma-delimited names of base classes.

A derived class can generally have any number of base classes.

```
class A : public C, public D, public E {. . .};
          └─────────────┬─────────────┘
                  derivation list
                   for class A
```

How Many Base Classes?

Invalid Syntax

There is, however, one restriction: every base class name must be unique on the derivation list. This is an example of an invalid syntax for multiple derivation. Class **c** occurs twice in the derivation list.

```
class A: public C, public D, public C// Error
{...};
```

Order of Names

The names of base classes can occur in any order. Any base class on the derivation list must meet either of the following conditions:

1 The base class must be defined,

or

2 There must exist a forward declaration for the base class.

The keywords **public, protected** and **private** which precede every base class defines the kind of derivation from the base class. If none of them is specified, the derivation is considered **private** by default.

```
// Example of private derivation
class ScrollableWindow : Window, ScrollBar {
...
  public:
    ScrollableWindow(Rect);
    ~ScrollableWindow();
...
};
```

In this example of derivation, all members of **Window** and **ScrollBar** become members of **ScrollableWindow** with private access. This means that the inherited members are inaccessible for a **ScrollableWindow** user.

Private Inheritance by Default

When inheriting from multiple base classes you must explicitly state whether inheritance is private, protected or public for each base class, otherwise private inheritance is assumed by default. For example:

```
class A: public B, C, protected D {...};
```

In this case, because we haven't explicitly stated how class **A** inherits from class **C**, it is private (not public, as it was from class **B**).

Try It Out - Multiple Inheritance

As an example of multiple inheritance, let's look at some code for drawing a circle around a text on the display screen. The figure opposite shows what might result from running this code:

Example of a Class Object Derived from Two Base Classes

As you can see from the task formulation, the solution is based on two concepts: 'circle' and 'text'. It would be possible, however, to restrict ourselves to the notion of circle by adding an attribute such as a text string to it.

However, circle and text are totally different notions. For example, among the text properties are font, character size, and so on, while the circle is characterized by its radius. You could have the notion of 'encircled text' derived from the notion of 'circle'. But it would be preferable to specify separate classes for different notions and then unite their properties in a derived class. You may want to use two separate classes, circle and text, to derive a third class 'encircled text'.

One other thing - circle and text are both graphic representations, and you should place the properties common to graphic representations in a separate class.

How It Works - The Picture Class

Let's begin with the definition of the class **Picture** to represent a graphic.

```
// Declaration of class Picture
// File picture.hpp

#if !defined(Picture_Class)
```

```
#define Picture_Class
// Include declaration of class Point
#include "point.hpp"

class Picture {
  protected:
    Point location;  // Picture coordinates
  public:
// Constructor
    Picture(Point &);
// Draw a picture
    virtual void Draw() = 0;
};
...
#endif
```

A **Picture** is characterized by its layout on the display screen (location). The location data member is an object of the **Point** class. The **Point** class defines the location of a point with the X-axis and Y-axis coordinates.

The Point Class

```
// Declaration of class Point
// File point.hpp

#if !defined(Point_Class)
#define Point_Class

class Point {
  private:
    int x;  // Point coordinates
    int y;
  public:
// Constructors
    Point(int, int);
    Point(Point &);
// Assignment of points
    Point & operator =(Point &);
// Get coordinates of point
    int IsX();
    int IsY();
};
...
#endif
```

This is the constructor of **Point** class:

```
// Constructors
Point :: Point(int aX, int aY)
{
```

```
  x = aX;
  y = aY;
}

Point :: Point(Point & p)
{
  x = p.x;
  y = p.y;
}
```

This is the assignment operator for the **Point** class:

```
Point & Point :: operator = (Point & p)
{
    x = p.x;
    y = p.y;
}
```

And finally, these are the selectors **IsX**() and **IsY**() for the **Point** class:

```
int Point:: IsX()
{
    return x;
}

int Point :: IsY()
{
    return y;
}
```

To complete the **Picture** class definition, let's define a constructor for the class.

```
// Constructor

Picture :: Picture(Point & p)
     : location(p)
{
}
```

You'll have noticed that Picture class member function Draw() is a pure virtual member and as such must be overridden in any derived classes that are to be instantiated. Picture is therefore an abstract base class, and objects of this class can't be instantiated.

Once we have defined the **Picture** class, we can use it as the base for our other classes: **Circle** and **GraphicText**.

The Circle Class

```cpp
// Declaration of class Circle
// File circle.hpp

#if !defined(Circle_Class)
#define Circle_Class

// include declaration of class Picture
#include "picture.hpp"
// Include graphics functions
#include <graphics.h>

class Circle : public Picture {

  protected:

    int radius;    // Radius of a circle in pixels
    int color;     // Color of a circle

  public:

// Constructor
    Circle(Point &, int, int);
// Draw a circle
    virtual void Draw();

};
...
#endif
```

This is the member function of **Circle**:

```cpp
// Definition of member function of class Circle
// File circle.hpp

class Circle : public Picture {
...
}
```

```cpp
// Constructor

Circle :: Circle(Point & loc, int rad, int col)
        : Picture(loc)
{
  radius = rad;
```

```
   color = col;
}

// Draw a circle

void Circle :: Draw()
{
  // Set drawing color
  setcolor(color);
  // Set fill color
  setfillstyle(SOLID_FILL, color);
  // Draw a circle
  circle(location.IsX(), location.IsY(), radius);
  // Fill a circle
  floodfill(location.IsX(), location.IsY(), color);
}
```

The GraphicText Class

```
// Declaration of class GraphicText
// File gtext.hpp

#if !defined(GraphicText_Class)
#define GraphicText_Class

// Include declaration of class Picture
#include "picture.hpp"
// Include graphics functions
#include <graphics.h>
// Include string functions
#include <string.h>

class GraphicText : public Picture {

  protected:

    char * text;    // String of a text
    int font;       // Font of a text
    int size;       // Size of a text
    int color;      // Color of a text

  public:

    // Constructor
    GraphicText(Point &, char *, int, int, int);
    // Destructor
    ~GraphicText();
    // Draw a text
    virtual void Draw();
```

```
};
...
#endif
```

These are the member functions of the **GraphicText** class:

```
// Definition of member function of class GraphicText
// File gtext.hpp

class GraphicText : public Picture {
...
}
```

```
// Constructor

GraphicText :: GraphicText(Point & loc, char * txt, int fnt,
                           int sz, int col)
              : Picture(loc)
{
  text = new char [strlen(txt) + 1];
  strcpy(text, txt);
  font = fnt;
  size = sz;
  color = col;
}

/// Destructor
GraphicText :: ~GraphicText()
{
  delete text;
}

// Draw a graphic text

void GraphicText :: Draw()
{
  // Get size of one character of the text
  int charSz = size / (8 * (strlen(text) + 1));

  // Set color of the text
  setcolor(color);
  // Set justification of the text
  settextjustify(CENTER_TEXT, CENTER_TEXT);
  // Output the text
  settextstyle(font, HORIZ_DIR, charSz);
  //
  outtextxy(location.IsX(), location.IsY(), text);
}
```

The CircumText Class

Finally, let's define a class which unites the properties of the circle and the text.

```cpp
// Declaration of class CircumText
// File ctext.hpp

#if !defined(CircumText_Class)
#define CircumText_Class

// Include declarations of classes Circle and GraphicText
#include "circle.hpp"
#include "gtext.hpp"

class CircumText : public Circle, public GraphicText {
  public:
// Constructor
    CircumText(Point &, int, int, char *, int, int);
// Draw a text into circle
    virtual void Draw();
};
// Member function of CircumText class
// Constructor
CircumText :: CircumText(Point & loc, int rC, int cC,
            char * tT, int fT, int cT)
        : Circle(loc, rC, cC),
        GraphicText(loc, tT, fT, 2 * rC, cT)
{
}
...
#endif
```

The `Circumtext` class constructor has no body since all the required actions are performed by the constructors of base classes.

```cpp
// Member function for displaying the text
// within circumference

// Draw a text into circle
void CircumText :: Draw()
{
// Circumference is drawn first
  Circle::Draw();
// Then text is written in
  GraphicText::Draw();
}
```

Now that we've defined our classes, let's look at how we can use objects of our final class:

```cpp
// Include graphic functions of Borland C++
#include <graphics.h>
// Include console i/o functions
#include <conio.h>

// Include declaration of class CircumText
#include "ctext.hpp"

main()
{
  int gdriver = DETECT,
      gmode;

  initgraph(&gdriver, &gmode, "");

  Point p = Point(getmaxx() / 2, getmaxy() / 2);
  CircumText cpp(p, 100, GREEN, "C++", DEFAULT_FONT,
                 WHITE);

  cpp.Draw();

  getch();

  return 0;
}
```

Using the Graphic Mode

Our **Draw** program contains references to some graphic functions from Borland C++. That is why the program is provided with a header file **GRAPHICS.H** with the declarations of graphic functions. The first graphic function used in the program is the **initgraph** function. This function switched the computer between text and graphic modes. To produce a picture on the screen, you should always use the graphic mode. The **closegraph** function is the reverse of **initgraph**. This function returns the computer back to the text mode.

For more detail on the graphic functions of Borland C++ compiler used in the program, you can refer to the appropriate compiler manual.

The hierarchy of classes used in the **Draw** program would appear like this:

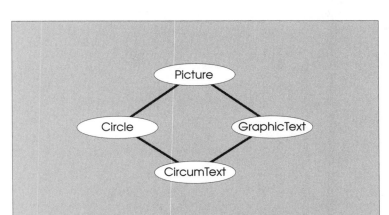

Multiple Derivation

Derivation of `Circle` and `GraphicText` from `Picture` is an example of single inheritance. Derivation of `CircumText` from the `Circle` and `GraphicText` classes is an example of multiple inheritance.

Derived Class Object

Unlike single inheritance, an object of a class produced by multiple inheritance will contain more than one inherited portion.

In the Draw program, we create an object of **CircumText** class which has been derived from two classes:

```
CircumText cpp(p, 100, GREEN, "C++", DEFAULT_FONT, WHITE);
```

Memory allocation for the object cpp of **CircumText** can be schematically represented as in the figure overleaf.

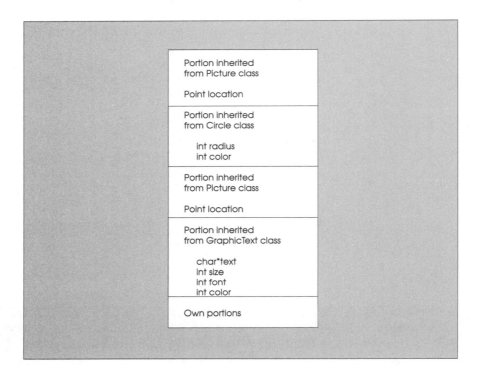

Portion inherited
from Picture class

Point location

Portion inherited
from Circle class

int radius
int color

Portion inherited
from Picture class

Point location

Portion inherited
from GraphicText class

char*text
int size
int font
int color

Own portions

Memory Allocation for an Object of Class Produced by Multiple Derivation

Accessing a Derived Class Member

To access members that have been inherited by a derived class from more than one base class, you should adhere to the same rules as those which pertain to members inherited from one base class.

One More Caveat

There is only one additional condition that might cause difficulties. When two or more base classes define member functions with the same signature or data members with the same name. If either of these conditions occurs, you should use the scope resolution operator to qualify the member to be accessed with the particular base class name.

Try It Out

We'll demonstrate this with the **Draw()** function of **CircumText** class, which we discussed earlier.

```
// Draw a text into circle
void CircumText :: Draw()
{
// Circumference is drawn first
  Circle::Draw();
// Then text is written in
  GraphicText::Draw();
}
```

How It Works

The **Draw()** function of **Circumtext** class works as follows: first it draws a circle and then places a text into the circle. To draw the circle, the **Draw()** function of the base class **Circle** is called. To draw the text, the **Draw**() function of the base class **GraphicText** is called. However, the two functions are named similarly in both base classes. Therefore, to call the **Draw()** function of the base class **Circle**, you should qualify it with the class name. For this, use the scope resolution operator:

```
Circle :: Draw();
```

You should do the same to call the **Draw()** function of the **GraphicText** class:

```
GraphicText :: Draw();
```

How It Breaks

You may wonder what would happen if we didn't use the scope resolution operator.

```
void CircumText :: Draw() {
  Draw();
  Draw();
}
```

In this case **Draw()** will be called from the current scope. The current scope is the **CircumText** class which has also a function named **Draw**. That is why the **Draw()** of **CircumText** will be called. In other words, the **Draw()** of **CircumText** will call itself which would result in an infinite loop. Which is less fun than it sounds.

Try It Out!

Ambiguity in Class Members Produced by Multiple Derivation

Let's consider what can become a source of ambiguity when accessing members of a class produced by multiple derivation.

We'll define a member function, **Move()**, which is used to move objects of our classes around the screen.

```
class Picture {
...
  public:
  virtual void Move(Point &) = 0;
};
...

class Circle : public Picture {
...
  public:
  virtual void Move(Point &);
};
...

class GraphicText : public Picture {
...
  public:
  virtual void Move(Point &);
};
...
```

The derived class **CircumText** inherits **Move** functions of both the **Circle** and **GraphicText** **classes**. If you now instantiate an object of the **CircumText** class as

```
CircumText ct(Point(300, 200), ...);
```

and try to move it over the screen:

```
ct.Move(Point(250,300));
```

The **Move** function call would result in the compiler generating an error message. This function call is ambiguous because the compiler is not aware from which base class **Move** function should be called. To eliminate this ambiguity, you must explicitly specify the name of the base class to which the **Move** function belongs *before the function call*:

```
ct.Circle :: Move(Point(250,300));
```

This **Move** function call causes only the circle to be moved. The text remains stable. To move both the circle and the text, we will provide a **Move** function for the **CircumText** class which moves both text and circle together:

```
class CircumText : public Circle, public GraphicText {
...
  public:
  virtual void Move(Point &);
};
...
```

```
void CircumText :: Move(Point & p) {
  Circle :: Move(p);
  GraphicText :: Move(p);
}
```

Order of Calling Constructors and Destructors for Derived Class Objects

Since an object of a derived class consists of several portions inherited from the base classes, the derived class constructor must initialize all inherited portions. To do this, the initialization list in the heading of the derived class constructor must name constructors of all base classes. For example, the **CircumText** constructor may be declared as follows:

```
// Constructor
CircumText :: CircumText(Point & loc, int rC, int cC,
        char * tT, int fT, int cT)
      : Circle(loc, rC, cC),
        GraphicText(loc, tT, fT, 2 * rC, cT)
{
}
```

Also the derived class constructor is responsible for passing arguments to the base class constructors.

When deriving from multiple classes, the constructors are called in the following order:

1 Constructors of base classes in the order they were specified.

2 Constructors for members that are class objects, if any, in the order they were declared.

3 The derived class constructor.

Let's look at the order of executing constructors for a **CircumText** class object being created:

```
CircumText ct(...);
```

In the case of the **CircumText** class the constructors would be called in the following order:

```
Point::Point()(a member of the Picture class)
Picture::Picture()
Circle::Circle()
GraphicText::GraphicText()
CircumText::CircumText()
```

The reason that the **Circle** class's constructor is called before the **GraphicText** class's constructor is because the **Circle** class was listed first in the list of base classes in the **CircumText** class's definition:

```
class CircumText : public Circle, public GraphicText {...};
```

When an object of **CircumText** class is destroyed, the destructors are called in the reverse order to that of the constructors.

Virtual Base Classes

Problems With Multiple Inheritance

When deriving from multiple base classes, you may come across certain difficulties that never occur in derivation from a single class.

Recall the inheritance hierarchy of the **CircumText** class.

```
class Circle : public Picture { ... };          (1)
class GraphicText : public { ... };       (2)
class CircumText : public Circle,
      public GraphicText { ... };  (3)
```

Although a class can only directly inherit from a base class once, it is possible for the same class to appear more than once further up the inheritance hierarchy (see the following figure):

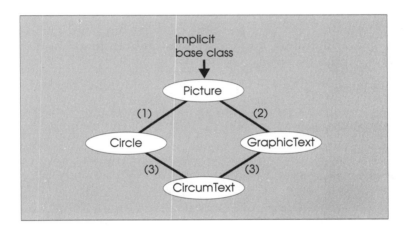

Implicit Base Classes in Multiple Derivation

The **CircumText** class has been derived from two classes: **Circle** and **GraphicText** (marked by 3). In their turn, the **Circle** class has been derived from **Picture** (marked by 1) and the **GraphicText** class has also been derived from **Picture** (marked by 2). Although the **Picture** class is not specified explicitly on the derivation list for **CircumText**, it will implicitly inherit the **Picture** twice: via **Circle** and via **GraphicText**. Thus an object of **CircumText** would contain two portions implicitly inherited from **Picture** class (see the earlier figure). A **CircumText** object would contain two copies of the location member of **Picture**.

Nitty Gritty - Two Problems with Multiple Inheritance

From the above we can conclude that multiple inheritance has two potential problems:

1 Waste of memory for extra members of the implicit base class. In this case extra memory is allocated for a second copy of the location data (the **Point** member of the **Picture** class).

2 Ambiguity exists when a member of an implicit base class is accessed.

Suppose you want to know the location of the 'encircled text' object on the screen. You could define the **IsLocation** member function in the **CircumText** class as follows:

```
class CircumText : public Circle, public GraphicText {
...
  public:
  Point IsLocation();
};
...

Point CircumText :: IsLocation() {
  return location;
}
```

However, the statement

```
return location
```

is ambiguous as it could refer to the **location** data member inherited via the **GraphicText** class (from the **Picture** class) or the **location** data member inherited via the **Circle** class (also from the **Picture** class).

To resolve the ambiguity the data member name must be qualified as either this:

```
return Circle :: location;
```

or this:

```
return GraphicText :: location;
```

In this case, we only really want one instance of the location data member, not two as our **CircumText** object can only be in one place at a time! To achieve this we must inherit from the **Picture** class in such a way that our **CircumText** class objects only contain one instance of the **Picture** class, not two which is the case at the moment.

The C++ language allows you to implement this by providing virtual base classes. Virtual base classes is a mechanism of class derivation which ensures that only one base class instance is created, no matter how often it occurs in the hierarchy.

Definition of a Virtual Base Class

A base class is defined as virtual by specifying the **virtual** keyword before the base class name in the derivation list for the new class.

The syntax of virtual base class definition is as follows:

```
class   derived-class-name:
            virtual[public|private|protected]
            base-class-name  [,...]
            {...};
```

Let's, for example, define the **Picture** class as virtual when defining the **Circle** and **GraphicText** classes:

```
// Derivation of class Circle from virtual base class
// Picture

#if !defined(Circle_Class)
#define Circle_Class

// include declaration of class Picture
#include "picture.hpp"

class Circle : virtual public Picture {
  protected:
    int radius; // Radius of a circle in pixels
    int color; // Color of a circle
  public:
// Constructor
    Circle(Point &, int, int);
// Draw a circle
    virtual void Draw();
};
```

```
...
#endif
```

and

```
// Derivation of of class GraphicText from virtual base
// class Picture

#if !defined(GraphicText_Class)
#define GraphicText_Class

// Include declaration of class Picture
#include "picture.hpp"

class GraphicText : virtual public Picture {
  protected:
    char * text;    // String of a text
    int font;       // Font of a text
    int size;       // Size of a text
    int color;      // Color of a text
  public:
// Constructor
    GraphicText(Point &, char *, int, int, int);
// Destructor
    ~GraphicText();
// Draw a text
    virtual void Draw();
};
...
#endif
```

The order of specifying the words **virtual** and **public** (**private** or **protected**) is irrelevant. Thus, for example, you could also declare the **Circle** class as follows:

```
class Circle: public virtual Picture {...};
```

If a base class is declared **virtual** while a new class is being derived, an object of the derived class will contain its own part and a pointer to the base part instead of the base part itself. The following figure shows the representations of objects from the **Circle** and **GraphicText** classes with virtual base class.

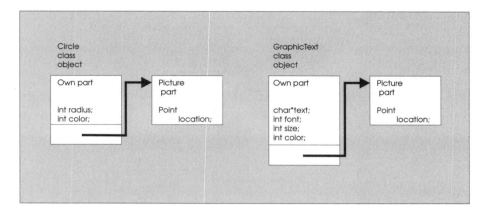

Memory Allocation for Derivation from the Virtual Class

Derivation of the **CircumText** class from the **Circle** and **GraphicText** classes is represented as before:

```
// Declaration of class CircumText

#if !defined(CircumText_Class)
#define CircumText_Class

// Include declarations of classes Circle and GraphicText
#include "vcircle.hpp"
#include "vgtext.hpp"

class CircumText : public Circle, public GraphicText {
  public:
// Constructor
    CircumText(Point &, int, int, char *, int, int);
// Draw a text into circle
    virtual void Draw();
};

    ...

#endif
```

However, the memory allocation for the **CircumText** object will appear differently than in the earlier figure. The object of **CircumText** class will now appear as follows overleaf:

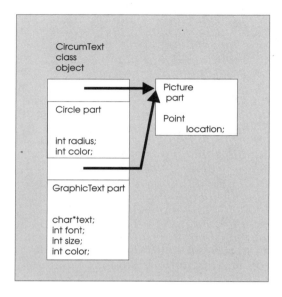

Memory Allocation for Multiple Derivation from a Single Virtual Base Class

Thus we have changed from the derivation hierarchy we saw earlier to the next derivation hierarchy (see below):

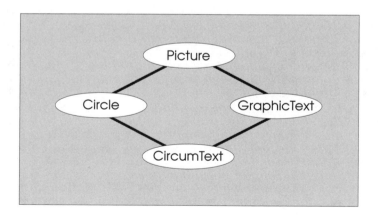

The Hierarchy of Multiple Derivation from a Single Virtual Base Class

Calling a Constructor of Virtual Base Class

You may well wonder how a constructor of a virtual base class should be called? What should the constructors of **Circle**, **GraphicText** and **CircumText** look like?

Normally, a derived class constructor must immediately call the constructor of immediate base class.

The **Circle** class constructor must contain a call for the constructor of the **Picture** base class in its heading.

```
// Constructor

Circle :: Circle(Point & loc, int rad, int col)
    : Picture(loc)
{
  radius = rad;
  color = col;
}
```

The **Circle** class constructor doesn't change when the **Picture** class is declared a virtual base class - nor does the **GraphicText** class constructor:

```
// Constructor

GraphicText :: GraphicText(Point & loc, char * txt, int fnt,
        int sz, int col)
      : Picture(loc)
{
  text = new char [strlen(txt) + 1];
  strcpy(text, txt);
  font = fnt;
  size = sz;
  color = col;
}
```

The derived class constructor is the same, irrespective of whether the immediate base class is virtual or not.

The situation is different for the **CircumText** class constructor with the **Picture** class being the virtual base class.

Because the **Circle** and **GraphicText** classes now 'share' the **Picture** class, neither is allowed to call the **Picture** class constructor. The reason is that if it *were* allowed, then the constructor could be called twice - not a good thing! For this reason, a class further down the inheritance hierarchy must call the **Picture** class's constructor, in our case the **CircumText** class.

The definition of the **CircumText** class constructor now appears as follows:

```
// Constructor

CircumText :: CircumText(Point & loc, int rC, int cC,
        char * tT, int fT, int cT)
    : Picture(loc),
      Circle(loc, rC, cC),
      GraphicText(loc, tT, fT, 2 * rC, cT)
{
}
```

> The modified code of the draw program is in **VDRAW.CPP** file on the disk.

Rules for Calling Constructors and Destructors

Here are the rules of calling constructors and destructors for a virtual base class:

Rule 1

Constructors for virtual base classes are called before any non-virtual base classes, regardless of the order they were declared in the derivation list.

If you wish to create an object of the **CircumText** class

```
CircumText ct(Point(320,240), 100, LIGHTBLUE,
            "C++", GOTHIC_FONT, WHITE);
```

the constructors for the base and derived classes will be called in the following order:

```
Point();   // Constructor of a member which is a
        // class object is called before the constructor
        // of the class with the object

Picture(); // Constructor of the virtual base class
Circle();   // Constructors of nonvirtual base classes are GraphicText();
```

```
// called in the order in which they were
    // specified

CircumText(); // Constructor of derived class is the last called
```

Rule 2

If there are multiple virtual base classes, the virtual base class constructors are called in the order in which they were declared in the derivation list.

The **CircumText** class has only one virtual base class.

Rule 3

Destructors of virtual base classes are always called after the non-virtual base class destructors.

Accessing a Member of a Virtual Base Class

When virtual base classes are used in derivation, the access rules remain the same as those for nonvirtual base classes:

Virtual Base Classes with Public and Private Derivations

Assume that the **Circle** class has been publicly derived from the **Picture** class and the **GraphicText** class has been privately inherited from the **Picture** class.

```
class Circle : virtual public Picture {
...
};

class GraphicText : virtual Picture {
...
};

class CircumText : public Circle, public GraphicText {
...
   Point IsLocation() { return location; }
};
```

One More Rule

Is it possible for the **CircumText** class to access the inherited members of the **Picture** virtual base class? That is, is the location data member accessible in the **IsLocation** function of the **CircumText** class?

The rule is that even if one of the branches used in derivation involving a virtual base class is private, the inherited members of the virtual base class are accessible unless all branch(es) in the derivation are private.

The inherited members of the **Picture** virtual base class are accessible in the **CircumText** class because the derivation branch from **Picture** to **Circle** remained public (see the following figure):

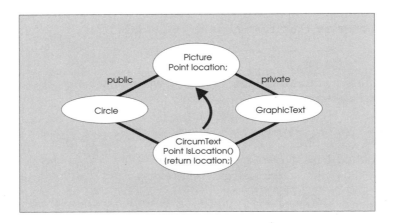

Public and Private Derivation for a Virtual Base Class

Thus the location data member is accessible from the **IsLocation**() function.

The Domination Principle

Let's examine the following inheritance hierarchy with virtual base class:

```
class A {
  protected:
    int a;
  public:
    A(int);
    void Print();
};

class B : public virtual A {
  protected:
    int b;
  public:
    B(int);
```

```
    void Print();
};

class C : public virtual A {
  protected:
    int c;
  public:
    C(int);
};

class D : public B, public C { ... };
```

Try It Out

Let's create an object of class **D**:

```
D obj;
```

A question arises - which function instance is called by the following statement:

```
obj.Print();
```

will it be the **Print** function of the class **A** or class **B**, or is it ambiguous ?

When inheriting from a base class which is not virtual, such function calls would be ambiguous and cause a compiler error message.

But there is no any ambiguity on derivation using virtual base class. In such a case, the dominance rule is applied. This rule dictates the member of a class (data member or member function) more distant from hierarchy base class is dominated. Thus, the **B** class **Print** function dominates over the **A** class **Print** function. This is why the **Print** function of **B** class will be called.

Try It Out!

Summary

You can create a new class from more than one existing class. This form of class derivation is called multiple derivation. The derived class inherits the data members and member functions of several base classes. The syntax for multiple derivation is as follows:

```
class  derived_class_name
    :  [public|private|protected]   base_class_name_1,
       [public|private|protected]   base_class_name_2
       [,  ...  ]
{
. . .
};
```

To access members that have been inherited by a derived class from multiple base classes, you should adhere to the same rules as these for the members inherited from one base class. However, when two or more base class define similarly named members you should qualify them by base class name using the scope resolution operator.

When deriving from multiple base classes, you may come across the situation when a derived class inherits the same base class more than once in the class hierarchy. To avoid having a multiple duplicated base class you can declare the base class as **virtual** using the following syntax:

```
class  derived_class_name   :
    virtual  [public|private|protected]  base_class_name
    [,  ...  ]
{
. . .
};
```

In this case, the derived class object will only contain a pointer to base class part instead of the whole virtual base class.

A virtual base class constructor is called by a distant derived class in the inheritance hierarchy, rather than by the immediately derived class. The virtual base class constructor is performed before any non-virtual base class constructors.

When virtual base classes are used in inheritance, the access rules remain the same as those for non-virtual base classes.

CHAPTER 11

Generic Classes and Functions (Templates)

In the examples we have used in the preceding chapters, you may have noticed that we used a number of very similar classes, each of which had to be individually defined. If we had a large number of similar classes, say a hundred, then it would be nice to be able to define the class once, rather than a hundred times. C++ provides a mechanism to do this through class templates. C++ also provides a similar mechanism for functions.

Class and function templates can be considered as meta-classes and functions. That is, they describe a group of classes and functions, but are not themselves a class or function.

In this chapter we'll review the geometric figure classes we used in Chapter 9 and the operand and operator classes we used in Chapter 4, and see how they could be implemented using templates.

We'll cover:

- Templates
- Function templates
- Template declaration syntax

Templates

Let's remind ourselves of the definitions of classes **Circle**, **Triangle** and **Rectangle** that we used in Chapter 9 for creating a list of geometric figures and evaluating the figure areas.

```cpp
// Circle class definition

class Circle : public Figure {
   protected:
      double radius;
   public:
      Circle (double);        // Constructor
      ~Circle() {}            // Dummy destructor
// Set a radius
      void SetRadius (double);
// Get a radius
      double GetRadius();
// Get a surface area
      virtual double Area();
};

// Circle class member function definition
// Constructor

Circle :: Circle (double r) {
   radius = r;
}

// Get a surface area of a circle
double Circle :: Area() {
   return 3.14159 * radius * radius;
}


// Triangle class definition
class Triangle : public Figure {
   protected:
      double height;
      double base;
   public:
      Triangle(double, double);    // Constructor
      ~Triangle() {}               // Dummy destructor
// Set sizes of a triangle
   void SetSize (double, double);
// Get a height of a triangle
   double GetHeight();
// Get a base of a triangle
   double GetBase();
```

```
// Get a surface area
   virtual double Area();
};

// Constructor
Triangle :: Triangle(double b, double h) {
   base = b;
   height = h;
}
// Get an area size of a triangle
double Triangle :: Area() {
   return base * height/2;
}


// Rectangle class definition
class Rectangle : public Figure {
   protected:
      double height;
      double width;
   public:
// Constructor
      Rectangle(double, double);
// Dummy destructor
      ~Rectangle() {}
// Set sizes of a rectangle
      void SetSize(double, double);
// Get a height of a rectangle
      double GetHeight();
// Get a width of a rectangle
      double GetWidth();
// Get an area size
      virtual double Area();
};

// Constructor
Rectangle :: Rectangle(double w, double h) {
   width = w;
   height = h;
}
// Get an area size of a rectangle
double Rectangle :: Area() {
   return width * height;
}
```

The definitions of these three classes are similar in their members, and in their definitions of member functions. The only difference is in the number of parameters required to evaluate the area. One parameter, a radius, is required for **Circle**, and two parameters, a height and a base, are required for **Triangle** and **Rectangle**. It is natural that the formula used for finding each figure area is distinct. The names of classes also differ, since they should naturally relate with the objects to be acted on.

Each of these three classes had to be individually defined. Imagine if we had a hundred such geometric figures - we would have to provide a hundred individual definitions, one for each.

The same is true of the set of, say, mathematical functions that must perform identical calculations for different types. Having no template mechanism, we would have to define a set of overloaded functions that differ in operand types and the return value type.

To demonstrate this we'll take a classical example of a **max** macro which lets us define the greater of the two arguments for different argument types. As you no doubt remember, to define a greater of the two arguments of **integer** type, for example, you can define the following function:

```
int max(int x, int y) {
    return (x > y) ? x : y;
}
```

For a **float** type argument, the function must appear as follows:

```
float max (float x, float y) {
    return (x > y) ? x : y;
}
```

The same should be done for every type required. As you know, this solution of the problem utilises the function overloading mechanism. This approach, however, doesn't relieve us of having to write as many function definitions as we need for the selected argument types.

In both cases mentioned above, a template is a way of defining a pattern (or a way of giving a generalized definition) of a class or function, from where specific class or function instances will be generated automatically (see the following figures).

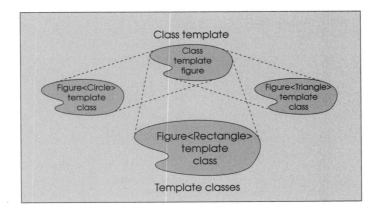

A Class Template and a Template Class

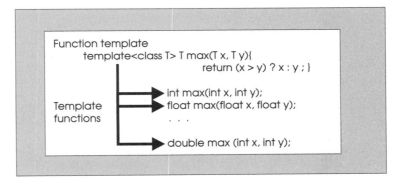

A Function Template and a Template Function

Class Templates

Let's try to define a generic class from which the required three classes could be created.

We'll name this generic class **Figure**. The generic class name will be used to produce a name for a specific class. To do this, the generic class name **Figure** is followed by the type name which is the value of argument for the class template parameter surrounded by angle brackets. Thus to specify the name of a template class for the figure **Circle**, we can use the following syntax:

```
Figure<Circle>
```

The names for classes **Triangle** and **Rectangle** will be respectively:

```
Figure<Triangle>
Figure<Rectangle>
```

However, if you want to use the words **Circle**, **Triangle** and **Rectangle** as type names, you must declare them as class names:

```
class Circle;
class Triangle;
class Rectangle;
```

The Template of a Template

Any definition of a class template begins with the **template** keyword which is followed by a class template parameter type list enclosed by angle brackets and by the **class** keyword (which indicates that we are defining a class template rather than the function). The generic class name (the class template name) then follows:

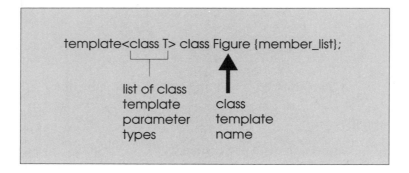

The Class Template Name

As for an ordinary class definition, the class template heading is followed by a list of generic class member declarations (data member and member function), enclosed in braces.

In our example, the parameter type list consists of a single parameter class T which is mandatory. The word class is a keyword which indicates that the type (class) name is used as an argument and T is an arbitrarily chosen designation (parameter name). If you want to reference a type to be passed as an argument in the body of class definition, you should use the name (T in the above example).

For example, if you want to declare a pointer to the class being defined as a template data member, use the following syntax:

```
T *   fig;   // Pointer to object type which is
             // a class template parameter
             // representing the name of specific class
or  type
```

There can be more than one template parameter, and they are comma-separated as in an ordinary parameter list, and can include default values as well. We'll discuss an example of multi-parameter class template later.

Defining the Body

We now turn our attention to defining the body of the generic for our example classes. For simplicity, we'll restrict ourselves to two member functions from the old classes **Circle**, **Triangle** (rectangular) and **Rectangle**: the constructor and the **Area** function which calculates the figure area. The remaining functions could be defined in a similar way.

Try It Out

Firstly, let's try to write a generic class with an ordinary constructor and a single **Area** function for the three types of figures. Since the area formulas used for the three figures are different, we must somehow identify the type of figure whose area is to be calculated. To do this, we introduce a data member with the name of **figure** type:

```
template<class T> class Figure {
   private:
      double dimen1;    // Radius for circle or
                // base for other figures
      double dimen2;    // Height of triangle or rectangle
      char * name;   // Pointer to name of figure kind
```

Try It Out!

Although we're not only going to have a single constructor for the three kinds of figures, but also distinguish among them, we introduce a parameter to define the type of figure (**FigureType**) in the constructor. We declare **FigureType** as an enumerator with the following values of figure types:

```
enum FigureType {C, Tr, Re};
```

We can now define our constructor as follows:

```
// Class template member function definition

template<class T> Figure<T> ::
 Figure(FigureType t, double a, double b = 0) {

   switch (t) {
      case C:    name = "Circle"; break;
      case Tr:   name = "Triangle"; break;
      case Re:   name = "Rectangle"; break;
      default:   name = "Unknown";
      }

   dimen1 = a;
   dimen2 = b;
}
```

The declaration of an object of **Figure<Circle>** class specifies two arguments: **c** is the figure type, and the number specifying the radius of circle. For example:

```
Figure<Circle> c(C,4);
```

The third argument can be omitted because there is a default value defined for it.

Notice the syntax for defining a generic class member function when the member function is to be defined outside the template body (opposite):

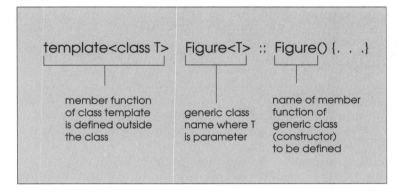

We'll discuss overloading member functions of a generic class and the syntax of the `::` operator later.

Now the **Area** function will evaluate the figure area depending on the value pointed by name:

```
template<class T>  double Figure<T> :: Area() {
   if (!strcmp(name, "Circle"))
      return 3.14159 * dimen1 * dimen1;
   if (!strcmp(name, "Triangle"))
      return dimen1 * dimen2 /2;
   if (!strcmp(name, "Rectangle"))
      return dimen1 * dimen2;
   return ERROR;
   }
```

How It Works - The Complete Program

Here is the complete program to evaluate the area of circle, triangle and rectangle:

```
// Class template definition for geometric figures
#include <iostream.h>
#include <string.h>
#define ERROR -1

enum FigureType {C, Tr, Re};
class Circle;
class Triangle;
```

```cpp
class Rectangle;

template<class T> class Figure {
   private:
      double dimen1;
      double dimen2;
      char * name;
   public:
      Figure(FigureType, double, double=0);
      double Area();
      char * NameOf();
};

// Class template member function definition

template<class T> Figure<T> ::
 Figure(FigureType t, double a, double b = 0) {

   switch (t) {
      case C:    name = "Circle"; break;
      case Tr:   name = "Triangle"; break;
      case Re:   name = "Rectangle"; break;
      default:   name = "Unknown";
      }

   dimen1 = a;
   dimen2 = b;
}

template<class T>   double Figure<T> :: Area() {
   if (!strcmp(name, "Circle"))
      return 3.14159 * dimen1 * dimen1;
   if (!strcmp(name, "Triangle"))
      return dimen1 * dimen2 /2;
   if (!strcmp(name, "Rectangle"))
      return dimen1 * dimen2;
   return ERROR;
   }

template<class T> char * Figure<T> :: NameOf() {
   return name;
}

int main() {
Figure<Circle> c(C, 4);
cout << "Area of " << c.NameOf() << ": " << c.Area() << '\n';
Figure<Triangle> t(Tr, 5, 4.5);
cout << "Area of " << t.NameOf() << ": " << t.Area() << '\n';
Figure<Rectangle> r(Re, 2.5, 3);
cout << "Area of " << r.NameOf() << ": " << r.Area() << '\n';
return 1;
}
```

The program result would appear as follows:

```
Area of Circle: 50.26544
Area of Triangle: 11.25
Area of Rectangle: 7.5
```

Forming the Class Name

In the **main** function we declare an object of specific (individual) class. This is almost the same as for an ordinary class, excluding the fact that the class name is formed from that of the class template, followed by an argument represented by the class name (to be produced from the class template), and enclosed by angle brackets. This instance of the class is referred to as a template class. We can further reference this class name as an ordinary class name. The difference is that the name of a template class must always include its argument list enclosed by angle brackets when used everywhere (except within its own class definition).

Notice that outside the context of a template definition, you can use only the instantiations of a template class (with actual values of type parameters).

```
int DoAction(Stack<Operand, long> & opd,
        Stack<Operator, char> & opt) { ... }
```

In a template function, you can specify either a particular instance of a template class or a generic (parameterized) class:

```
template<class T, class T1> int Stack<T, T1> ::
                Push (T1 n) { ...}
```

Using typedef to Define a Synonym of a Template Class Name

The name of a template class with angle brackets can appear fairly complicated. Using a declaration with a typedef you can declare an alternative name as a synonym for the existing name with angle brackets. For example:

```
typedef Figure<Circle> fc;
typedef Figure<Triangle> ft;
typedef Figure<Triangle> fr;
```

Then the **main** function can be simplified as follows, but the result will be the same:

```cpp
int main() {
typedef Figure<Circle> fc;
typedef Figure<Triangle> ft;
typedef Figure<Rectangle> fr;

fc c(C, 4);
cout << "Area of " << c.NameOf() << ": " << c.Area() << '\n';

ft t(Tr, 5, 4.5);
cout << "Area of " << t.NameOf() << ": " << t.Area() << '\n';

fr r(Re, 2.5, 3);
cout << "Area of " << r.NameOf() << ": " << r.Area() << '\n';
return 1;
}
```

The full program is then:

```cpp
// Class template definition for geometric figures
#include "iostream.h"
#include "string.h"
#define ERROR -1

enum FigureType {C, Tr, Re};
class Circle;
class Triangle;
class Rectangle;

template<class T> class Figure {
   private:
      double dimen1;
      double dimen2;
      char * name;
   public:
      Figure(FigureType, double, double=0);
      double Area();
      char * NameOf();
};

// Class template member function definition

template<class T> Figure<T> ::
 Figure(FigureType t, double a, double b = 0) {

   switch (t) {
      case C:    name = "Circle"; break;
      case Tr:   name = "Triangle"; break;
      case Re:   name = "Rectangle"; break;
```

```
        default:  name = "Unknown";
        }

   dimen1 = a;
   dimen2 = b;
 }


template<class T>  double Figure<T> :: Area() {
   if (!strcmp(name, "Circle"))
      return 3.14159 * dimen1 * dimen1;
   if (!strcmp(name, "Triangle"))
      return dimen1 * dimen2 /2;
   if (!strcmp(name, "Rectangle"))
      return dimen1 * dimen2;
   return ERROR;
   }

template<class T> char * Figure<T> :: NameOf() {
   return name;
}



int main() {
typedef Figure<Circle> fc;
typedef Figure<Triangle> ft;
typedef Figure<Rectangle> fr;

fc c(C, 4);
cout << "Area of " << c.NameOf() << ": " << c.Area() << '\n';

ft t(Tr, 5, 4.5);
cout << "Area of " << t.NameOf() << ": " << t.Area() << '\n';

fr r(Re, 2.5, 3);
cout << "Area of " << r.NameOf() << ": " << r.Area() << '\n';
return 1;
}
```

Function Templates

In the same way as we defined a class template to derive specific class instances (template classes) for multiple similar classes, we can define a function template for multiple similar functions. This is especially convenient when lexically the same function must ensure processing of different data types. A typical example of this function is finding the larger of the two objects, comparison, sorting performed on objects of various types.

Let's go back to the class of geometric figure list discussed in Chapter 9.

```cpp
// FigureList class definition
class FigureList {
   public:
      static FigureList * head;        // Head of list
   private:
// Pointer to a figure
      Figure * obj;
// Pointer to the next element of the list
      FigureList * next;
   public:
      FigureList(Figure *);        // Constructor
      ~FigureList();               // Destructor
// Add a figure to a list
      FigureList * Add(Figure *, FigureList *);
// Destroy a list of figures
      void Destroy(FigureList *);
// Print area size of all figures in a list
      void Print(FigureList *);
 };

FigureList * FigureList:: head = 0;

// Constructor
FigureList :: FigureList(Figure * fp){
   obj = fp;
   next = 0;
   if (head == 0)
      head = this;
}

// Destructor
FigureList :: ~FigureList() {
   Destroy(head);
}

// Add a new figure to the list
FigureList * FigureList :: Add(Figure * f, FigureList * p) {
   if (p == 0)
      p = new FigureList(f);
   else
      p -> next = Add(f, p->next);
   return p;
}

// Destroy a list of figures
void FigureList :: Destroy (FigureList * p) {
   if (p != 0) {
      Destroy (p->next);
```

```
      }
   }

   // Print area size of all figures in the list
   void FigureList :: Print(FigureList * p) {
      Figure * fp;
      if (p != 0) {
         fp = p->obj;
         cout << fp->Area() << '\n';
         Print (p->next);
      }
   }

   double GetArea(Figure & obj) {
      return obj.Area();
   }

   int main () {
      Circle c(4);
      cout << " Area of circle: " << GetArea(c) << '\n';
      FigureList flist(&c);
      Rectangle r(2.5, 3);
      cout << " Area of rectangle: " << GetArea(r) << '\n';
      flist.Add (&r, flist.head);
      Triangle t(5, 4.5);
      cout << " Area of triangle: " << GetArea(t) << '\n';
      flist.Add (&t, flist.head);

      flist.Print (flist.head);
      return 1;
   }
```

Using Polymorphism at Run-time

The basic idea behind this example is using the virtual function mechanism (polymorphism) to resolve the call at run time, depending on which class object the function was called for.

> We used the property of a hierarchy of classes - a pointer or reference to a derived class object can be automatically converted to a pointer or reference to a base class.

Try It Out - Rewriting the Add Function

Let's rewrite the **Add** function which adds a figure to the list of figures using a function template.

Try It Out!

The heading of a function template definition resembles that of a class template definition. However, unlike a class template definition it has the type of value returned by the function and the function heading:

```
// Add a new figure to the list
template<class T> FigureList * Add(T & f, FigureList * p)
  {
    if (p == 0)
       p = new FigureList(&f);
    else
       p -> next = Add(f, p->next);
    return p;
}
```

How It Works

To instantiate which **Add** function we want to apply, we substitute the reference to type **T** specified in the function template definition with an object of class **Circle**, **Triangle** or **Rectangle** in the function call. A specific instance of a function template is referred to as a template function. The process of type substitution is referred to as template instantiation. Function template instantiation occurs when you call a function as in our example or when you take the function address.

```
// Figure list using a function template for the add function

int main () {
...
   Rectangle r(2.5, 3);
   Add (r, flist.head);
...
   Triangle t(5, 4.5);
   Add (t, flist.head);
...
}
```

The full program is as follows:

```
// Figure class defines general notion
// "plane geometric figure"
#include "iostream.h"

class Figure {
   public:
// Constructor
      Figure() {}              // Dummy constructor
// Destructor
```

```
     ~Figure() {}            // Dummy destructor
// Get an area
     virtual double Area();
};

// Figure class member functions definition

double Figure :: Area() {
   return 0;
}

// Circle class definition

class Circle : public Figure {
   protected:
      double radius;
   public:
      Circle (double);        // Constructor
      ~Circle() {}            // Dummy destructor
// Set a radius
      void SetRadius (double);
// Get a radius
      double GetRadius();
// Get an area
      virtual double Area();
};

// Circle class member function definition
// Constructor

Circle :: Circle (double r) {
   radius = r;
}

// Set a radius of a circle
void Circle :: SetRadius (double r) {
   radius = r;
}

// Get a radius of a circle
double Circle :: GetRadius () {
   return radius;
}

// Get a surface area of a circle
double Circle :: Area() {
   return 3.14159 * radius * radius;
}

// Triangle class definition
class Triangle : public Figure {
```

```cpp
   protected:
      double height;
      double base;
   public:
      Triangle(double, double);    // Constructor
      ~Triangle() {}               // Dummy destructor
// Set sizes of a triangle
   void SetSize (double, double);
// Get a height of a triangle
   double GetHeight();
// Get a base of a triangle
   double GetBase();
// Get an area
   virtual double Area();
};

// Constructor
Triangle :: Triangle(double b, double h) {
   base = b;
   height = h;
}

// Set sizes of a triangle
void Triangle :: SetSize(double b, double h) {
   base = b;
   height = h;
}

// Get a base of a triangle
double Triangle:: GetBase() {
   return base;
}

// Get a height of a triangle
double Triangle :: GetHeight() {
   return height;
}

// Get an area size of a triangle
double Triangle :: Area() {
   return base * height/2;
}

// Rectangle class definition
class Rectangle : public Figure {
   protected:
      double height;
      double width;
   public:
      // Constructor
      Rectangle(double, double);
```

```cpp
       // Dummy destructor
       ~Rectangle() {}
       // Set sizes of a rectangle
       void SetSize(double, double);
       // Get a height of a rectangle
       double GetHeight();
       // Get a width of a rectangle
       double GetWidth();
       // Get an area size
       virtual double Area();
};

// Constructor
Rectangle :: Rectangle(double w, double h) {
   width = w;
   height = h;
}

// Set (change) sizes of a rectangle
void Rectangle :: SetSize(double w, double h) {
   width = w;
   height = h;
}

// Get a width of a rectangle
double Rectangle :: GetWidth() {
   return width;
}

// Get a height of a rectangle
double Rectangle :: GetHeight() {
   return height;
}

// Get an area size of a rectangle
double Rectangle :: Area() {
   return width * height;
}

// FigureList class definition
class FigureList {
   public:
      static FigureList * head;        // Head of list
//   private:
// Pointer to a figure
      Figure * obj;
// Pointer to the next element of the list
      FigureList * next;
   public:
// Constructor
      FigureList(Figure *);
```

```cpp
// Destructor
    ~FigureList();
// Destroy a list of figures
    void Destroy(FigureList *);
// Print area size of all figures in a list
    void Print(FigureList *);
 };

FigureList * FigureList:: head = 0;

// Constructor
FigureList ::   FigureList(Figure * fp)
{
   obj = fp;
   next = 0;
   if (head == 0)
      head = this;
}

// Destructor
FigureList :: ~FigureList() {
   Destroy(head);
}


// Destroy a list of figures
void FigureList :: Destroy (FigureList * p) {
   if (p != 0) {
      Destroy (p->next);
   }
}

// Print area size of all figures in the list
void FigureList :: Print(FigureList * p) {
   Figure * fp;
   if (p != 0) {
      fp = p->obj;
      cout << fp->Area() << '\n';
      Print (p->next);
   }
}


// Add a new figure to the list
template<class T> FigureList * Add(T & f, FigureList * p)
 {
   if (p == 0)
      p = new FigureList(&f);
   else
      p -> next = Add(f, p->next);
   return p;
```

```
}

double GetArea(Figure & obj) {
   return obj.Area();
}

int main () {
   Circle c(4);
   cout << " Area of circle: " << GetArea(c) << '\n';
   FigureList flist(&c);
   Rectangle r(2.5, 3);
   cout << " Area of rectangle: " << GetArea(r) << '\n';
   Add (r, flist.head);
   Triangle t(5, 4.5);
   cout << " Area of triangle: " << GetArea(t) << '\n';
   Add (t, flist.head);

   flist.Print (flist.head);
   return 1;
}
```

The result of executing the program is as follows:

```
Area of circle: 50.26544
Area of rectangle: 7.5
Area of triangle: 11.25
50.26544
7.5
11.25
```

In the template definition body, you can use the formal parameter type declared in the parameter type list of a function template as well as the name of a built-in type or user-defined class.

> The only restriction to the use of formal parameters is the requirement that each of them must appear in the function signature at least once. The function template can also use parameters of normal type.

Checking Argument Types

When a template function is called (instantiated) argument types are checked against parameter types of the function template the same as it is done for the arguments in the ordinary function call and parameters in its prototype.

Firstly, the appropriate template parameter is checked to see whether it is a parameterized type (that is, declared with the **class** keyword). If it is parameterized, the actual argument type of the template function is defined. Then the formal parameter and the actual argument are type-checked by discarding the appropriate type modifiers.

If, for example, a formal parameter of the function template

```
template<class T> T max(T * x, T * y)
```

has been declared as

```
T * x
```

and an actual argument is of the following type

```
int *
```

the formal parameter **T** is associated with the **int** type, and for the case of

```
int **
```

with the **int*** type.

If a formal parameter occurs in the argument list of a template function more than once, every occurrence of the type name **T** is associated with the type with which it has been associated on the first parameter occurrence. In our example, the actual argument for parameter y must be of **int** type (for the case of **int** *).

If the function instance generated by the compiler is not appropriate for some **T**, we can have it overloaded by another function or template function with the same name.

Overloading resolution is performed in the following steps:

1 The compiler looks for a function instance with an exact match of arguments.

2 If the compiler failed to find such an instance, it tries to find a function template to generate a template function with matching arguments.

3 If the function template isn't found, the compiler tries to apply the ordinary function resolution rules.

If the compiler can find an exact match in more than one way at step **1** an ambiguity arises causing an error message to be issued.

At step **2**, there is no attempt at type conversion. Only the template function with exact matching arguments that can be generated from the function template would be appropriate.

Declarations and Definitions

Normally, there can be many declarations but only one definition of a function or class template in a program. That is, no definition is required for a specific instance of a function or class template. A template function definition is generated automatically when invoking or taking the address of a template function. A template class is generated when the template class name is used, for example, when declaring an object of the class. That is, in our examples, when this declaration is encountered at compile-time:

```
Figure<Circle> c(4);
```

the definition for the **Figure<Circle>** template class is created.

When the compiler encounters a template function call

```
Add (r, flist.ead);
```

where **r** is an object of **Rectangle** class, the definition of the template function is created for the **Rectangle** type argument.

It's also possible to declare and define your own function for a specific type, if the function needs to perform specific actions for the type.

For example, if you want to perform some additional operations while adding a **Circle** object to the figure list, you can use the following definition syntax:

```
FigureList  *  Add  (Circle  &, FigureList * p) { body of
function  other  than  function  template}
```

Defining Function Templates

A function template can only be defined globally. However, if you have defined a class template, every member function of the class template will be implicitly a template function. To overload this member function, you must see that the definition of overload member function outside the class starts with the template class name in the left-hand side of the scope resolution operator:

```
Figure<Circle> :: Figure(double a) { ... }
Figure<Triangle> :: Figure(double a, double b) { ... }
Figure<Rectangle> :: Figure(double a, double b) { ... }
```

Similarly, you can give your own definition for a specific template class. For example:

```
template<class T> class Figure {body of class template};
class Figure<Circle> {body of template class for Circle type};
```

In this case the template class definitions automatically generated at compile-time will be used for the figures **Triangle** and **Rectangle**, while the definition provided by you will be used for the **Circle** figure.

A specialized template class definition can only follow a class template definition. If a specialized template class instance is defined, each member function used in the template must be defined explicitly. The template class member functions are not automatically instantiated.

A class template can only be declared globally.

Member Function Templates

Member functions of a class template are implicitly function templates. Therefore, when we declared the member functions:

```
Figure (FigureType, double, double=0);
double Area();
char * NameOf();
```

in the earlier example, we declared the templates of member functions where the class template argument **T** is an implicit argument of member function templates.

As you can see, the constructor template shared by three different figures doesn't appear to be good enough. To define a specific template function instance for ourselves, let's declare two constructor prototypes and define three constructors for each figure type:

```
template<class T> class Figure {
   private:
       double dimen1;
       double dimen2;
       char * name;
   public:
       Figure(double);
       Figure(double, double);
       double Area();
       char * NameOf();
};

// Class template member function definition

Figure<Circle> ::  Figure(double a) {
   name = "Circle";
   dimen1 = a;
 }

Figure<Triangle> ::  Figure(double a, double b) {

   name = "Triangle";
   dimen1 = a;
   dimen2 = b;

}

Figure<Rectangle> ::  Figure(double a, double b) {
```

```
    name = "Rectangle";
    dimen1 = a;
    dimen2 = b;
}
```

Now the constructor we defined (with the name pointer set to the **"Circle"** string) will be called wherever an object of the **Figure<Circle>** class is declared. The constructors called for a declared object of the **Figure<Triangle>** and **Figure<Rectangle>** will respectively set the name pointer to the **"Triangle"** and **"Rectangle"** string.

Since there is no need to pass the **FigureType** parameter to a constructor, the **main** function will appear as follows:

```
int main() {
typedef Figure<Circle> fc;
typedef Figure<Triangle> ft;
typedef Figure<Rectangle> fr;

fc c(4);
cout << "Area of " << c.NameOf() << ": " << c.Area() << '\n';

ft t(5, 4.5);
cout << "Area of " << t.NameOf() << ": " << t.Area() << '\n';

fr r(2.5, 3);
cout << "Area of " << r.NameOf() << ": " << r.Area() << '\n';
return 1;
}
```

Notice that the constructor name for **Figure** has no **T** argument specified in its declaration or definition. This is an implicit argument of member function templates. This argument is defined by the class of object for which the member function is called.

Value Typing

A constructor (the same as a destructor) is a member function that has no return value type. If a member function returns any value type, the return value type for a defined member function template or a template member function must be specified in the function heading between the **template<template_argument_list>** specifier and the class template name. This can be demonstrated with our example of template definition for the **Area** member function (opposite):

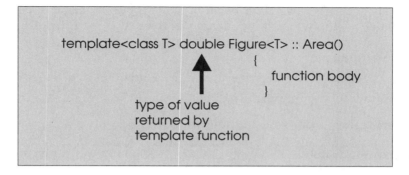

A Template Definition

Template Declaration Syntax

The syntax of a class or function template declaration can appear as follows:

```
template-declaration:
    template<template-argument-list> declaration

template-argument-list:
    template-argument
    template-argument-list, template-argument

template-argument:
    type-argument
    argument-declaration

type-argument:
    class  identifier
```

Whether the template declared applies to a class or a function is specified by the syntax of declaration following the template argument type list, enclosed in angle brackets. The entries in the template argument type list might appear as:

```
class  identifier
```

or be an ordinary declaration of an argument type. A name appearing in declaration of the template declaration is referred to as a template name.

Template Names

A class template name must be unique in a program and mustn't be used for other templates, classes, functions, objects or types within the same scope.

To instantiate a class, use the following syntax:

```
template-class-name:
    template-name<template-arg-list>

template-arg-list:
    template-arg
    template-arg-list,  template-arg

template-arg:
    expression
    type-name
```

To define a specific class you must append a list of argument values enclosed in angle brackets to the template name where the template argument appearing as *class identifier* must be associated with a class or type name and the ordinary argument declarations must be associated with expressions.

For example:

```
template<class T, int size> class buf;
```

is a declaration of class template where:

`<class T, int size>` is the list of class template argument types where the first argument is the class or type name and the second argument is an ordinary argument declaration.

```
buf<char, 512> x;
```

is a declaration of object **x** of the template class where **buf<char, 512>** is the template class name.

`<char, 512>` is a template class argument list associated with the **buf** class template declared above. **char** is the type name substituted for the class **T** parameter in the template parameter list. **512** is a constant value associated with the second non-type parameter in the template parameter list.

> Non-type template parameters are usually associated with a constant expression, object address or function.

Argument types in a template class name must coincide with those specified in the template argument list of the class template declaration.

Class Template with Multiple Arguments

Although the examples discussed up till now use only one class template argument, the list of arguments can contain multiple arguments to represent data types (as the first argument **"class   T"**) or values. The values supplied for non-type arguments must be constant expressions.

The classes **OperandStack** and **OperatorStack** defined for the simple calculator program could be the candidates for a class template with multiple arguments.

These classes were declared as follows:

```
class OperandStack {
   private:
      long stack[MAXDEPTH];
      int top;
   public:
      OperandStack();
      int Push(long);
      long Pop();
};
```

```
class Token;
class OperatorStack {
   private:
      char stack[MAXDEPTH+1];
      int top;
   public:
      OperatorStack();
      int Push(char);
      char Pop();
```

```
        void Clear(OperandStack &);
        int isHigherStack(char);
        int isHigherOrEqual(char);
        int DoAction(OperandStack &);
};
```

For one thing, these declarations differ in the stack entry types (**long** for operand stack and **char** for operator stack) as well as argument and return value types for member functions **Push** and **Pop** - for another, in class names. A reference to the class name **OperandStack** is an argument of the functions **Clear** and **DoAction**.

Without going into detail on other differences between these classes, let's have a look at a class template definition with two arguments each of which represents a type name. We'll restrict ourselves to only constructor, member functions **Push**, **Pop** and **DoAction** which allow us to put operands and an operator, to the operand and operator stacks respectively, to perform operations. Let's denote the names of classes **Operand** and **Operator** by **T** and the stack entry type by **T1: long** (for operands) and **char** (for operators).

A declaration for the **Stack** class template can appear as follows:

```
class Operand;
class Operator;
template<class T, class T1> class Stack {
    private:
        T1 stack[MAXDEPTH];
        int top;
    public:
        Stack();
        int Push(T1);
        T1 Pop();
        int DoAction (Stack<Operand, long> &);
};
```

To define the **Push** member function that is also a function template, you can write the following:

```
template<class T, class T1> int Stack<T, T1> ::
    Push(T1 n) {
        if (top < MAXDEPTH)
            stack[top++] = n;
        else
            return ERROR;
    return OK;
    }
```

T1 is the type (**long** or **char**) of entry to be placed on stack depending on the **T** stack class.

Take a closer look at the arguments of the template function **DoAction**:

```
template<class T, class T1> int Stack<T, T1> ::
   DoAction(Stack<Operand, long> & opd) {
      T1 op2;
      switch (stack[top - 1]) {
            case '+':
                    opd.Push(opd.Pop() + opd.Pop());
                    break;
            case '*':
                    opd.Push(opd.Pop() * opd.Pop());
                    break;
            case '-':
                    op2 = opd.Pop();
                    opd.Push(opd.Pop() - op2);
                    break;
            case '/':
                    if ((op2 = opd.Pop()) != 0)
                       opd.Push(opd.Pop() / op2);
                    else
                       Err_rep(3);
                    break;
            case '(':
            case ')':
                    break;
      }
      Pop();
      return OK;
}
```

We can't specify here the type designation **T** or **T1** as we did for the **Push** function since we call the function for an object of class **Stack<Operator, char>** using **Operator** as the type for the first function argument and we must pass an object of class **Stack<Operand, long>** as an argument to the **DoAction** function.

This function can't be generated automatically from the template. That is why we explicitly programmed the required function instance by specifying the template class name

```
Stack<Operand, long>
```

as an argument type.

Here is the **main** function:

```
int main() {
typedef Stack<Operand, long> OperandStack;
typedef Stack<Operator, char> OperatorStack;

   OperandStack opd;
   OperatorStack opt;

   opd.Push(2);
   opd.Push(3);
   opt.Push('+');
   opt.DoAction(opd);
   cout << opd.Pop() << '\n';
   return 1;
}
```

The results of program execution will be 5.

Friends

The **DoAction** function of the above example is a member function of a template class used to operate on object of another template class. As we noted in Chapter 5 where the situation is discussed, we can declare the **DoAction** function a friend.

A function declared friend in a class template definition isn't an implicit template function but it can be explicitly declared and defined as a template.

Try It Out - Be My Friend

Let's declare the **DoAction** function a friend to the **Stack** class template and globally define it as a template function.

```
class Operand;
class Operator;
template<class T, class T1> class Stack {
   private:
      T1 stack[MAXDEPTH];
      int top;
   public:
      Stack();
      int Push(T1);
      T1 Pop();
```

```
friend int DoAction (Stack<Operand, long> &, Stack<Operator, char> &);
};
```

...

```
int   DoAction(Stack<Operand, long> & opd, Stack<Operator, char> & opt) {
      long op2;

      switch (opt.stack[opt.top - 1]) {
            case '+':
                  opd.Push(opd.Pop() + opd.Pop());
                  break;
            case '*':
                  opd.Push(opd.Pop() * opd.Pop());
                  break;
            case '-':
                  op2 = opd.Pop();
                  opd.Push(opd.Pop() - op2);
                  break;
            case '/':
                  if ((op2 = opd.Pop()) != 0)
                     opd.Push(opd.Pop() / op2);
                  else
                     Err_rep(3);
                  break;
            case '(':
            case ')':
                  break;
      }
      opt.Pop();
      return OK;
}
```

Template Classes Under Derivation

A template class can be used as the base class from which an ordinary class or class template can be derived.

Static Members and Variables

Every template class or template function generated from a template has its own instance of static members or variables. However, only one static member or variable instance is represented in memory to be shared by all objects of the same template class, and the local static variable retains its value on exit from the function (see the figure overleaf):

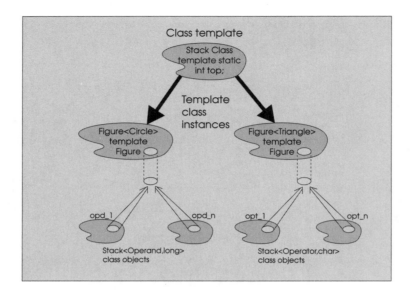

Static Members of Template Classes

Type Equivalence

You may wonder if a template class name references the same class or different classes when the class template has more than one argument.

Two template class names reference the same class if the template class names are identical and their arguments have identical values.

For example, let's declare the class template buffer:

```
template<class T, int sz> class buffer;
```

Then the declarations:

```
buffer<int, 2*512> x;
buffer<int, 1024> y;
buffer<char, 1024> z;
```

have **x** and **y** of the identical type, that is, they represent objects of the same class, and **z** represents an object of another class.

The Advantages of Using Templates

If you have some experience in C programming, and the preprocessor macro facility, you may wonder if we could achieve the same result through macro definition?

Actually, you can resolve the problem of multiple function definition by using a macro definition:

```
#define max(x, y) ( (x > y) ? x : y)
```

However, using macro definition circumvents the type-checking mechanism which is a very important feature of object-oriented programming, and indeed, of safe programming. Macro expansion facility allows the `max(x,y)` macro to be used to compare types of arguments `x` and `y` which are incompatible. Another drawback of using the macro definition facility is the fact that macro expansion can occur even when you don't want it to. For example:

```
class Compare {
   public:
      int max(int, int);
...
};
```

Our intent here was to declare a class member function but the macro expansion facility flagged it as error at compile time.

Using a function template is a more reliable and controllable solution to the problem:

```
template<class T> T max(T x, T y) {
   return (x > y) ? x : y;
}
```

The `T` argument can be of any type: built-in or class. The compiler generates only the appropriate template function instances according to the argument type actually used in the function call:

```
float x, y;
Figure<Circle> c1, c2;

float z = max(x, y);
Figure<Circle> c3 = max(c1, c2);
```

For an object of class you defined by yourself, for example, **Figure<Circle>**, the only thing you have to do is to define **operator >**.

Thus, function templates provide a mechanism which lets you take advantage of the compactness of macro solution without sacrificing any of the benefits provided by C++ as a strongly-typed language.

Another benefit of using class templates is the fact that you can operate on object types which are known at compile-time, rather than pointers to a base type as in the case of derived classes with virtual functions.

Let's go back to the example of the geometric figure list of Chapter 9 that we already discussed under the heading, *Function Templates*.

In the source version of the program using the **Area** virtual function in the **Figure** base class, we redefined the function in each of the three classes (**Circle**, **Triangle**, and **Rectangle**) derived from the **Figure** base class.

```
// Figure class defines general notion
// "plane geometric figure"
#include "iostream.h"

class Figure {
   public:
// Constructor
      Figure() {}            // Dummy constructor
// Destructor
      ~Figure() {}           // Dummy destructor
// Get a surface area
      virtual double Area();
};

// Figure class member functions definition

double Figure :: Area() {
   return 0;
}
```

...

```
// Get a surface area of a circle
double Circle :: Area() {
   return 3.14159 * radius * radius;
}
```

...

```
// Get an area size of a triangle
double Triangle :: Area() {
   return base * height/2;
}
```

. . .

```
// Get an area size of a rectangle
double Rectangle :: Area() {
   return width * height;
}
```

The required instance of **Area** function is dynamically defined at program run-time. With the class template approach, the required function instance belongs to a template class that is explicitly derived at compile-time, according to the class object declaration.

Let's discuss another aspect of creating the figure list in the source version of the program: using a pointer to a base class as a parameter of the **Add** function that adds a geometric figure to the list.

```
// Add a new figure to the list
FigureList * FigureList :: Add(Figure * f, FigureList * p) {
   if (p == 0)
      p = new FigureList(f);
   else
      p -> next = Add(f, p->next);
   return p;
}
```

When an **Add** function is called:

```
int main () {
   Circle c(4);
   cout << " Area of circle: " << GetArea(c) << '\n';
   FigureList flist(&c);
   Rectangle r(2.5, 3);
   cout << " Area of rectangle: " << GetArea(r) << '\n';
   flist.Add (&r, flist.head);
   Triangle t(5, 4.5);
   cout << " Area of triangle: " << GetArea(t) << '\n';
   flist.Add (&t, flist.head);

   flist.Print (flist.head);
   return 1;
}
```

the pointer to the geometric figure type is converted to the pointer to the base type thereby complicating control over the process for you as a programmer.

The class template solution allows you to completely retain control and use a reference to an object of class known at compile time in the **Add** function call.

Summary

When you need to define lots of nearly identical classes to solve a problem, you can facilitate program design without losing run-time efficiency by using class templates.

A specific class instance is automatically generated at compile-time whenever the class object declaration is encountered. A specific class instance derived from the class template is referred to as a template class.

A function template can be defined for a set of nearly identical functions that differ in argument types. A specific function instance is generated from the function template wherever a function call is encountered, and is referred to as a template function.

You can redefine a specific instance of a template class or template function if the template class or function type requires specific features.

A class template member function is implicitly a template function which is implicitly passed the type which is the class template argument, as its argument.

A class template definition begins with the template keyboard followed by the class template parameter list enclosed in angle brackets. When a specific class is created, the class template name is appended the specific type name enclosed in angle brackets. No other template class definition is required.

```
// Class template definition
template <class T> class Figure { ... };
// Template class definition
Figure<Circle> c(4);
```

Unlike the macro approach which circumvents the type-checking mechanism, the mechanism of class and function template mechanism ensures type-safe programming.

CHAPTER 12

Exception Handling

The chapter describes the mechanism for exception handling in C++ programs. An exception is an abnormal situation which occurs during program execution due to conditions which are outside the control of the programmer, such as files not being present, or lack of memory.

The normal 'C' way to deal with such problems is to write code to check to see if the result of a function like **malloc()** returns an error code, then act accordingly. However, this leads to more complicated programs which are harder to maintain.

The C++ exception handling facilities represent an alternative approach to coping with error situations. This approach allows the separation of error handling code from main program code and makes the program readable and structured.

Exception handling in C++ is based on:

 ▶ The ability to throw an exception when an abnormal situation occurs in the program execution

 ▶ Specification of an exception handler to provide exception identification and code to deal with the situation.

In this chapter we'll cover:

 ▶ What an exception is

 ▶ How to handle it

 ▶ Try, throw, and catch

 ▶ Unhandled exceptions

 ▶ Exception class hierarchies.

What's an Exception?

An exception is an abnormal situation that might occur at run-time.

These abnormal situations can occur owing to a number of different reasons, all of which are out of the programmer's control. For example, any user input could cause an exception. Disk and memory operations are also classic examples of parts of the computer which the programmer would love to have more control over.

Let's take the following code fragment - although not a true exception (it's really a bug), it serves to illustrate the point.

```
int a = 5;
int b = 0;
int c = a/b;    // Abnormal situation
```

A better example would be to write:

```
int a,b;
cin >> a >> b;
int c = a/b;    // Only results in an exception if b = 0
```

Among other situations that might force the program to behave abnormally are:

- Arithmetic underflows and overflows
- Subscript out of array boundaries.

What To Do

Any of the above error situations could lead to a program (or even operating system) failing. To avoid program failure, the programmer must provide for exception handling. This is generally a sequence of steps for checking the results of operations. Let's look, for example, at the case of the **new** operator. An exception can occur if, when using the **new** operator, you ignore the fact that the **new** operator can't always allocate the requested memory. For example:

```
char * s = "Exceptions are abnormal situations at program run time";
char * s2;
s2 = new char[strlen(s) + 1];    // Unsuccessful memory allocation
strcpy(s2, s);                   // Abnormal situation
```

An attempt to copy into an unallocated memory area is an example of an exception.

Coping With Exceptional Circumstances

When the **new** operator fails to allocate memory, it returns a **NULL** pointer. So as to avoid attempting to use a **NULL** pointer (and causing untold grief), we need to check the return value of **new** against **NULL**.

A couple of examples follow which use normal methods to handle the situation where a **NULL** pointer appears.

Firstly, we'll explicitly check for unsuccessful memory allocation:

```
char * s = "Exceptions are abnormal situations at program run time";
char * s2 = new char[strlen(s) + 1];
if (s2 != NULL)
   strcpy(s2, s);
else
{
   cout << "Unsuccessful memory allocation";
   exit(-1);
}
```

Now, we'll use the **assert()** macro from the standard C library **ASSERT.H**:

```
#include <assert.h>
#include <string.h>

void main()
{
   char * s = "Exceptions are abnormal situations at program run time";
   char * s2 = new char[strlen(s) + 1];
   assert(s2 != NULL);
   strcpy(s2, s);
}
```

In this case, if the expression **(s2 != NULL)** evaluates as false (that is, **s2** pointer is **NULL**), the **assert()** macro prints out the following diagnostic message:

```
Assertion failed: s2 != NULL, file assert.CPP, line 8
```

and invokes the **abort()** function to issue the message:

```
Abnormal program termination
```

to terminate the program.

> If you want to know how we got the message, we changed the program to **assert(s2 == NULL);** then fiddled the output!

421

Classes and Exceptions

Any user-defined data types and classes are open to causing exceptions. We can demonstrate this with the **Rational** class of Chapter 10 which defines a rational number:

```
class Rational
{
private:
    long n;   // Numerator
    long d;   // Denominator
public:
    Rational(long, long);
    Rational(long);
    ...
};
```

A rational number is the ratio of the numerator and denominator. Thus, in regard to the **Rational** class, an exception would occur when the rational number denominator is zero. For example:

```
Rational r(2, 7);        // Valid rational number
Rational r2(3, 0);       // Invalid rational number
Rational r3 = r + r2;    // Abnormal situation
```

You may ask why it is the addition of two rational numbers, of which one has a zero denominator, that leads to an exception. The answer is in the way the + operator for the **Rational** class is defined:

```
Rational & Rational :: operator + (Rational & r)
{
    n = n * r.d + d * r.n;
    d = d * r.d;
    reduce();
    return *this;
}
```

A rational number is always represented by an irreducible fraction. Thus, once the numerator and denominator have been evaluated, the addition function invokes the **reduce()** function to reduce the rational number to an irreducible fraction.

```
void Rational :: reduce()
{
    long num, num2, rem;
    int sign = 1;
    if (n < 0)
        {
```

```
      sign = -1;
      n = n * sign;
   }
   if (n > d)
   {
      num = n;
      num2 = d;
   }
   else
   {
      num = d;
      num2 = n;
   }
   do
   {
      rem = num % num2;
      num = num2;
      num2 = rem;
   } while (rem > 0);

   n = n / num;
   d = d / num;

   n = n * sign;
}
```

If the denominator of a **Rational** instance is zero, then on executing **Reduce()** an exception occurs, because the modulus operator will attempt to divide by zero. Similarly, an exception might occur for a **Rational** class instance with the zero numerator. To avoid these exceptions, we should test for either parts of the rational number being zero. This test can be included into the **Rational** class constructor:

```
Rational :: Rational(long num, long den)
{
   if (num == 0)
   {
      cout << "Numerator of rational number can not be zero\n"
      abort();
   }
   if (den == 0)
   {
      cout << "Denominator of rational number can not be zero\n"
      abort();
   }

   n = num;
   d = den;

   reduce();
}
```

Exception Handling

An abnormal situation which occurs at run-time might lead to termination of the program. However, the exception handling mechanism can catch the exception and handle it, that is, it can perform certain actions before the program terminates abnormally. This may be a diagnostic message which lets you know what it is that has caused the program to behave abnormally.

Only exceptions caused by events generated from within the program are handled. An event which is generated from outside the program and leads to program termination isn't considered to be an exception. For example, the events generated by a keyboard are not exceptions to be handled by the C++ exception handling mechanism, although some compilers do allow for these kind of errors.

The Exception Handling Mechanism

Let's discuss the C++ exception handling mechanism.

An exception generally occurs at some point where the normal flow of the program is interrupted due to invalid data. In C++, the area of the code where an exception may occur is associated with **try**. Within the **try** block, if an exception occurs, then the **throw** statement passes control of the program to the exception handler. The exception handler is specified by the **catch** statement. Once the exception has been handled by the **catch** handler, the program terminates. Schematically this is:

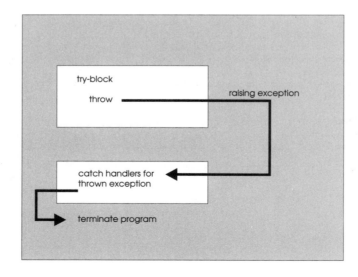

Exception Handling Scheme

Let's demonstrate exception handling with an example of the **Rational** class. For the **Rational** class, there are the following two exceptions possible:

1 Zero numerator

2 Zero denominator.

Let's introduce a class to define exceptions characteristic of the **Rational** class.

```
enum RationalError
{
   ZeroNumerator,
   ZeroDenominator
};

class RationalException
{
// What kind of exception
   RationalError err;
public:
// Constructor
   RationalException(RationalError);
// Response to exception
   void Response();
};
```

The constructor of **RationalException** class is as follows:

```
RationalException :: RationalException(RationalError code)
{
   err = code;
}
```

The **Response()** function specifies the steps to be taken for exceptions associated with the objects of the **Rational** class. It issues a diagnostic message on the cause of an exception.

```
void RationalException :: Response()
{
   switch(err)
   {
     case ZeroNumerator:
       cout << "Numerator of rational number cannot be zero";
       break;

     case ZeroDenominator:
       cout << "Denominator of rational number cannot be zero";
   }
}
```

When a rational number is created by the **Rational** class constructor, exceptions associated with the class of rational numbers will be thrown:

```
Rational :: Rational(long num, long den)
{
   if (num == 0)
      throw RationalException(ZeroNumerator);
   if (den == 0)
      throw RationalException(ZeroDenominator);
   n = num;
   d = den;
// Reduce the rational number to irreducible fraction
   reduce();
}
```

Finally, here is the code for catching and handling the exceptions that might be encountered while using rational numbers.

```
#include <iostream.h>
...
void main()
{
// Try block
   try
   {
      Rational r(1, 5);
      Rational r2(3, 0);
      Rational r3 = r * r2;
      cout << "First rational number: " << r << '\n'
         << "Second rational number: " << r2 << '\n'
         << "Multiplication of two rational numbers: "
         << r3;
   }

// Catch handler
   catch(RationalException & r)
   {
      r.Response();
   }

   cout << "\nEnd of program";
}
```

The result of running this program is:

```
Denominator of rational number cannot be zero
End of program
```

Error Handling Keywords

Thus the C++ error handling mechanism requires the use of three keywords:

1 `try`

2 `catch`

3 `throw`

Syntactically, this can be represented as follows:

```
try
{
   if(exception_condition)
      throw exception_type;
}

catch(exception_type)
{
   handler
}
```

The **try** block is a compound statement. It consists of a sequence of program statements that can generate exceptions. Exceptions can be generated only on the **try** block. Within the **try** block, there has to be a **throw** statement that passes control to the **catch** block. The *handler* are statements which provide all the necessary code to report and deal with the problem.

Let's have a close look at the three components of the C++ exception handling mechanism.

Exception Identification: The try Block

The **try** block begins with the **try** keyword followed by a sequence of program statements enclosed in braces.

```
try
{
    statements
}
```

The **statements** specified in the **try** block form the program code that can generate exceptions and where the generated exceptions will be watched for. For example:

```
try
{
    Rational r(1, 5);
    Rational r2(3, 0);
    Rational r3 = r * r2;
}
```

In the above example, the **try** block consists of three statements involved in exception watching. Each new instance of the **Rational** class uses the **Rational** constructor, in which is the exception is watched for. In this case, the exception is due to either of the arguments being zero, in which case the **throw** statement is used to indicate an exception has occurred.

Throwing an Exception: The throw Statement

An exception can only be thrown in the **try** block. Normally, this is done as a result of a condition. When the condition is met, we need to pass program execution to the exception handler. We do this by using the **throw** statement.

```
Rational :: Rational(long num, long den)
{
    if (num == 0)
        throw RationalException(ZeroNumerator);
    if (den == 0)
        throw RationalException(ZeroDenominator);
    n = num;
    d = den;
// Reduce the rational number to irreducible fraction
    reduce();
}
```

The **throw** statement specifies a value to be passed to the point of code where an exception will be handled. This value is referred to as the exception name. This name will be used to find the right handler for the exception.

The constructor of **Rational** class generates an exception to indicate that an attempt to create a rational number has been made using zero. If this were allowed, then the **Reduce()** method would cause a division by zero error.

Both **throw**s contain a call for the constructor of **RationalException** class. The generated instance of **RationalException** type will be passed to a matching exception handler.

We have used the argument passed to the constructor to indicate the type of exception that has occurred and it is an instance of the **RationalException** class which is passed to the handler.

An Implicit Throw

You may have noticed that the actual **throw** statement doesn't occur in the **try** block directly, but rather in a function (the **Rational** constructor) called from within the **try** block. This is called an implicit throw. If the throw is directly in the **try** block, then this is explicit. The following program illustrates this:

```
#include <iostream.h>

void function(int Error)
{
    throw Error;    // Implicit throw
}

void main()
{
    int Error;
    cin >> Error;

    try
    {
        if(Error % 2 == 0)
            throw Error;    // Explicit throw
        else
            function(Error);
    }
    catch(int error_code)
    {
        cout << "Error code " << error_code << " was entered";
    }
}
```

This program also serves to illustrate another point: the **throw** argument can be of any type, providing the **catch** parameter is of the same type as **thrown** (or can be converted from the **thrown** type to the **catch** type).

Handling an Exception: The catch Statement

If an exception has been thrown in the **try** block, the program flow is interrupted and the following steps are taken:

> The executable code searches for an exception handler that accepts the same type as the thrown exception.

> If a handler is found, program control is transferred to the handler.

An exception handler is specified by the **catch** keyword. The **catch** statement must immediately follow the **try** block. Also, you can have more than one handler, provided that the handlers follow on from each other. The C++ language requires that at least one handler specified by **catch** should be available for the **try** block.

```cpp
#include <iostream.h>
#include <ctype.h>

void main()
{
    int Error;
    cin >> Error;

    try
    {
        if(isalpha((char)Error))
            throw (char)Error;
        else
            throw Error;
    }
    catch(int error_code)
    {
        cout << "Error code " << error_code << " was entered";
    }
    catch(char error_code)
    {
        cout << "Error code " << error_code << " was entered";
    }
}
```

Example output from this program is:

```
5
Error code 5 was entered
```

or

```
68
Error code D was entered
```

The code compares the type of the thrown name against each of the **catch** statement parameters that follow the **try** block. The mechanism for this is similar to function overloading. The handlers are evaluated sequentially after the **try** block. If there is an exact match, then that handler is used, and none of the subsequent handlers are tested.

Classes can be used in the same way as in the rational number program. In that program, the expression in the **throw** clause is evaluated as an instance of the **RationalException** class. The **catch** parameter is a reference to an instance of the **RationalException**. Therefore, a type match exists here, hence the handler specified by **catch (RationalException & r)** will be called to handle an exception associated with the rational number class.

Loss of Flexibility

The **catch** statement may contain simply the type, rather than an *instance* of the type, as it is the type which is used to find a match. However, doing this means that we do remove some flexibility from the exception handler. For instance, we would be able to handle the **RationalException** but be unable to know the cause of the exception as we would no longer have an instance to work from.

The **catch** can have a third possibility:

```
catch (...)
{
...
}
```

In this case the ellipses, after the word **catch**, indicate that this handler is for any type.

In the rational example, the handler specified by **catch** responds to an exception by issuing a diagnostic message to indicate the cause that led to the exception. For this, the handler is passed an instance of the **RationalException** class. The **Response()** method for the passed instance was then executed.

Leaving Out the Cause of the Exception

We could have simplified the program by leaving out the cause of the exception. For example, we could simplify the **RationalException** class to be empty:

```
class RationalException{};
```

The **Rational** constructor can also be simplified by using the default, compiler supplied constructor for **RationalException**:

```
Rational :: Rational(long num, long den)
{
    if (num == 0 || den == 0)
        throw RationalException();
    n = num;
    d = den;
// Reduce the rational number to irreducible fraction
    reduce();
}
```

The catch block then becomes:

```
catch(RationalException)
{
    cout << "invalid rational number\n";
}
```

There is yet another stage of simplification available to us. If there is only one type of exception that can occur in a **try** block, then we could use ellipses. This situation occurs in the rational case. The only type of exception we check for is if one of the two numbers is zero. This means we no longer need the **RationalException** class at all. We simplify the **Rational** constructor to be the following:

```
Rational :: Rational(long num, long den)
{
    if (num == 0 || den == 0)
        throw 0;
    n = num;
    d = den;
// Reduce the rational number to irreducible fraction
    reduce();
}
```

and the **catch** to be the following:

```
catch(...)
{
    cout << "invalid rational number\n";
}
```

After the exception handler has executed, program control is transferred to the statement that follows the last **catch** block. Control is never returned to the statement following the **throw**.

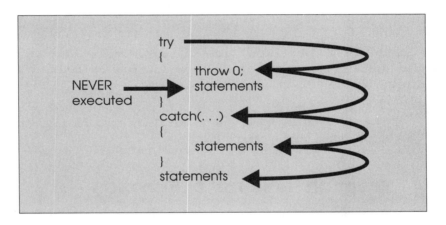

Program Flow Owing to an Exception

Important Issues With try, throw, and catch

There are some important things you need to know about using **try**, **throw**, and **catch**.

> ▶ The **try** blocks can be nested. If an exception is thrown in the inner **try** block, its handler is searched for from the end of the block, as normal. If a matching handler is not found, the enclosing **try** block's handlers are searched. The procedure is performed for every enclosing **try** block. If no handler is found, the pre-defined **terminate()** function will be executed. We'll discuss this function later.

> ▶ Exception handlers are compared in strict sequential order and this can't be changed. Therefore, the order of the handlers is very important.

For example:

```
try
{
...
}
catch(...)
{
...
}
catch(int)    // Never called
{
...
}
```

The handler specified by **catch   (int)** would never be executed, since the handler **catch(...)** responds to all types. Therefore, it should be the last one in the list.

▶ A **goto** statement can be used to transfer control out of a **try** block or handler. You can never use a **goto** statement for transferring control *into* a **try** block or handler.

Throw Exception List for a Function

The C++ language lets you define exceptions that a function can throw explicitly or implicitly. The syntax of the function will be as follows:

```
Rational  multiply()  throw  (RationalException);
```

The following expression:

```
throw (RationalException)
```

is referred to as a throw list for **multiply()** function. The throw list means that the **multiply()** function can only throw a **RationalException** type exception.

The same throw list must be both declared and defined for the **multiply()** function.

Here is the **multiply()** function definition:

```
Rational multiply() throw (RationalException)
{
   long n, d;

   cout << "Enter numerator and denominator of valid rational number: ";
   cin >> n >> d;
   Rational r = Rational(n, d);

   cout << "Enter numerator and denominator of invalid rational number: ";
   cin >> n >> d;
   Rational r2 = Rational(n, d);

   return r * r2;
}
```

Let's rewrite the **try** block by using the **multiply()** function call.

```
Rational multiply() throw(RationalException)
{
...
}

void main()
{
   try
   {
      cout << multiply();
   }
   catch(RationalException & r)
   {
      r.Response();
   }

   cout << "\nEnd of program";
}
```

The **multiply()** function call in the body of **try** block means that the only exception to be thrown is **RationalException**. If, within the function, we throw another type of exception, then this results in the **terminate()** function being used.

The throw list for the function can be empty. For example:

```
void  multiply()  throw();
```

This syntax means that the function won't throw an exception, that is, if an exception is thrown then it doesn't get passed back to the handlers at the end of the **try** block, but still results in the termination of the program execution. The syntax can also mean that the **multiply()** function can handle any exception generated within it by itself. For example:

```
Rational multiply() throw ()
{
   long n, d;

   try
   {
      cout<<"Enter numerator and denominator of first rational number: ";
      cin >> n >> d;
      Rational r(n, d);

      cout<<"Enter numerator and denominator of second rational number: ";
      cin >> n >> d;
      Rational r2(n, d);

      return r * r2;
   }
   catch(RationalException & r)
   {
      r.Response();
      return Rational r(1,1);
   }
}
```

Obviously, with this version of **multiply()**, if the user enters an incorrect rational number, then the function returns a number of 1, which could be the correct result. The only way the user knows that they have entered the wrong information is because of the message.

The meaning of the declaration:

```
void multiply() throw();
```

is somewhat different from the declaration:

```
void multiply();
```

The first declaration means that the function won't throw exceptions, while the second declaration means that the function *can* throw an exception.

Unexpected and Unhandled Exceptions

You may wonder what would happen if an exception other than those specified in the handler list occurs, or what would happen if a matching handler is not found for the thrown exception? The first kind of exception is referred to as unexpected exception. The second kind is referred to as an unhandled exception.

Unexpected Exceptions

For an unexpected exception, the pre-defined **unexpected()** function is called. By default, this function calls another pre-defined function, **terminate()**, to terminate the program. You can replace the pre-defined **unexpected()** function with your own function. To register the replacement function the **set_unexpected()** function is used:

```
Rational multiply() throw (int)
{
...
}

void ownUnexpected()
{
   cout << "Called own unexpected function\n";
   terminate();
}

void main()
{
    set_unexpected(ownUnexpected);
...
}
```

In this example, the **set_unexpected()** function sets the **ownUnexpected()** as a function to be called whenever an unexpected exception occurs.

Here is the program output:

```
Enter numerator and denominator of valid rational number: 1 7
Enter numerator and denominator of invalid rational number: 2 0
Called own unexpected function
Program Aborted
```

> The own function called for when an unexpected exception occurs must meet the following condition: the function must not return control to the program. In our case, the ownUnexpected() function calls the terminate() function to terminate the program.

Unhandled Exceptions

When an unhandled exception occurs, the program calls a pre-defined **terminate()** function, which terminates the program.

You can write you own function to terminate the program. Like the **unexcepted()** function, the **set_terminate()** function must be called to register the new termination function:

```
void ownTerminate()
{
    cout << "Called own terminate function\n";
    exit(-1);
}

main()
{
    set_terminate(ownTerminate);
    ...
}
```

If you do write your own termination function, then you must make sure that the function terminates the program execution, either by calling the **exit()** function, as we have, or the **abort()** function.

Here is the program output:

```
Called own terminate function.
```

Constructors, Destructors and Exception Handling

If an exception is thrown in the **try** block, then the destructor is called for every object that was created within the **try** block, before control is passed to the handler.

We can show this by adding a simple destructor to our **Rational** class:

```
class Rational
{
private:
   long n;
   long d;
public:
   Rational(long, long);
   Rational(long);
   ~Rational()
   {
      cout << "Destructor of class Rational called\n";
   };
...
};
```

This is the original **main** function for the rational program:

```
main()
{
   try
   {
      Rational r(1, 5);
      Rational r2(3, 0);

      Rational r3 = r * r2;
...
}
```

Before the exception occurs an instance of the **Rational** class is successfully created. Hence, the destructor of that instance is called, destroying it. The program produces the following output:

```
Destructor of class Rational called
Denominator of rational number can't be zero
End of program
```

This is owing to the rules of scope. The trailing **}** causes any instances created since the leading **{** to be destroyed, regardless of whether or not there has been an exception.

Exception Class Hierarchy

To conclude this chapter we'll write a more complex example of exception handling. We'll begin by defining the class **MatrixOfRational**:

```
class MatrixOfRational
{
private:
// Size of matrix
   int rows;
   int cols;
// Pointer to array of rational numbers
   Rational * elements;
public:
   MatrixOfRational(int, int);
   ~MatrixOfRational();
   Rational & operator () (int, int);
   MatrixOfRational & operator + (MatrixOfRational &);
   friend ostream & operator << (ostream &, MatrixOfRational &);
};
```

We will allocate memory for the instances of the **Rational** class which makes up the matrix in the matrix constructor. This memory will then have to be released in the destructor.

For the **MatrixOfRational** class, the following exceptions are possible:

▶ Unsuccessful attempt to get memory for the elements of the matrix. This exception may be thrown by **MatrixOfRational** class constructor.

▶ Attempting to access elements outside of the matrix dimensions. This exception may occur when matrix element is referred in **operator()** function.

▶ Illegal matrix size. This exception may occur in **operator+** function when adding one matrix to another.

Let's introduce the **MatrixOfRationalException** class to describe exceptions associated with a matrix of rational numbers. We define the class as a derivation from the already known class **RationalException**:

```
enum RationalError
{
   ZeroNumerator,
   ZeroDenominator,
   NoMemory,
```

```
   OutOfMatrixBoundary,
   InvalidMatrixSize
};

class RationalException
{
   virtual void Response();
...
};

class MatrixOfRationalException : public RationalException
{
public:
   MatrixOfRationalException(RationalError);
   virtual void Response();
};

MatrixOfRationalException :: MatrixOfRationalException(RationalError code)
   : RationalException(code)
{}

void MatrixOfRationalException :: Response()
{
   switch(err)
   {
      case NoMemory:
         cout << "Memory allocation failed\n";
         break;
      case OutOfMatrixBoundary:
         cout << "Out of boundary of matrix of rational numbers\n";
         break;
      case InvalidMatrixSize:
         cout << "InvalidMatrixSize\n";
         break;
   }
}
```

Now we can define the **MatrixOfRational** class member functions:

```
MatrixOfRational :: MatrixOfRational(int r, int c)
{
   rows = r;
   cols = c;
   if ((elements = new Rational [rows * cols]) == 0)
      throw MatrixOfRationalException(NoMemory);
}

MatrixOfRational :: ~MatrixOfRational()
{
   delete elements;
```

```
}

Rational & MatrixOfRational :: operator () (int i, int j)
{
   if ((i < 0) || (i >= rows) ||(j < 0) || (j >= cols))
      throw MatrixOfRationalException(OutOfMatrixBoundary);

   return *(elements + i * rows + j);
}

MatrixOfRational & MatrixOfRational :: operator+ (MatrixOfRational & m)
{
   int i, j;

   if ((rows != m.rows) || (cols != m.cols))
      throw MatrixOfRationalException(InvalidMatrixSize);

   for (i = 0; i < rows; i++)
      for (j = 0; j < cols; j++)
         elements[i, j] = elements[i, j] + m(i, j);

   return *this;
}

ostream & operator << (ostream & out, MatrixOfRational & m)
{
   int i, j;

   for (i = 0; i < m.rows; i++)
      for (j = 0; j < m.cols; j++)
      {
         out << m(i, j);
         if (j == m.cols - 1)
            out << '\n';
         else
            out << ' ';
      }
   out << '\n';

   return out;
}
```

If you were paying close attention (wake up at the back!), then you would have noticed that the constructor and the **()** and **+** operator functions each contain the **throw** statement. It's in these functions that we check for the exception conditions.

This is demonstrated in the following example:

```
...
void main()
{
    try
    {
        MatrixOfRational m(3, 3);

        m(0, 0) = Rational(1, 6);
        m(0, 1) = Rational(4);
        m(0, 2) = Rational(5, 6);
        m(1, 0) = Rational(7, 6);
        m(1, 1) = Rational(1, 4);
        m(1, 2) = Rational(2, 6);
        m(2, 0) = Rational(1, 9);
        m(2, 1) = Rational(3, 4);
        m(2, 2) = Rational(3, 6);

        cout << m;

        m(2, 3) = Rational(1, 2);

        cout << m;
    }
    catch(MatrixOfRationalException & m)
    {
        m.Response();
    }
    catch(RationalException & r)
    {
        r.Response();
    }

    cout << "\nEnd of program";
}
```

Here is the program output:

```
1/6 4/1 5/6
7/6 1/4 1/3
1/9 3/4 1/2

Out of boundary of matrix of rational numbers

End of program
```

We have used two handlers in this program as we have two different types of exception class:

1 The first is responsible for exceptions arising from instances of the **MatrixOfRational** class.

2 The second is responsible for the previously discussed **Rational** class instances.

The order of the handlers is important in this program. Suppose we had used the following order:

```
catch(RationalException &)
{
...
}
catch(MatrixOfRationalException &)
{
...
}
```

When exception occurs, the **catch** exception handlers are looked through in sequence, one after another. If the handler matching the name of thrown exception is found, it is executed. In our example, the exception appears in a matrix rather than the rational numbers, that is, the exception type is **MatrixOfRationalException**. The **catch** handler is chosen if its argument type matches exactly the exception type, or can be cast to exception type using standard conversions. The conversion from a derived class to the base class is standard.

As the **MatrixOfRationalException** class is derived from the **RationalException**, it can be converted to **RationalException**. Hence, independent of what type is thrown, the first handler will be always executed.

Summary

Exceptions and exception handling are a method of dealing with problems that occur within the code. An exception is a condition that if true, and is not dealt with, causes the program to fail. Exception handling is a method of dealing with the problem cleanly.

Having said that, it doesn't allow you to deal with an exception in such a way as to correct the mistake and continue with the program. In other words, exceptions are not designed to handle erroneous user input. It would be very annoying for the user if every time they entered something wrong, they got an error message and were dumped back at the prompt!

The places where exceptions could be sensibly used are in class libraries, particularly if they are to be used by other programs. No matter how much information you give about the **Rational** class, for instance, you can bet your bottom dollar someone will get it wrong!

In the final chapter, we will cover file and stream input and output.

CHAPTER 13

File and Stream Input
and Output

The C++ language doesn't define any built-in Input/Output (I/O) functions, but it *does* let you use a wide range of facilities provided in the **iostream** library. The facilities discussed in the chapter belong to this library.

At a low level, a file is treated as a sequence of bytes, or else as a stream of bytes. On one hand, the I/O library controls transfer of these bytes - and from this point of view, there is no notion of *type* for input/output data. From the user's point of view, a file consists of different data types: **character**, **integer**, **floating**, and so on. The I/O library controls conversions between sequences of bytes and different types.

In this chapter we'll cover:

- The input/output library
- How C++ defines input and output
- User-defined types and input and output
- Formatting output
- Manipulators
- More about files
- Arrays.

The Input/Output Library

The I/O library specifies a range of operations for reading and writing built-in types. To perform I/O for an object of user-defined type, you should expand the I/O operations by using the basic facilities.

Several classes are used to implement I/O. These include **istream** (input stream) and **ostream** (output stream), as well as **iostream** which is derived from the two.

> The **iostream** lets you create bi-directional streams.

Insertion and Extraction

An output operator is designated by **<<** and is sometimes referred to as the insertion into a stream. An input operator is designated by **>>** and is referred to as the extraction operator.

In either case, the point of the operator sign shows the direction in which data is to be transferred.

```
>> example
```

In the above example, data is extracted from the stream and placed *into* the variable **example**.

```
<< example
```

Here, data is inserted into the stream *from* the variable **example**.

Input and Output of Built-in Types

To accomplish input/output, a C++ program uses the header file **iostream.h**, which contains definitions of certain classes and objects which support input/output methods. Standard implementations of C++ open create four I/O objects on code startup. These are:

1 **cin** for conventional input, and corresponding to **stdin** in C (generally, a keyboard).

2 **cout** for conventional output, and corresponding to **stdout** in C (generally, terminal).

3 **cerr** for conventional error output, and corresponding to **stderr** in C (generally, terminal).

4 **clog** for the buffered version of **cerr** (no equivalent in C).

These standard streams can be reassigned to other devices or files.

The **cout** is an object of **ostream** class. This class is used to control formatted and unformatted output. Class **ostream** defines **operator** **<<** for achieving built-in type output.

Concatenation of Output Operations

```
class ostream {
...
  public:
    ostream & operator << (char *);
    ostream & operator << (int);
    ostream & operator << (long);
    ostream & operator << (double);
};
```

Thus the statement **cout** **<<** **x** passes the value of variable **x** to object **cout** of class **ostream** to be output. The **operator** **<<** function returns a reference to the **ostream** object for which it has been called. Therefore, another output operator may be performed on the result of output operation, that is, output operations may be concatenated:

```
int x;
cout << "x = " << x << "\n";
```

Taking account of the fact that **operator** **<<** is evaluated from left to right, this code will be interpreted as follows

```
((cout.operator << ("x = ")).operator << (x)).operator << ("\n");
```

The instance of operator **<<** function called depends on the type of argument passed.

Outputting Binary Data - put and write

It may be convenient to use the **put** and **write** functions declared in the **ostream** class for outputting binary data.

```
ostream & ostream :: put(char ch);
ostream & ostream :: write(const char *buf, int n);
```

The function **put()** puts a single character on **ostream**, whereas **write** passes the specified number of bytes.

Concatenating put and write

Since functions **put** and **write** return a reference to an output class object, they may be concatenated. For example,

```
cout.put('0x7').put('0x7').put('0x7').put('\n');
```

or

```
char *str = "Hello";
cout.put('\t').write(str, strlen(str)).put('\a').put('\n');
```

How C++ Defines Input and Output

C++ defines input the same as output. Class **istream**, with the overloaded **operator >>** for standard types, is associated with input.

```
class istream {
...
  public:
    istream & operator >> (char *);
    istream & operator >> (char &);
    istream & operator >> (short &);
    istream & operator >> (int &);
    istream & operator >> (long &);
    istream & operator >> (float &);
    istream & operator >> (double &);
...
};
```

The **cin** object of **istream** class is used for input from the assigned device. For example:

```
int x;
cin >> x;
```

Depending on the way variable **x** is declared, the memory area named **x** is loaded with either an integer, a floating-point number, a character, or a character string.

Concatenation of Input Objects

The **operator >>** function returns a reference to specific objects of **istream** class, that is, input operations can be concatenated. For example,

```
cin >> x >> d >> c;
```

This will be interpreted as:

```
((cin.operator>>(x)).operator>>(d)).operator>>(c);
```

The get Function

The values entered must comply with the declared type and are separated by a blank. Alternatively, you can use the set of overloaded **get** functions.

```
class istream {
...
  istream & get(char &);
  istream & get(char *p, int n, int z = '\n');
...
};
```

Using these functions, you can enter any character, including white spaces. The **get(char &)** function simply reads a character and places it in its argument. The second **get** function of the overloaded function set can perform more complicated work. It reads and puts characters, whose count doesn't exceed that specified by the second argument, at the address specified by the first argument.

By default the **get** function reads no more than **n** characters into not more than one string. The latter limitation is determined by the third argument, specifying a delimiting character, which, when read, stops the function operation. It is '**\n**' by default. However, you can set it to another character by specifying three arguments when calling the function. The delimiter remains in the input stream and is the first character to be read, if not skipped in some way. For example:

```
char buffer[512];
cin.get(buffer, 512, '\v');
```

451

This **get** function will read no more than 512 characters into the buffer, but stops reading on occurrence of a vertical tabulation symbol **(\v)**. In this case the first character to be read from **cin** by the next read operation will be '**\v**'. Note that the **get** functions return a reference to the class object **istream** for which they were called. Therefore, they can be concatenated into a chain.

For example:

```
char str[10];
char ch, ph;
cin.get(ch).get(str, 10).get(ph);
```

From the **cin** stream, values will be entered into variables **ch**, **str** and **ph**. Some more functions may be useful for organization of input/output.

Other Functions for Organizing Input/Output

The following function puts the character back to **iostream**.

```
putback(char c);
```

The following function puts back the next character (or EOF), but does not delete it from the stream.

```
peek();
```

The following function skips the specified number of characters and stops when it finds the **Delim** character. If no arguments have been specified, the **ignore()** function skips one character and stops by default when it finds the **EOF**.

```
ignore(int Limit = 1, int Delim = EOF);
```

Stream State

Any stream is in some definite state at every time. Error and non-standard conditions are handled whilst taking into account the state. The stream may assume one of the states defined by the **io_state** enumeration in class **ios**.

```
class ios {
...
  public:
    enum io_state {
    goodbit = 0x00,
    eofbit  = 0x01,
    failbit = 0x02,
    badbit  = 0x04,
    hardbit = 0x08
    };
...
};
```

The variable of enumeration type **io_state** is set to one state or another depending on the last operation termination:

Setting	What It Means
goodbit	No error bits set. The operation terminated successfully.
eofbit	End of file. No characters to be entered.
failbit	The last operation terminated abnormally. The stream can be used, but the error bit must be cleared.
badbit	An attempted input/output terminated abnormally. The stream can basically be used upon resetting the error condition.
hardfail	Is set when there is an unrecoverable error in the stream.

The difference between states **failbit** and **badbit** is negligible. The **failbit** state implies that the stream is not destructed and no characters are lost. The **badbit** state implies that the stream might be basically destructed.

If the stream is in **goodbit** or **eofbit** state, the last input/output was a success. The **goodbit** state means that the next operation may be performed and successful. When the stream is in any other state, any further attempt at reading it will be unsuccessful.

Once the error state (**failbit**, **badbit**, **hardfail**) has been set for the stream, all read attempts will be ignored until the appropriate bit is cleared in the stream state variable. To clear the stream variable, you can use the member function **ios::clear(J)**. The member function **ios::clear(J)** simply sets the state variable to integer specified by argument **J**.

For example, `ios::clear(0)` clears all error bits, except for **hardfail** bit, which can't be cleared because it is associated with an equipment malfunction.

> **Stream state should be verified after each input/output operation. This is good programming style, since unsuccessful input/output can later provoke to many errors.**

To verify the stream call the **rdstate()** member function. This function returns the error state as a value **int**. The value can then be examined in each situation.

```
switch (cin.rdstate())
  {
    case ios::goodbit :
      cout << "Last operation on cin is a success\n";
      break;
    case ios::eofbit :
      cout << "End of file \n";
      break;
    case ios::failbit:
      cout << "Input/output error occurred\n";
      break;
    case ios::badbit:
      cout << "Error, characters may be lost in cin\n";
      break;
    case ios::hardfail:
      cout << "Unrecoverable error in cin \n";
      break;
  }
```

Alternative Remedies - eof, fail, bad, and good

An alternative approach to stream state checking is the use of functions **eof()**, **fail()**, **bad()**, and **good()**. These are member functions of class **ios** that check the appropriate bits and return the truth (non-zero) for on bit or false for off bit (see the following table):

Member function	Action
int rdstate()	Returns the current error state
void clear(int i=0)	Sets state variable to 1
int good()	Returns nonzero if no error bits are on; otherwise, returns zero

continued

Member function	Action
int eof()	Returns non-zero if eofbit is set, otherwise, returns zero
int fail()	Returns non-zero if failbit, badbit or hardfail is set; otherwise, returns zero
int bad()	Returns non-zero if badbit and hardfail are set; otherwise, returns zero

A stream state can also be checked as an ordinary logical expression. This demonstrates the beauty and elegance of C++. For example:

```
if (cin >> ch)
  cout << "Character entered\n;"
```

or

```
if (!cin)
  cerr << "Input error\n";
```

The expression **cin >> ch** is an ordinary logical expression whose value may be either non-zero (TRUE), or zero (FALSE). This is possible because class **ios** defines two overloaded operators:

```
int operator! ();
```

or

```
operator void * ();
```

Operator void ()

The **operator void * ()** function defines conversion from type **stream** to type **pointer** to **void**. This conversion operation returns zero (false), if bits **failbit**, **badbit** or **hardfail** are set on. Otherwise, non-zero (truth) is returned.

> Note that in many implementations the end of file (eofbit) state is not handled as an error and therefore cannot be checked in this way.

To recognize the end of file state, you can use either **rdstate()** or **eof()** function. This will guarantee the portability of the code. The overloaded negation operator (!) returns non-zero (truth) if the stream is in any of states **failbit**, **badbit** or **hardfail** - otherwise, it returns zero (false).

It should be noted that conversion of a stream object into pointer to **void** type is used only at logic checking and has no other practical application. Such an approach tests the stream for error. To qualify the state, you must use one of the member functions from the previous table.

Input and Output of User-Defined Types

File **<iostream.h>** contains overloaded input/output operations for built-in types, but the C++ language allows the user to define new types, which are as efficient and convenient as the built-in types. As we already know, handling built-in and user-defined types is done using operator overloading. Have a look at a user-defined type:

```
class String {
    int sz;
    char *str;
  public:
    String();
    String(char *);
    String(int);
  friend String & operator +(const String &, const String &);
  friend String & operator -(const String &, const String &);
  ...
};
```

Then if you have, for example, a **String** class object:

```
String s("string");
```

you must have an appropriate member function or friend function to print the object **s** contents. For example:

```
void String :: print()
{
  cout << "\t" << sz << "\t" << str << "\n";
}
```

Try It Out - Printing an Object

To print an object, call the following function:

```
cout << "s = ";
s.print();
```

The result is

```
s = 6        String
```

There is another way of printing object **s**. With the **operator <<** overloaded for class **String**, as it has been done for + and -, you can use it the same as for any built-in type, thereby retaining a uniform style. This can be achieved as follows:

```
ostream & operator << (ostream &r, String s)
{
  return r << "\t" << s.sz << "\t" << s.str << "\n";
}
```

Now you can print the object in a normal way:

```
cout << "s = " << s;
```

The result is the same. You can then concatenate the new user **operator** **<<** with the already existing output operations since the operator function returns a reference to the class object **ostream**.

How It Works

The function must be declared as a friend of class **String** (rather than its member) because an object of another class is placed in the left-hand side of the output operation. A member function (as it has been mentioned earlier) is passed the **this** pointer as the first argument in an implicit way, whereas the output **operation** **<<** must receive the reference to the class **ostream**.

The user type input is defined the same as output. The sole difference between them is that the second parameter is a reference, which is obligatory for the input operation. For example:

```cpp
istream & operator >> (istream &r, String &s)
{
  char buf[256];
  for (int i = 0; i < 256; i++)
      buf[i] = '\0';// Array initialization
  r >> buf;
  if (r)
      s = String(buf);
  return r;
}
```

Local array **buf** must be initialized.

By testing **if(r)** you ensure that variable **s** will be successfully set to the input value only upon successful input of characters (stream state **goodbit**). The fact that the operator returns a reference to class **istream** makes it possible to concatenate a new input operation with the already existing operations. For example:

```cpp
int x;
double y;
String G;
cin >> x >> y >> G;
```

Formatted Output

The **iostream** library contains the facilities that make it possible to display data in one notation or other with different precision and adjusted left or right. The formatted output facilities also allow you to control other format elements. All these subtleties are defined by certain functions and flags specified by the bits of format state variable in class **ios**:

```cpp
class ios {
...
  public:
    enum {
          skipws=0x0001,
// Skip blanks on input
          left  =0x0002,
// Adjust on the left boundary
          right =0x0004,
// Adjust on the right boundary
          internal=0x0008,
//
```

```
         dec     =0x0010,
// Decimal notation
         oct     =0x0020,
// Octal notation
         hex     =0x0040,
// Hexadecimal notation
         showbase=0x0080,
// Show notation base
         showpoint=0x0100,
// Show decimal point
         uppercase=0x0200,
// Print hexadecimal uppercase
         showpos =0x0400,
// Print "+" before positive numbers
         scientific=0x0800,
// For floating numbers use
// notation with E: 1.2345E2
         fixed     =0x1000,
// For floating numbers use
// notation 123.45
         unitbuf   =0x2000,
// Flush all streams after input
         stdio     =0x4000
// Flush all streams after output
         };
```

By using the overloaded functions **setf** and **unsetf**, you can set or reset any flag. Thus, for example, decimal notation is used by default. You can change the notation base for octal or hexadecimal by using the **setf()** function. This function is overloaded:

```
setf(long);
setf(long,long);
```

The first argument specifies the bit to be set. It may be one of the flags specified in an enumeration. To include more than one flag, concatenate the flags by the bitwise operator *³* (OR). Some flags can't be specified at the same time. For example, you can't use the octal and hexadecimal notation at the same time. By simply specifying:

```
setf(oct);
...
setf(hex);
```

you will have both flags included.

The same applies to the form for displaying floating-point numbers. You can never use the ordinary and scientific notation at the same time. In such cases, you should use the second overloaded function **setf()**. In this function instance, a group of flags to be reset prior to setting bits specified by the first argument is passed as the second argument (see the following table). Either of the two values also defined in the **ios** class may be passed as the second argument.

Argument	Flag to be Cleared	Flag Action
ios::basefield	ios::hex/ios::oct/ios::dec	Integer
ios::floatfield	ios::fixed/ios::scientific	Floating point
ios::adjustfield	ios::left/ios::right/ios::internal	Display format

This way of setting the flags prevents you from setting two flags at a time. Therefore, to set the hexadecimal notation, you can write

```
cout.setf(ios::hex, ios::basefield);
```

The above function resets all bits associated with notation to zero and then sets the required bit. Similarly, once the **setf** function has been called:

```
cout.setf(ios::scientific, ios::floatfield);
```

floating-point numbers will be printed out in scientific notation.

Left and Right Adjustment

By default, any value printed is right-adjusted. With the left flag set, the value will be left-adjusted at printing. This can be performed as follows:

```
cout.setf(ios::left, ios::adjustfield);
```

The remaining flags can be set by the **setf** function with a single argument. The **setf** function returns the previous state of format flags as a numeric **long**. This state, once saved, can be easily restored. For example:

```
long old_stform = setf(ios::left, ios::adjustfield);
...
setf(old_stform, ios::adjustfield);
```

The number of characters displayed by default is that which is required for correct representation of the value, that is, a numeric isn't padded with blanks on the right or left. Therefore, when the output field width has not been defined, it would be meaningless to set the left or right flag for the field, since the field length equals the number of characters in a numeric, and the value is adjusted both on its left and right boundaries.

Try It Out - the width Function

However, you can specify the output field width yourself using the member function **width()**. **width()** is overloaded and has two prototypes:

```
int ios::width(int w);
int ios::width();
```

The first instance sets the output field width in the variable **w** and returns the previous width. Note that with the number of positions specified in the **width()** function being insufficient, no truncation occurs and all characters of the numeric are printed out. If the output field width specified is greater than that required for a numeric, the value will be added with blanks at the left. If the left flag is set as on in this case, the numeric will be added with blanks at the right. For example:

```
#include <iostream.h>
main()
{
int count1 = 8978, count2 = 7834;
int old_wd = cout.width(10);
cout << count1;
old_wd = cout.width(10);
cout << count2 << "\n";
cout.width(old_wd);
cout << count1 << count2 << "\n";
}
```

This results in the following:

```
      8978      7834
89787834
```

How It Works

The above code sets the field width of 10 positions with the default state being saved in the variable **old_wd**. The output operator **count <<** prints variable values adjusted on the right field boundary and padded with blanks to 10 at the left. The function width then restores the default state by using the variable **old_wd** where the default format value has been saved. The output field width is zero by default, that is, only meaningful digits will be printed out without any blanks padding at the right or left. Therefore, the values of two variables are printed out together.

The Other Prototype of width

The **width()** function has one more prototype which is passed no arguments. Such a function changes nothing but returns the current value of the output field width. Note that the field width, thus set, will be reset to **0** after any output operator performs. For example:

```
int a, b;
cout.width(7);
cout << a << b << "\n";
```

In this example, the field width of **7** is in effect only for variable **a**. Variables **b** and **\n** will use the field width by default for output.

The Member Function fill()

As we've already said, if by using the **width()** function, the output field width programmed exceeds the required minimum, the value will be padded with blanks at the left or right. A blank is by default a pad character. By using the member function **fill()**, you can change the pad character. For example:

```
#include <iostream.h>
main()
{
  int L = 7834;
  cout << "\n";
  cout.fill('#');
  cout.width(8);
  cout << L;        // ####7834 is printed
  cout << "\n";
  L = 7834;
  cout.fill('#');
  cout.width(8);
// left flag is used
  cout.setf(ios::left, ios::adjustfield);
  cout << L;        // 7834#### is printed
}
```

When manipulating floating-point numbers, you can select the notation for the number to be output. By setting flags **ios::fixed** and **ios::scientific**, you can select between normal or scientific notation for the number:

```
cout.setf(ios::fixed, ios::floatfield);
```

The Member Function precision()

The floating point number is output in ordinary notation. You are given control over the precision of the numeric to be output by specifying the number of digits after the point. You can do this by using the member function **precision()**. In a similar way to the preceding two functions, this function can be overloaded and has two prototypes:

```
int precision(int);
int precision();
```

- The first format is used to set the number of digits to be printed after the decimal point. This function returns the precision that has been used prior to changing.

- The second format doesn't change the precision, it simply returns the current number of digits to be printed after the point.

By default, six precision digits are output after the point. The trailing zeros, even if explicitly specified, are discarded. For example:

```
cout << 55.7700 << "\n";
```

produces

```
55.77
```

If the decimal point is followed only by zeros, both zeros and the decimal point are discarded. For example:

```
cout << 77.00 << "\n";
```

produces

```
77
```

If you want to print all the trailing zeros after the decimal point, set the **ios::showpoint** flag. For example:

```
cout.setf(ios::showpoint);
cout << 77.0000 << "\n";
```

This produces

```
77.000000
```

Six digits of precision are output by default.

Let's change the precision setting:

```
cout.setf(ios::showpoint);
cout.precision(12);
cout << 77.00 << "\n";
cout << "Now " << cout.precision() << "digits is printed after the
point\n";
```

This code displays on the screen

```
77.000000000000
```

12 digits are now printed after the point.

By calling **cout.precision(12)**, you selected 12 digits to be printed after the point. Flag **showpoint** ensures printing of 12 digits after the point, even if these are the trailing zeros.

By calling **precision()** without arguments, you specify the current precision. Thus by combining member functions of the **ios** class and flags defined for the class, you can organize the formatted input/output.

Manipulators

There is an alternative way of organizing formatted input/output, and that is by using the mechanism of overloaded functions called **manipulators**. The use of manipulators simplifies the coding of formatted input/output. They can be inserted into an output chain by the **<<** or **>>** operators.

Try It Out - Parameters and Manipulators

Manipulators can be parameterized or non-parameterized. For the parameterized manipulators to be used, insert the directive:

```
#include <iomanip.h>
```

To select notation setting, use the following manipulator functions: **dec** for decimal, **hex** for hexadecimal, **oct** for octal. For example:

```
int a = 256, b = 72;
cout << a << hex << a << oct << a << "\n";
```

How It Works

In such a statement, a number will be sequentially displayed first in decimal, then in hexadecimal and finally in octal notation. **dec**, **hex** and **oct** are manipulator functions without parameters, therefore, the **<iomanip.h>** file need not be used for them. The following table summarizes manipulator functions and their actions.

Name	Action	Remarks
dec	Sets decimal notation	Used for I/O
hex	Sets hexadecimal notation	Used for I/O
oct	Sets octal notation	Used for I/O
ws	Enables to enter white space characters	Used for input only
endl	Inserts new line character and flushes stream	Used for output only
ends	Inserts terminating null character	Used for output only
flush	Flushes stream ostream	Used for output only
setbase(int)	Sets notation parameter to 0, 8, 10 or 16	Used for output. 0 is default. Means decimal for output and use of C rules for integer literals.
resetiosflags (long)	Resets format bits for input/output stream specified by argument	Used for I/O
setiosflags (long)	Sets format bits for input/output streams specified by argument	Used for I/O

continued

465

Name	Action	Remarks
`setfill(int)`	Sets filling character	Used for I/O
`setprecision (int)`	Sets precision for floating type	Used for I/O
`setw(int)`	Sets field width to **n**	Used for I/O

Changing the Output Width

The parametrized manipulator `setw()` is passed the value `int` that defines the width of output field as the argument. To make use of the manipulator, insert the following directive

```
#include <iomanip.h>.
```

For example:

```
#include <iostream.h>
#include <iomanip.h>
main()
{
int i = 255;
cout << setw(10) << hex << i << setw(5) << dec << i << "\n";
}
```

This code produces the following:

```
ff        255
```

Changing the Floating Point Precision

By using the manipulator functions, you can alter the floating-point precision:

```
#include <iostream.h>
#include <iomanip.h>
main()
{
  cout << setprecision(10) <<
    "       " << 10.11111111111111 << "\n";
}
```

This code displays the following:

```
Current precision: 10     10.1111111111
```

The manipulator **setprecision(int)** has set the floating-point precision to 10.

Insertion of White Space

By using the manipulator **ws**, you can enter a blank. For example:

```
char sp;
cin >> ws >> sp;
```

Any white space character inserted will be placed to the variable **sp**.

> If no special facilities are provided, input/output will be buffered in C++. This improves the efficiency of the program run, but complicates the writing of interactive programs.

The flush Manipulator, and endl

Such programs are intended to perform alternative actions depending on the character entered, irrespective of whether the buffer is full or not. What you need to do is supply the functions which might flush the buffer at any instant. You can do this with **flush** manipulator.

```
cout << "Enter name : \n" << flush;
```

You can also use the manipulator function **endl**. It accomplishes line feed and buffer flush. The subsequent two lines are practically equivalent.

```
cout << z << "\n" << flush;
cout << z << endl;
```

Initializing

When a program starts running, four streams are automatically initialized and linked to the appropriate default files (units): **cin**, **cout**, **cerr** and **clog**. If you want to initialize some other streams and associate them with certain files, do it explicitly.

Any stream to be initialized may be either input stream, output stream or both. The input stream is always an object of class **ifstream** derived from **istream**. The output stream is always an object of class **ofstream** derived from class **ostream**. The input/output stream is an object of class **fstream** derived from class **iostream**. Any of the classes supplies the constructors to associate a class object with each specific file. For example:

```
ifstream in("data");
```

The code declares object **in** of class **ifstream** and passes the name of the file to be opened to it. An input stream named **"in"** is created and associated with the file named **"data"**. The constructor of class **ifstream** provides for opening the **"data"** file. In the above example, the file is opened with the default options, that is, the read file in text mode. You can change the setting by passing additional arguments to the constructor. Similarly, you can create an output stream. To do so, declare an object of class **ofstream**:

```
ofstream out("data");
```

To make the classes **ifstream, ofstream** and **fstream** accessible, you must also include the directive **#include <fstream.h>** in addition to the directive **#include <iostream.h>**. The file **fstream.h** specifies the classes, comprising the set of constructors and member functions to perform open, create and control for input/output files. If the specified file can't be opened, the associated stream sets to error state. The error state check procedure has been discussed earlier.

The set of constructors supported by the classes allows the stream to be initialized without associating it with any files. You can associate the stream with a file later by using the member function **open()**. Then close the file with the stream remaining initialized, thereby allowing another file to be associated with the stream. For example:

```
ifstream in;
// Initialize stream
in.open("data");
// Associate stream "in" with file "data"
in.close();
// Close file. Stream released
in.open("code");
// Associate stream "in" with file "code"
```

You may use standard facilities for write/read performed on the file. For example:

```
#include <iostream.h>
#include <fstream.h>
#include <stdlib.h>
main()
{
  char ch;
  ofstream out ("data");
  if(!out)
    {
    cerr << "File open error \n";
    exit(16);
    }
  while (cin.get(ch))
    out.put(ch);
  return(0);
}
```

The above code reads characters from the default input unit and puts them into the opened file **"data"**. You can also use the operators **<<, >>.**

```
#include <iostream.h>
#include <fstream.h>
#include <stdlib.h>
main()
{
  char ch;
  ofstream out ("data");
  if(!out)
    {
    cerr << "File open error \n";
    exit(16);
    }
  while (cin >> ch)
    out << ch;
  return(0);
}
```

Text Mode

By default a file is opened in text mode. That is, the pair of characters - carriage return and line feed - is replaced with a single new line character at reading. On output any new line character is replaced with a pair of characters - line feed and carriage return.

Opening in Binary Mode - open()

If you don't want conversions of this kind, open the file in binary mode. To open a file, use the member function **open()**, which is declared as follows:

```
void open(char * name, int = ios :: out, int prot = filebuf::openprot);
```

The **open** function is declared in such a way in the class **ofstream**, and it similarly is declared in the **ifstream** class.

```
void open (char * name, int = ios::in, int prot = filebuf::openprot);
```

These functions differ in the second argument that's referred to as open mode. The available modes of opening a file are collected in the declaration of the **open_mode** enumeration type.

```
class ios {
...
  public:
    enum open_mode { in, out, ate, app, trunc, nocreate,
    noreplace, binary };
    };
```

The meaning of each mode is presented in the following table:

Mode	Action
ios::in	Open file for input (for ifstream class object is used by default)
ios::out	Open file for output (for ofstream class object is used by default)
ios::ate	Open file to add to the end. If no file exists, create it
ios::app	Open file to append to the end of file
ios::trunc	Recreate the file, if it already exists
ios::nocreate	If no file exists, set the error state
ios::noreplace	If file already exists, set the error state
ios::binary	Open file in binary mode

If more than one mode is to be specified at opening, it must be bitwise **ORed** ([3]). For example:

```
ofstream out ("data", ios::binary³ ios::app³ ios::nocreate)
```

More About Files

The above declaration of an output stream opens the file named **"data"** in the binary mode for adding to the end of file. If the specified file isn't available on the disk, the function will set the error state for the output stream without creating a new file. If the same file is to be used both for input and output, create the stream as an **fstream** class object. For example:

```
fstream inout("data", ios::in³ ios::app);
```

Such declaration connects the in/out stream with file **"data"** that has been opened both for reading and appending. It should be noted that if the file opened where the **ios::out** mode already exists, the file content will be destroyed. Sometimes, when using the file, you need to know the next file position to be involved in an input/output operation. Also, the current file position often needs resetting. You can do this using the following functions:

```
tellg()

tellp()

seekg()

seekp()
```

The **tellg()** function specifies the current file position to be read. The **tellp()** function specifies the current file position to be written into. For example

```
fstream inout("data", ios::in³ ios::app);
streampos i = inout.tellg();
```

When the above operation is performed, the variable **i** will contain the current position to begin the next read. The **streampos** type is defined by the **typedef** in file **<fstreampos.h>**:

```
typedef long streampos;
```

The **seekg()** function sets the file position pointer to the specified number of bytes in the specified direction for the write operation.

Similarly, **seekp()** sets the file pointer for the read operation. The **seekg()** function has the following prototype:

```
seekg(streampos p, seek_dir d = ios::beg);
```

seek_dir is the enumeration comprising three elements:

> **ios::beg** - relative to the beginning of file
>
> **ios::cur** - relative to the current position
>
> **ios::end** - relative to the end of file.

The second argument defines what is to be used as a relative point for resetting the file pointer to the number of positions specified by the first argument. This may be a negative number. For example:

```
ifstream in("data", ios::binary);
in.seekg(-20, ios::end);
```

The pointer to the file position is set to the twentieth position from the end. Starting from the position, the next read is performed.

Input/Output for an Array

The iostream library supports **incore** operations performed on character arrays. For this, the **ostrstream** class which provides the functions of output to a character array and the **istrstream** class which provides the function of reading from a character array are defined. The **ostrstream** and **istrstream** classes are derived from **ostream** and **istream**, respectively. Thus every function of the **istream** class is available for the **istrstream** class. This is the same for **ostrstream** and **ostream**.

> The functions defined in `istrstream` and `ostrstream` classes support in-memory formatting, similar to the `sscanf` and `sprintf` functions, but much more flexible.

To define an object of any of the above classes, you should include **strstrea.h** in your program.

```
#include <strstrea.h>
```

Inserting Files into Arrays

Thus, for example, once the file is read, you can insert it into a character array. In other words, once you have defined an object of class **ostrstream,** you can treat it as an input 'device'. Since the 'device' is associated with a pre-allocated array, this is the array which is used as an 'output device'.

Similarly, once you have defined an object of the class **istrstream** and associated it with an array, you thereby associated the input stream with the array.

For the classes **istrstream** and **ostrstream**, the input **(>>)** and output **(<<)** operators are overloaded and (as we noted earlier) all functions of parent classes are available. Therefore, we can perform I/O for an array in a usual way.

```
ostrstream buf;
char x;
buf << x;
```

or

```
buf.put(x);
```

The Member Function str()

Once you have performed data output to an object of class **ostrstream**, you can work with the object as with a normal array by applying the member function **str()** to the object which returns a pointer to the array associated with the class object.

```
char* pbuf = buf.str();
```

The **pbuf** pointer is initialized to the address of array related to the **buf** object in the class **ostrstream**.

When the **str** member function is called, the programmer regains control over the array and the class **ostrstream** is no longer responsible for its object. This means that once the **str** function has been performed on an object, the object can't be used for output. Thus you must complete output before calling the **str** function.

Moreover, when an object of class **ostrstream** goes out of scope and no **str** function is applied to it, the destructor of **ostrstream** is automatically called to release the array memory. If the **str()** function has been applied to the object, it is up to you to ensure that the array is deleted by explicitly using the **delete** operator. For example:

```
delete pbuf;
```

Associating Class Objects with Allocated Arrays

There is another way of using an object of class **ostrstream**, and that is to associate this class object with the previously allocated array. In this case the constructor of class **ostrstream** must take arguments. The first argument is a pointer to **char**, that is, a pointer to the previously allocated array. The second argument of **long** type must specify the array size in bytes. The third argument must specify the mode: **ios::app** or **ios::out**. Depending on the third argument, the string will either have a terminating null character or not. If the third argument value is **ios::app**, the terminating null character is present. Otherwise, it is not!

Note that you must use the **seekp()** function in order to move to the starting position of an array. For example:

```
#include <iostream.h>
#include <strstrea.h>
char * function(char *item, int count)
{
  const Len = 512;
  char buffer[Len];
// Stream defined for output to array
  ostrstream outs(buffer, Len, ios::out);
// Positioning at the beginning of array
  outs.seekp(ios::beg);
// Member output
  outs << item << " member output ";
  cout << endl;
  return buffer;
}
```

Once the function for output to an array has been defined, you can use it for normal output to the screen.

```
main()
{
  cout << function("String", 55) << "\n";
}
```

Thus with the complex-format string defined, you can use it by passing arguments to the array to generate, for example, reports with complicated structure.

Similarly, you can use the input string class (**istrstream**) that is an analog of **sscanf** function:

```
istrstream work;
...
work >> x;
```

A constructor of class **istrstream** can take two arguments. The first argument is a pointer to a previously allocated array. The second argument is the array size in bytes.

For example:

```
#include <iostream.h>
#include <strstrea.h>
float function(char *str, int num)
{
  float temp;
  istrstream(str, num) >> temp;
  return temp;
}
```

This function can now be used to convert a character string into a floating-point number, for example, by keying characters into the internal representation of floating-point numbers.

Summary

In addition to conventional I/O facilities defined in C, the C++ language implementation provides the **iostream** class library to input and output for a stream of bytes. You can input and output both built-in type and user-defined class objects without using the **printf** function.

Class **iostream** library also defines I/O operations on files treated as input or output streams.

The variable of enumeration type **io_state** should be used to check whether or not an I/O operation has successfully completed.

The **iostream** class library has a set of member functions (manipulators) allowing data to be entered or output in different representation formats.

You can also consider an array as a stream and perform I/O operations for it in the same way as for input or output devices.

As it has been noted, input/output facilities are not defined within the C++ language, therefore there may be some differences from the above discussed in various implementations. However, the general approach to the input/output implementation remains the same. All implementations support input/output for console, disk file handling, and resetting the current position. Besides, provision is made for the buffer control facilities and the stream state analysis. To make the usage of input/output facilities more efficient, have a look at the publications which deal with specific implementation.

APPENDIX

Changes to the C++ Language

Authors of good books on C++ have a particularly difficult task because the language is still considered to be under development. During the process of standardizing C++, numerous minor problems surface that need fixing. Most of these fixes involve a more precise definition that will increase reliability and remove ambiguity in code. Some changes just make something possible that was not previously allowed. Changes to a language operation are carefully considered by national and international panels and committees. Extensive discussions and tests are monitored within the programming industry before any alterations are implemented.

An example of such a change is the one that allows explicit template function instantiation. This means that future compilers will support a wider range of template function definitions.

Note that it takes time for compiler writers to catch up with changes, even when they are members of either ANSI X3J16 (the US committee on standardizing C++ - membership open to non-US nationals/companies) or their own national committee for C++ standardization (such as the UK C++ panel).

The problem is made worse by the existence of a number of talented compiler developers who are not members of any C++ standardization committee. Without such membership they assume that the 'Annotated Reference Manual ' defines C++. It doesn't!

This same problem is faced by many authors. Some are either members of X3J16 or have access through their employers. Most have to rely on whatever they can find published in journals such as 'The Journal of C Translation' and 'C++ Report'.

Minor Changes

There are some changes, fortunately very few, that are correcting aspects of the language as a result of experience and programmer demand. Arguably, only two of these will impact most ordinary C++ programmers (as opposed to specialist library designers, or those involved in large projects using very advanced idioms).

1   The change in the scope rule for a variable declared in the **init** clause of a **for** statement. The new scope rule specifies that such a variable goes out of scope on exit from the body of the **for** statement. When compilers implement this change, they will have to issue a warning in a situation such as:

```
int i =0;
void fn(){
    for(int i=0;i<10;i++){ // whatever
    }
    cout<<i; // required warning, i is outer scope version
}
```

There are further enhancements that allow other declarations in iterations, but this is the only one that affects existing code. Fixing the code is easy, just move the declaration to immediately before the **for** statement.

2   The specification for an **enum** has been tightened up. The range of valid values for an **enum** is now effectively from the minimum to the maximum value of the specified set. Actually, it is slightly larger because it's specified in terms of the minimum bit-field that can represent that range (possible as offsets from a value). This means that existing uses of **enums** to provide named bit values will work correctly. Values outside the required range are undefined.

3   Explicit conversion to an **enum** is now legal (it wasn't before!) and an attempt to convert an integral value outside the **enum**'s range is undefined (that is, an error that the compiler is not required to diagnose).

If you want to provide operators for your **enums** you can do so as long as the relevant operator is not restricted to definition in a class scope (assignment is, so you can only use default assignment, with explicit conversion if needed).

Major Changes

The original mandate handed to the X3J16 and WG21 groups (the ISO committee working in parallel with X3J16) included templates and exception handling.

1 The fuller specification for templates is unlikely to affect existing code, it largely better defines the facilities and extends them.

2 Exception handling is far more problematic as it impacts on all existing code. Once an exception can be thrown, there are substantial implications. Resource management in an EH environment needs care, to ensure that resources are not lost when an exception is thrown. Of course, if no exception is thrown you might reasonably expect your code to function as previously. This is NOT true because of changes that have resulted from re-specifying the new operators. (See below.)

3 More recent experience has caused the introduction of **RTTI** (run time type information) because existing practice was resulting in a multitude of vendor or library specific tools to support some form of RTTI functionality. The only impact RTTI has on existing code is that some could be re-written to use it.

4 A fourth major extension is the introduction of something called **'namespace'** to resolve the growing problem of name clashes between different vendor libraries. This has a minor impact on existing code - don't use the global scope operator unless it is needed to resolve an ambiguity.

Some authors have recommended use of the global scope operator. This is simply to make explicit that a function, used in the definition of a member function, is not itself a member function. This use of the global scope operator is now suspect, and might cause errors in future compilations of code using it. There might be a remote possibility that it would change the meaning of the code.

The Impact of EH and new

ANSI X3J16/WG21 determined that the dynamic memory assignment operators (**new**, **new[]**) will give an "out of memory exception" if insufficient memory is available.

Despite considerable discussion, no acceptable way has yet been found to support both the original and the new mechanisms for handling out-of-memory. The conclusion, is that programs (and program idioms) that rely on **new** and **new[]** returning a null-pointer, will not function correctly in the future.

Attempts to fix this via the **new_handler** only make matters worse, as it hijacks the use of the **new_handler** mechanism in a way that is likely to introduce further inconsistencies. It's true that you can restore the return of a null-pointer by such a mechanism (if the compiler supports it) but you cannot, in addition, provide your own handlers in the traditional way.

In simple terms, the effects of introducing exception handling (which was required by the mandate for standardization) coupled with a requirement that **new** and **new[]** operators should throw an exception if there's insufficient memory, breaks all existing code.

There are many positive aspects to this change (and the introduction of a specific operator **new[]** which can now be replaced by an in-class version) but the transitional stage will cause problems to both programmers and authors.

New Keywords

The following are currently reserved as keywords (note that a keyword is more than a reserved word, it is a word that has significance to the parser) in addition to those listed in the ARM.

bool	const_cast	dynamic_cast	false
mutable	namespace	reinterpret_cast	static_cast
true	typeid	using	wchar_t

Note that both **bool** and **wchar_t** are full built-in types and not provided as **typedef**s.

As a result of deliberations concerning problems incurred by certain national character sets, the following have also effective keyword status:

`bitand`	`and`	`bitor`
`or`	`xor`	`compl`
`and_eq`	`or_eq`	`xor_eq`
`not`	`not_eq`	

The use of a double underscore in an identifier is reserved to implementors for support of name-mangling algorithms. Otherwise its use should be avoided - although a compiler is not required to diagnose it.

The following digraphs are also provided for use by those with nationally restricted character sets:

```
<%  %>  <:  :>  %:
```

(in the same manner as %:% is used as a preprocessing token equivalent to ##).

INDEX

W

The Book

The Beginner's Guide To C++

The ideal start for the newcomer to the

world of programming languages. This

Beginner's Guide contains comprehensive

coverage of the language syntax. You will

The Beginner's Guide to C++

master procedural programming in easy stages, and then learn object

Author - O. Yaroshenko

oriented programming - **the essential programming** methodology of the future.

ISBN - 1-874416-26-5

The Series

BEGINNER'S GUIDE TO ....

These guides are designed for beginners to the particular language

or to programming in general. The style is friendly and the emphasis

is on learning by doing. The chapters focus on useful examples

that illustrate important areas of the language. The wealth

of examples and figues help make the transition from

beginner to programmer both easy and successful.

The Book

The Revolutionary Guide to OOP

Using C ++   Benefit from the authors' years

of experience using C and C++ in some of the

most complex and demanding programming

The Revolutionary Guide to OOP Using C++

environments around today. This book aims to

Authors - V. Olshevsky

ease the difficulties in making the transition from

A. Ponomarev

C to C++, and will show you the power of object-oriented C++.

ISBN - 1-874416-18-4

The Series

REVOLUTIONARY GUIDE TO .....

Learning the programming techniques

of the industry experts with the

Revolutionary Guides. This series guides you

through the lastest technology to bring your skills

right up to date. Example applications are used to illustrate new

concepts and to give you practical experience in the language.

WIN FREE BOOKS

TELL US WHAT YOU THINK!

Complete and return the bounce back card and you will:

- Help us create the books you want.
- Receive an update on all Wrox titles.
- Enter the draw for 5 Wrox titles of your choice.

FILL THIS OUT to enter the draw for free Wrox titles

Name _____

Address _____

_____

_____

_____ Postcode/Zip _____

Occupation _____

How did you hear about this book ?
- ☐ Book review (name) _____
- ☐ Advertisement (name) _____
- ☐ Recommendation
- ☐ Catalogue
- ☐ Other _____

Where did you buy this book ?
- ☐ Bookstore (name) _____
- ☐ Computer Store (name) _____
- ☐ Mail Order
- ☐ Other _____

What influenced you in the purchase of this book ?
- ☐ Cover Design
- ☐ Contents
- ☐ Use of Color
- ☐ Other (please specify)

How did you rate the overall contents of this book ?
- ☐ Excellent
- ☐ Good
- ☐ Average
- ☐ Poor

What did you find most useful about this book ?
_____

What did you find least useful about this book ?
_____

Please add any additional comments. _____
_____

What other subjects will you buy a computer book on soon ?

What is the best computer book you have used this year ? _____

Please do not put me on your mailing list ☐

WROX PRESS INC.

Wrox writes books for you. Any suggestions, or ideas about how you want information given in your ideal book will be studied by our team. Your comments are always valued at WROX.

Free phone from USA 1 800 814 3461
Fax (312) 465 4063

Compuserve 100063,2152.
UK Tel. (4421) 706 6826   Fax   (4421) 706 2967

Computer Book Publishers

NB. If you post the bounce back card below in the UK, please send it to:
Wrox Press Ltd. 1334 Warwick Road, Birmingham, B27 6PR

NO POSTAGE
NECESSARY
IF MAILED
IN THE
UNITED STATES

BUSINESS REPLY MAIL
FIRST CLASS MAIL   PERMIT#64   CHICAGO,IL.

POSTAGE WILL BE PAID BY ADDRESSEE

WROX PRESS
2710 WEST TOUHY AVE
CHICAGO IL 60645-3008
USA